PHILADELPHIA

MAIN LINE CLASSICS II

Cooking Up a Little History

The Junior Saturday Club of Wayne

A PHILANTHROPIC ORGANIZATION

Published by
The Junior Saturday Club of Wayne
P.O. Box 521
Wayne, Pennsylvania 19087

Copyright© March, 1996

Manufactured in the United States of America
First Printing: March, 1996   10,000 copies
Second Printing: October, 1996   15,000 copies

Library of Congress Number: 96-83136
ISBN: 0-9650818-0-X

Edited and Manufactured by
Favorite Recipes® Press
P.O. Box 305142
Nashville, Tennessee 37230
1-800-358-0560

Preparation times do not include chilling or cooking time.

Proceeds from the sale of **MAIN LINE CLASSICS II**
will be used to support individuals and charitable
organizations throughout the Philadelphia area.

Additional copies of **MAIN LINE CLASSICS II** may be obtained
by sending $18.95 each plus $3.50 for postage and
handling (PA residents add $1.14 sales tax) to:

MAIN LINE CLASSICS II
P.O. Box 521
Wayne, Pennsylvania 19087
(610)-688-3252

TABLE OF CONTENTS · 3

✦

MAIN LINE CLASSICS II

is dedicated to

all the people in the Philadelphia area

whom we continue to educate, serve and support

so that they can

improve their quality of life

and the lives around them.

✦

(opposite) William Penn holding the Welsh Tract Charter, stands in front of the Merion Friends Meetinghouse. Built in 1695 by Welsh Quakers, it is the oldest recorded place of worship continuously used in the United States. The building was constructed in the form of a cross and supported with two-foot-thick jointed stone walls housing small leaded windows. Penn preached here in 1701, but few could understand him because he spoke English, not Welsh.

PENN AT MERION MEETING

In the late 1600s Sir William Penn, a British
Navy admiral, was owed a debt of 20,000 pounds sterling by
Charles II, King of England. For his loyal service, the obligation
was paid with a grant of sparsely populated land north of
Maryland to his 36-year-old son, William Penn. On March 4,
1681, with 50,000 acres and deed in hand, William Penn, the
persuasive salesman, went to work establishing a colony.

A visionary, Penn had four major objectives: first,
to prove that people could live together and govern themselves
in peace, in what he termed a "Holy Experiment"; second, to
create a community in which a person's word was as good as his
land; third, to give people the freedom to worship as they pleased;
and finally, to make the Province a profitable venture.

The Welsh Quakers were the first people attracted
to Penn's idea and they promptly reserved 40,000 acres of land.
They were all gentlemen of the highest social caste in Wales, and
because they owned or worked most of the land, the "Welsh
tract" became its name. The new settlers were preceded by the
Lenni-Lenape Indians, the "original people," who had inhabited
the area for some twelve thousand years. When Penn arrived in
Pennsylvania, he bought their land to ensure a strong friendship
and dictated a careful policy of trade and equal privileges for the
Indians' protection. It was to become one of Penn's greatest
achievements; he held their loyalty for many years, and the full
support of the Indian Council until his death. Penn's colony,
conceived as a haven for Quakers and others dedicated to
religious freedom, soon became America's first "melting pot,"
with a wide variety of people of different religions, ethnic
cultures, and economic backgrounds. They came to work, pray,
and build a new life in this beautiful valley of the New World.

HOT ALMOND CHEESE DIP

1/3 cup mayonnaise
8 ounces cream cheese, softened
1 cup shredded sharp Cheddar cheese
1 cup shredded Swiss cheese
4 scallions, minced
Ground nutmeg to taste
3/4 cup slivered almonds, toasted

✦ Combine mayonnaise, cream cheese, Cheddar cheese, Swiss cheese, scallions and nutmeg in bowl; mix well. Stir in almonds. Spoon into baking dish.
✦ Bake, uncovered, at 350 degrees for 30 minutes. Serve immediately with crackers.
✦ Toasted almonds may be sprinkled over top instead of stirred into dip.

Preparation time: 15 minutes   15 servings

HOT CRAB MEAT DIP

16 ounces cream cheese, softened
6 tablespoons mayonnaise
1/4 cup white wine or vermouth
1 tablespoon Dijon mustard
1/2 teaspoon sugar
Pinch of salt
16 ounces fresh crab meat, drained

✦ Combine cream cheese, mayonnaise, white wine, mustard, sugar and salt in double boiler. Stir over hot water until thoroughly blended and heated through. Add crab meat, stirring until blended and heated through.
✦ Spoon mixture into chafing dish. Serve hot with bland crackers.

Preparation time: 30 minutes   12 servings

CREAM CHEESE JALAPENO DIP

8 ounces cream cheese, softened
1/2 (10-ounce) jar hot taco sauce
2 green onions, minced
1 (4-ounce) can green chiles, chopped
Dash of cumin
Scallions and cherry tomatoes

✦ Combine cream cheese, taco sauce, green onions, green chiles and cumin in bowl; mix well. Spoon into serving bowl.
✦ Garnish around edge of dip with scallions and cherry tomatoes.
✦ Serve with tortilla chips or corn chips.

Preparation time: 10 minutes   10 servings

SPICY THREE-CHEESE DIP

8 ounces mild Cheddar cheese, shredded
8 ounces sharp Cheddar cheese, shredded
8 ounces Monterey Jack cheese, shredded
1/2 cup almonds, toasted
2 cups sour cream
11/2 jalapeños, minced
1/2 cup raisins (optional)
1/2 teaspoon cumin

✦ Layer half the cheeses, almonds, sour cream, jalapeños, raisins and cumin in 21/2-quart baking dish. Repeat layers.
✦ Bake at 375 degrees for 30 minutes. Serve immediately with crackers.

Preparation time: 30 minutes   8 servings

The Dutch were the first Europeans to arrive in Chester County. They came to fortify their existing trading posts, not to settle the land. Their disregard for the Native Americans resulted in the bloody massacres of 1643 and 1664. William Penn was determined not to repeat their mistakes in his new settlement.

TANGO DIP

2 cups mayonnaise
1 cup cottage cheese
3/4 cup chopped onion
1 1/2 tablespoons horseradish
1 1/2 tablespoons Worcestershire sauce
1 1/2 teaspoons caraway seeds
1 tablespoon garlic powder
1 teaspoon salt
1 teaspoon Tabasco sauce
1/2 teaspoon seasoned salt

✦ Combine all ingredients in blender container. Process until smooth. Spoon into serving bowl.
✦ Serve with corn chips or crackers.

Preparation time: 10 minutes   16 servings

INCREDIBLE SHRIMP DIP

16 ounces cream cheese, softened
1 tablespoon fresh lemon juice
2 tablespoons Worcestershire sauce
2 tablespoons mayonnaise
1/4 cup finely minced white ends of scallions
8 ounces tiny cocktail shrimp
1/2 (12-ounce) bottle chili sauce
6 ounces fresh or 1 (6-ounce) can crab meat

✦ Combine cream cheese, lemon juice, Worcestershire sauce, mayonnaise, scallions and shrimp in bowl; mix well. Chill, covered, overnight.
✦ Spread cream cheese mixture in serving dish; cover with chili sauce. Sprinkle crab meat over top. Garnish with sliced tops of scallions. Serve with bland unsalted crackers.

Preparation time: 20 minutes   12 servings

TEX-MEX SHRIMP DIP

1 pound large, peeled, cleaned shrimp
1 teaspoon fresh lemon juice
3 tablespoons minced fresh cilantro
2 to 3 cloves of garlic, minced
1 fresh jalapeño, seeded, minced
1 bunch scallions, finely chopped
1/2 teaspoon cayenne
Tabasco sauce, paprika and salt to taste
16 ounces Monterey Jack cheese, shredded
16 ounces cream cheese, softened
Flour tortillas

✦ Poach shrimp in water with lemon juice for 4 minutes; drain. Chop coarsely in food processor.
✦ Combine with seasonings in bowl; mix well.
✦ Blend Monterey Jack cheese and cream cheese in food processor. Add to shrimp mixture; mix well. Line baking dish with overlapping tortillas. Spoon in shrimp mixture.
✦ Bake at 350 degrees for 15 to 20 minutes or until bubbly. Broil until tortillas are light brown. Garnish with chopped tomatoes. Serve with tortilla chips.
✦ May prepare a day ahead and chill until baking time.

Preparation time: 30 minutes   8 servings

AVOCADO AND CORN SALSA

1 cup fresh corn, cooked, drained
1/3 cup each chopped red and yellow bell peppers
1/3 cup chopped tomato
3 tablespoons chopped fresh cilantro
3 tablespoons fresh lemon juice
1 1/2 tablespoons finely chopped shallots
1/2 to 1 jalapeño, minced
1 cup finely chopped peeled avocado
Salt and pepper to taste

✦ Combine corn and next 7 ingredients in bowl; toss gently to mix. Chill, covered, for up to 8 hours.
✦ Add chopped avocado and seasonings just before serving.

Preparation time: 30 minutes   16 servings

The Welsh tract was planned as a "barony state" in which Penn presided over all—Welsh Quakers, English, and Native Americans. Each group within the settlement elected its own officers and juries so that all causes, quarrels, crimes and disputes could be settled by people speaking the same language.

PESTO

1 cup mayonnaise

1 cup loosely packed
fresh parsley leaves

3 tablespoons
fresh basil leaves

2 tablespoons
freshly grated
Parmesan cheese

$1/2$ teaspoon finely
chopped garlic

$1/4$ cup finely
chopped walnuts

✦

Process mayonnaise,

parsley, basil, cheese

and garlic in blender

or food processor

until smooth. Mix in

walnuts. Chill until

serving time.

CRUDITES WITH PESTO

3 red bell peppers
3 green bell peppers
2 yellow bell peppers
3 small bags baby carrots
1 bunch celery
1 bunch broccoli
1 head clauliflower
2 small bags radishes
Pesto (at left)

✦ Cut vegetables into pieces suitable for finger foods
for dipping.
✦ Serve with Pesto for dipping.

Preparation time: 1 hour   20 to 30 servings

CORN AND RED PEPPER RELISH

2 large red bell peppers, chopped
$1/4$ cup olive oil
2 cups chopped onions
4 teaspoons chopped garlic
2 cups corn, fresh or frozen, thawed, drained
$1/4$ cup sugar
6 tablespoons cider vinegar
$1/2$ teaspoon dry mustard
Cayenne pepper to taste
1 teaspoon salt
3 tablespoons chopped fresh cilantro

✦ Sauté red peppers in olive oil in skillet for 3 to 4 minutes.
Add onions and garlic; sauté for 3 minutes. Add corn.
Sauté for 2 minutes. Dissolve sugar in vinegar in bowl.
Add to corn mixture. Add mustard, cayenne and salt.
Cook for 5 minutes or until liquid evaporates, stirring
constantly. Remove from heat. Chill for up to 24 hours;
stir in cilantro. Serve with white corn chips.
✦ For more colorful relish, substitute 1 green bell pepper
for 1 red bell pepper.

Preparation time: 30 minutes   20 servings

ELLEN'S FABULOUS SALSA

1 (25-ounce) can peeled whole tomatoes
1/4 large onion, chopped
1/2 green bell pepper, chopped
1 tablespoon red wine vinegar
1/4 teaspoon salt
1/8 teaspoon cayenne
1/2 tablespoon chili powder
11/2 tablespoons sugar
1/2 cup chopped fresh parsley or cilantro

✦ Process tomatoes in food processor container until coarsely chopped. Texture should be chunky. Add onion, pepper, vinegar, salt, cayenne, chili powder, sugar and parsley; process until mixed. Chill until serving time.
✦ May store in the refrigerator for at least 1 week.

Preparation time: 20 minutes   8 servings

CHEESY BACON ROUNDS

1 pound bacon, crisp-cooked, crumbled
1 cup mayonnaise
11/4 cups shredded sharp Cheddar cheese
4 scallions, finely chopped
3/4 tablespoon sherry
11/2 teaspoons white wine
1 teaspoon Worcestershire sauce
1 package plain Melba rounds

✦ Combine bacon, mayonnaise, cheese, scallions, sherry, wine and Worcestershire sauce in bowl; mix well. Spread evenly on Melba rounds; place on rack in broiler pan. Broil for 1 to 3 minutes or until bubbly.

Preparation time: 20 minutes   16 servings

The Gilmore Mansion in Merion was built in 1899 in the French Gothic style. In 1921 the Episcopal Academy opened its suburban campus there.

HOLLANDAISE SAUCE

4 egg yolks

2 tablespoons fresh lemon juice

Salt to taste

1/2 cup melted butter

✦

Process egg yolks, lemon juice and salt in blender until well mixed. Add melted butter in a fine stream, processing constantly. Pour into microwave-safe bowl. Microwave on High for 20 seconds. Mix until creamy. Microwave on High for 20 seconds longer or until sauce is thickened.

ASPARAGUS TOASTIES

12 fresh asparagus spears
Honey mustard spread
12 thin slices fresh bread, crusts removed
3 tablespoons melted butter
Fresh parsley
Hollandaise Sauce (at left)

✦ Remove and discard tough ends of asparagus. Cook asparagus in boiling water for 1 to 2 minutes or until tender-crisp; drain and cool.

✦ Spread honey mustard on bread. Place 1 piece asparagus on each slice of bread. Roll diagonally to enclose asparagus, kneading ends of bread to hold. Wrap in parchment paper. Chill until baking time.

✦ Brush toasties with melted butter; place on baking pan. Bake at 350 degrees for 5 to 8 minutes or until brown, turning occasionally. Remove to serving plate. Garnish with fresh parsley.

✦ Serve with Hollandaise Sauce for dipping.

Preparation time: 15 minutes   12 servings

HAM AND TORTILLA ROLL-UPS

1 (10-count) package flour tortillas
2 bunches green onions
1 (6-ounce) can pitted black olives, drained
8 ounces low-salt boiled ham
16 ounces cream cheese, softened
Tabasco sauce to taste
Salsa

✦ Let tortillas come to room temperature. Process green onions, olives and ham in food processor until minced. Add to cream cheese in bowl; mix well. Stir in Tabasco sauce.

✦ Spread mixture on tortillas to edges; roll to enclose filling. Place in sealable plastic bag. Freeze for 10 minutes.

✦ Cut tortillas into diagonal slices. Serve on serving platter with salsa. Garnish with cilantro.

Preparation time: 20 minutes   20 servings

BRIE EN CROUTE

2 sheets frozen puff pastry, thawed
1 (8-inch) round Brie cheese
Apricot preserves
1/4 cup whipping cream
1 egg yolk

✦ Roll puff pastry dough into 24-inch circle. Place cheese
in center; spoon a generous amount of preserves on top
of cheese. Gather pastry together to enclose cheese, tying
excess dough at center with cotton twine to hold. Trim
excess dough; place cheese on parchment-lined baking
sheet. Chill for 1 hour or longer.
✦ Beat cream and egg yolk in bowl. Brush mixture
over pastry.
✦ Bake at 400 degrees for 35 to 40 minutes or until pastry
is puffed and golden brown. Reduce oven temperature
during baking if pastry browns too rapidly.
✦ Remove to wire rack to cool. Serve warm or at room
temperature with crackers.

Preparation time: 30 minutes   8 servings

BAKED BRIE IN PHYLLO

2 tablespoons peach or raspberry preserves
2 (4- to 6-ounce) packages Brie cheese wedges
6 sheets frozen phyllo dough, thawed
1/2 cup melted butter
Fresh dillweed and grapes

✦ Spread preserves on top of cheese. Wrap each piece of
cheese in several sheets of phyllo dough brushed with
melted butter, turning with addition of each sheet for
even wrapping. Cover unused dough with damp cloth to
prevent drying. Brush outside of dough with melted
butter. Place on shallow baking pan; cover. Chill until
baking time.
✦ Bake at 425 degrees for 18 to 20 minutes or until
golden brown. Let stand for 10 minutes. Top with fresh
dill and grapes. Serve with sliced fruit and a glass of wine.

Preparation time: 15 minutes   16 servings

The 300-ton ship
that carried Penn to
the New World in
1682 was christened
the "Welcome."

William Penn named the first English settlement in Pennsylvania "Chester" for the city that one of his fellow Quaker passengers had left to come to the New World.

FETA CHEESE SPREAD

1/2 cup mayonnaise
12 ounces cream cheese, softened
8 ounces feta cheese, crumbled
1 clove of garlic, minced
1/4 teaspoon dried dill
1/4 teaspoon dried marjoram
1/4 teaspoon dried basil
1/4 teaspoon dried thyme
1/4 teaspoon salt

✦ Combine mayonnaise, cream cheese, feta cheese, garlic, dill, marjoram, basil, thyme and salt in food processor container. Process until well blended. Spoon into crock. Chill until serving time. Serve with crackers.

Preparation time: 15 minutes   12 servings

GOAT CHEESE WITH TOMATOES

6 sun-dried tomato halves
1 teaspoon pressed garlic
2 tablespoons olive oil
1 tablespoon chopped fresh rosemary
1 French baguette
Olive oil
1 (10-ounce) package goat cheese

✦ Cover tomatoes with boiling water in bowl; let stand for 5 minutes. Drain tomatoes; chop. Combine tomatoes, garlic, 2 tablespoons olive oil and rosemary in bowl; mix well. Chill, covered, for up to 4 hours.
✦ Cut baguette into thin slices; brush with olive oil. Place on baking sheet.
✦ Bake at 350 degrees for 8 minutes or until light brown.
✦ Place goat cheese on serving plate; spread marinated tomatoes over top. Serve with toasted baguette slices.

Preparation time: 15 minutes   8 servings

GOAT CHEESE AND PESTO TORTE

8 ounces cream cheese, softened
12 ounces Montrachet goat cheese
1 cup butter, softened
1 cup basil pesto
1 cup drained, minced sun-dried tomatoes

✦ Combine cheeses and butter in bowl; beat until well blended and fluffy. Line 8-inch cake pan with dampened cheesecloth, leaving enough on sides to cover top.
✦ Layer 1/3 of the cheese mixture, 1/2 of the pesto, 1/3 of the cheese mixture, remaining pesto and remaining cheese mixture in cake pan. Cover with plastic wrap; fold cheesecloth over top. Chill for 1 hour to 3 days.
✦ Fold back cheesecloth from top of torte; remove plastic wrap. Invert torte on serving plate; remove cheesecloth. Top with sun-dried tomatoes.
✦ Serve with bland crackers. Nice colorful presentation for the holidays.

Preparation time: 15 minutes   16 servings

MARINATED MOZZARELLA

1 3/4 cups olive oil
2 tablespoons fresh rosemary, crumbled
2 large cloves of garlic, slivered
16 ounces whole-milk mozzarella cheese
Salt to taste
4 large sprigs of fresh rosemary

✦ Combine olive oil, dried rosemary and half the garlic in saucepan. Simmer for 2 minutes, stirring occasionally. Cool to room temperature.
✦ Cut cheese into 3/4-inch cubes. Place cheese and remaining garlic in 1-quart jar with tightfitting lid. Strain olive oil mixture through sieve into jar. Add salt; push fresh rosemary sprigs down into jar.
✦ Chill, covered, for 24 hours or longer. Garnish with cherry tomatoes and rosemary sprigs. Serve cheese at room temperature with crackers.
✦ For a spicier version, add 2 tablespoons garlic olive oil.

Preparation time: 12 minutes   6 servings

The recorded sale of land from the Lenni-Lenape Indians to William Penn was on the 12th of April, 1682.

MONTRACHET BITES

16 slices French bread
8 ounces Montrachet goat cheese
1 (4-ounce) jar marinated roasted peppers

✦ Place bread on baking sheet. Broil for 1 to 2 minutes on each side or until light brown.
✦ Spread cheese generously on each bread slice. Cut peppers into 1-inch pieces; sprinkle over cheese. Place on serving platter.
✦ May substitute marinated sun-dried tomatoes for peppers.

Preparation time: 10 minutes   8 servings

SALMON AND SMOKED GOUDA PATE

7 ounces smoked Gouda cheese, shredded
3 ounces cream cheese, cubed
3 tablespoons milk
1/4 cup margarine, softened
1/3 cup mayonnaise
1/4 cup chopped green onions
2 tablespoons fresh lemon juice
1/4 teaspoon garlic salt
Several dashes of Tabasco sauce
1 (14-ounce) can plus 1 (7-ounce) can salmon
1/3 cup sliced almonds, toasted

✦ Combine softened cheeses and milk in food processor container. Process until blended. Spoon into bowl.
✦ Place margarine in food processor. Process until fluffy. Add mayonnaise, green onions, lemon juice, garlic salt, Tabasco sauce and salmon. Process until well blended.
✦ Line bottom and sides of 4x8-inch loaf pan with plastic wrap. Sprinkle almonds in pan; add half the salmon mixture, spreading evenly. Add cheese mixture; spread remaining salmon mixture on top. Cover with plastic wrap. Chill for 6 to 24 hours.
✦ Remove cover. Invert onto lettuce-lined salad plate; remove plastic wrap. Garnish with lemon slices. Serve with crackers.

Preparation time: 30 minutes   16 servings

SMOKED TUNA MOUSSE

1 cup ricotta cheese
1 cup (3¹/₂-ounces) coarsely flaked smoked tuna
2 tablespoons prepared horseradish, drained
1 tablespoon chopped fresh dill
2 teaspoons fresh lemon juice
Salt and freshly ground pepper to taste
2 tablespoons chopped scallions

✦ Place ricotta cheese in food processor container. Process until consistency of sour cream. Combine cheese, half the tuna, horseradish, dill, lemon juice, salt and pepper in bowl; mix well. Fold in remaining tuna and scallions. Spoon into ramekins. Chill until serving time.
✦ Serve with crackers or sliced baguette.

Preparation time: 15 minutes   10 servings

SMOKED TUNA PATE

1 pound smoked tuna, skinned, flaked
12 ounces cream cheese, softened, chopped
6 tablespoons unsalted butter, softened, chopped
1 medium red onion, minced
¹/₄ cup chopped fresh dill
2 tablespoons drained capers
3 tablespoons fresh lemon juice
2 tablespoons cognac
Freshly ground pepper to taste

✦ Beat tuna, cream cheese and butter in mixing bowl until well mixed. Add onion, dill, capers, lemon juice, cognac and pepper. Mix well but do not overbeat; pâté should have some texture.
✦ Chill in serving bowl for several hours to mellow flavors. Serve with crackers or French bread slices.

Preparation time: 15 minutes   3 cups

The name Merion
has two origins in
the Welsh language:
"Merionethshire"
refers to a dairy
farm, "Meriawn" to
a Welsh chieftain
who lived around
800 B.C. in the
mountainous region
of North Wales.

✦

Bala Cynwyd is
named for a town
in Wales.

CHICKEN AND BACON BITES

12 ounces boneless skinless chicken breasts
1/4 cup orange marmalade
2 tablespoons soy sauce
1/2 teaspoon ground ginger
1/4 teaspoon garlic powder
12 slices bacon, partially cooked
1 (8-ounce) can whole water chestnuts

✦ Rinse chicken; pat dry. Cut into 24 bite-size pieces.
Marinate chicken in mixture of marmalade, soy sauce,
ginger and garlic powder in shallow dish, covered, in
refrigerator for 30 minutes or longer.

✦ Cut bacon slices into halves. Cool slightly. Cut water
chestnuts into halves. Drain chicken. Wrap bacon to
enclose 1 piece chicken and 1 piece water chestnut;
secure with wooden pick. Place on rack in broiler pan.

✦ Broil 4 to 5 inches from heat source for 3 to 5 minutes
or until cooked through, turning once.

Preparation time: 15 minutes   6 servings

CREAM CHEESE CHICKEN BITES

8 ounces cream cheese, softened
1/2 teaspoon each fresh lemon juice and dried basil
1/4 teaspoon onion salt
1/8 teaspoon dried oregano
1 cup finely chopped cooked chicken
1/3 cup finely chopped celery
1 (2-ounce) jar chopped pimento, drained
2 (8-count) cans crescent dinner rolls
1 egg, beaten
1 1/2 teaspoons sesame seeds

✦ Combine first 8 ingredients in bowl. Separate dough into
rectangles; seal perforations. Spread with chicken mixture,
leaving 1/2 inch space on one long edge. Roll each from
long edge to enclose filling; seal edges and brush with egg.
Sprinkle with sesame seeds; cut each roll into 4 pieces.
Place seam side down on lightly greased baking sheet.

✦ Bake at 375 degrees for 15 to 20 minutes or until
golden brown.

Preparation time: 30 minutes   8 servings

SPICY GARLIC CHICKEN PIZZA

16 ounces boneless skinless chicken breasts
1/2 cup sliced green onions
2 cloves of garlic, minced
2 tablespoons rice or white wine vinegar
2 tablespoons reduced-sodium soy sauce
1 tablespoon olive or vegetable oil
1/2 teaspoon crushed red pepper
1/4 teaspoon black pepper
1 tablespoon olive oil
1 tablespoon cornstarch
1 (16-ounce) package pizza bread or focaccia
1/2 cup shredded Monterey Jack cheese
1/2 cup shredded mozzarella cheese
2 tablespoons pine nuts, toasted

✦ Rinse chicken; pat dry. Cut into 1/2-inch pieces. Combine
half the green onions, garlic, vinegar, soy sauce, 1
tablespoon oil and peppers in bowl; mix well. Add
chicken, stirring to coat. Chill, covered, for 30 minutes.
Drain, reserving marinade.

✦ Sauté chicken in 1 tablespoon hot oil in skillet for 3 or 4
minutes or until center is no longer pink. Stir cornstarch
into reserved marinade. Add to chicken. Cook until thick
and bubbly, stirring constantly. Spoon onto top of bread
on baking sheet. Sprinkle with cheeses.

✦ Bake, uncovered, at 400 degrees for 10 to 12 minutes.
Sprinkle with remaining green onions and pine nuts.
Bake for 2 minutes longer. Cut into wedges. Serve hot.

Preparation time: 45 minutes   8 servings

MUSTARD GLAZE

1/2 cup packed brown sugar

1/3 cup Dijon mustard

3 tablespoons cider vinegar

1 tablespoon molasses

2 teaspoons dry mustard

✦

Combine all glaze ingredients in saucepan. Bring to a boil over medium heat, stirring frequently. Cool slightly.

ROSEMARY BABY BACK RIBS

5 pounds pork baby back ribs
3 teaspoons fresh rosemary
3 to 4 medium cloves of garlic, minced
Salt and pepper to taste
Mustard Glaze (at left)

✦ Have butcher cut pork ribs in half lengthwise. Rub both sides of ribs with rosemary and garlic; sprinkle with salt and pepper. Arrange on baking pan.
✦ Bake meat-side up, at 350 degrees for 1 hour. Remove from pan, brush ribs with glaze and grill for 15 minutes, turning often.
✦ Serve ribs with remaining glaze.

Preparation time: 20 minutes   12 to 16 servings

SUPER BOWL REUBEN ROLLS

1/3 cup mayonnaise
1 1/2 tablespoons Dijon mustard
1/2 teaspoon caraway seeds
6 ounces corned beef, finely chopped
6 ounces Swiss cheese, shredded
1 cup drained sauerkraut
1 package refrigerator pizza crust dough

✦ Combine mayonnaise, mustard, caraway seeds, corned beef and cheese in bowl; mix well. Rinse sauerkraut; drain. Pat dry with paper towels. Add to mixture; toss to mix.
✦ Unroll dough on large ungreased baking sheet, stretching to 12x14-inch rectangle. Cut dough lengthwise in half.
✦ Spoon half the mixture onto each rectangle, spreading to 1 inch from edges. Roll as for jelly roll from long side to enclose filling; pinch dough to seal edges. Arrange seam side down 3 inches apart.
✦ Bake at 400 degrees for 10 minutes or until golden brown. Let stand for 5 minutes. Cut into 1-inch slices.
✦ May slice a little thicker and serve for lunch.

Preparation time: 10 minutes   20 servings

GINGER SAUSAGE BALLS

1½ pounds bulk sausage
1 medium clove of garlic, minced
2 tablespoons chopped candied ginger
2 teaspoons minced fresh ginger
2 egg yolks
2 egg whites, stiffly beaten
1 cup bread crumbs
Marmalade Horseradish Sauce (at right)

✦ Combine sausage, garlic, gingers and egg yolks in bowl;
  mix well. Fold in egg whites and bread crumbs. Shape
  into small balls; place on baking sheet.
✦ Bake at 375 degrees for 18 minutes. Serve with
  Marmalade Horseradish Sauce. May freeze after baking
  for 8 minutes and bake for the remaining 10 minutes
  just before serving.

Preparation time: 30 minutes   16 servings

CRAB PIZZA APPETIZER

½ cup mayonnaise
1 teaspoon fresh lemon juice
¼ teaspoon curry powder
⅛ teaspoon salt
8 ounces fresh backfin crab meat
1 cup shredded Swiss cheese
1 thin partially baked pizza crust
1 tablespoon chopped green onions

✦ Mix mayonnaise, lemon juice, curry powder and salt in
  bowl. Add crab meat and cheese; mix well. Chill, covered,
  until baking time. Place pizza crust on baking pan.
  Spread crab mixture over top; sprinkle with green onions.
✦ Bake at 450 degrees for 9 to 10 minutes or until topping
  is puffed and brown. Cut into small wedges. Serve
  immediately. Slide pizza directly onto oven shelf for last
  minute or two of baking for a crisp crust.

Preparation time: 15 minutes   8 servings

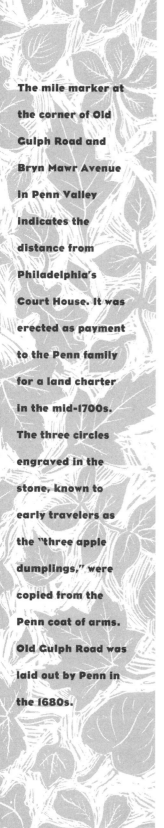

SPICY CRAB SPREAD

11 ounces cream cheese, softened
2 tablespoons chopped onion
2 tablespoons Worcestershire sauce
2 tablespoons mayonnaise
2 tablespoons fresh lemon juice
1/2 (12-ounce) bottle chili sauce
4 ounces fresh crab meat
Fresh Italian parsley

✦ Process cream cheese, onion, Worcestershire sauce, mayonnaise and lemon juice in food processor until mixed. Spoon onto serving plate; spread chili sauce over top. Sprinkle with crab meat; garnish with Italian parsley.
✦ Serve with crackers.

Preparation time: 30 minutes   8 servings

CLAMS CASINO BAKE

1 can minced clams
1/2 teaspoon fresh lemon juice
1 small onion, finely chopped
1 clove of garlic, minced
1/4 green bell pepper, finely chopped
1/4 cup butter
1/2 teaspoon dried oregano
Dash each of cayenne and Tabasco sauce
1/2 teaspoon dried parsley
4 slices bacon, crisp-cooked, crumbled
1/4 cup bread crumbs
Mozzarella cheese, shredded
Parmesan cheese, shredded
Paprika to taste

✦ Simmer clams with liquid and lemon juice in saucepan for 15 minutes, stirring constantly.
✦ Sauté onion, garlic and green pepper in butter in skillet. Add seasonings, parsley, bacon, bread crumbs and clams; mix well. Spoon into lightly greased 6-inch casserole. Sprinkle with cheeses and paprika.
✦ Bake at 400 degrees for 15 minutes. Serve with crackers.

Preparation time: 30 minutes   6 servings

SCALLOP PUFFS

1 pound fresh bay scallops, cut into quarters
2 teaspoons freshly grated lemon peel
3 cloves of garlic, minced
3 tablespoons unsalted butter
3 tablespoons chopped fresh dill
2 cups shredded Swiss cheese
2 cups mayonnaise
Pepper to taste
12 dozen (1-inch) white bread rounds, toasted
Paprika to taste

✦ Sauté scallops with lemon peel and garlic in butter in medium skillet for 2 to 3 minutes or until scallops are cooked through. Add dill. Cook for 30 seconds longer. Cool to room temperature.
✦ Stir cheese, mayonnaise and pepper into scallop mixture, mixing well. Chill, covered, for up to 3 days.
✦ Place heaping teaspoon of scallop mixture on rounds; sprinkle with paprika. Place on rack in broiler pan.
✦ Broil for 2 to 3 minutes or until golden brown.

Preparation time: 20 minutes   48 servings

SMOKED SALMON CROUTONS

2 tablespoons honey mustard
1 tablespoon Dijon mustard
1 tablespoon finely chopped red onion
1 tablespoon drained capers
2 teaspoons minced fresh dill
1 French bread baguette
Olive oil
4 ounces soft mild goat cheese
3 ounces thinly sliced smoked salmon

✦ Mix honey mustard, Dijon mustard, onion, capers and dill in bowl. Cut baguette into 12 diagonal slices 3/8 inch thick; place on baking sheet. Brush bread with olive oil.
✦ Bake at 350 degrees for 10 minutes or until toasted. Cool to room temperature.
✦ Layer cheese, mustard mixture and salmon on toast. Garnish with fresh dill.

Preparation time: 20 minutes   4 servings

SHRIMP WRAPPED IN BACON

1/2 cup olive oil
2 tablespoons Champagne vinegar
3 tablespoons chopped fresh dill
2 cloves of garlic, minced
1 pound large shrimp, peeled with tails intact
5 thin slices lean bacon

✦ Mix oil, vinegar, dill and garlic in bowl. Add shrimp. Chill, covered, for 8 to 10 hours; drain.

✦ Cut each bacon slice into thirds. Wrap shrimp in bacon; secure with wooden pick.

✦ Grill over hot coals for 7 to 8 minutes or until bacon is crisp and shrimp are cooked through. May also cook under hot broiler for 4 minutes on each side.

Preparation time: 15 minutes   8 servings

MARINATED SHRIMP

1/2 cup olive or vegetable oil
3 tablespoons red wine vinegar
3 tablespoons fresh lemon juice
1/3 cup chopped fresh parsley
1 clove of garlic, halved
1 bay leaf
1 teaspoon dry mustard
1 tablespoon chopped fresh basil
1 teaspoon salt
1/4 teaspoon pepper
2 pounds medium shrimp with tails, cooked, peeled
1 medium red onion, sliced
2 small lemons, sliced
1/2 cup sliced, pitted black olives

✦ Combine oil, vinegar, lemon juice, parsley, garlic, bay leaf, dry mustard, basil, salt and pepper in jar with tightfitting lid. Cover; shake well to mix. Layer shrimp, onion slices, lemon slices and black olives in bowl.

✦ Pour marinade over shrimp layers, tossing gently to coat. Chill, covered, for 8 hours, tossing occasionally.

✦ Drain shrimp. Arrange on lettuce-lined serving plate. Garnish with lemon slices.

Preparation time: 30 minutes   10 servings

SHRIMP AND JALAPENO CHEESE

1 pound large shrimp, cooked, peeled
3 pickled jalapeños, seeded
12 ounces cream cheese, softened
1 clove of garlic, minced
3 tablespoons chopped fresh cilantro
1/2 teaspoon salt
3/4 teaspoon chili powder
Pepper to taste
Multi-grain crackers
Stuffed green olives, sliced
Cherry tomatoes, cut into halves

✦ Coarsely chop shrimp. Chop jalapeños. Mix shrimp, jalapeños, cream cheese, garlic, cilantro, salt, chili powder and pepper in bowl. Chill until serving time.
✦ Place 1 teaspoon of shrimp mixture on each cracker. Garnish with olives and tomatoes. Serve immediately.

Preparation time: 30 minutes   30 servings

CURRIED SHRIMP PAPAYA

1 cup mayonnaise
1/4 teaspoon ground ginger
1/2 teaspoon curry powder
1 clove of garlic, minced
1 teaspoon honey
1 tablespoon fresh lime juice
2 ripe papayas, cut into halves
3/4 pound fresh shrimp, cooked, peeled

✦ Mix mayonnaise, ginger, curry powder, garlic, honey and lime juice in bowl. Fill papaya halves with shrimp; top with dollop of mayonnaise mixture.

Preparation time: 10 minutes   4 servings

To populate his settlement, William Penn included a condition in his bill of sale to the Welsh that their families be "seated" on the land in a completed structure within three years of purchase. Those who did not meet these terms lost their land rights and Penn was free to sell the land again. His word was final.

ZESTY ORANGE SHRIMP

1 cup mayonnaise
1 tablespoon dry sherry
$2^1/4$ teaspoons freshly grated orange peel
2 pounds large shrimp, peeled, deveined
3 tablespoons unsalted butter
3 tablespoons olive oil

✦ Combine mayonnaise, sherry and orange peel in bowl; mix well. Chill, covered, until serving time.
✦ Sauté shrimp in butter and olive oil in skillet until cooked to taste. Chill until serving time.
✦ Serve shrimp with mayonnaise for dipping. Garnish with orange segments and Italian parsley.

Preparation time: 25 minutes 12 servings

ROASTED ITALIAN PEPPERS

Red bell peppers
Olive oil to taste
Minced fresh garlic, parsley and basil to taste
Salt to taste
Cream cheese, softened
Assorted crackers

✦ Roast desired number of red peppers in 300-degree oven or on grill until skins turn completely black.
✦ Place hot peppers in brown paper bag made of non-recycled paper; close tightly. Let stand until cool. (This will help skins to loosen.)
✦ Remove skins, discard seeds and slice peppers into strips. Freeze peppers in desired amounts in sealable plastic bags if desired.
✦ Combine desired amount of freshly roasted or thawed peppers with desired amounts of olive oil, garlic, parsley and basil; toss lightly.
✦ Serve with cream cheese and crackers.

Preparation time: 45 minutes Variable servings

Welsh, one of the oldest languages still spoken, was prevalent in the Philadelphia region in the seventeenth century. In 1814, the genealogist Rev. Joseph Harris surmised in his book Seren Comer that Welsh was the spoken language of Adam and Eve.

SPICED PECANS

1 egg white
1 tablespoon water
1 pound pecans
1/3 cup sugar
3/4 teaspoon salt
1 teaspoon ground cinnamon
1/4 teaspoon ground cloves
1/4 teaspoon ground nutmeg

✦ Beat egg white and water in bowl with whisk until fluffy.
  Add pecans; toss to coat. Mix sugar, salt, cinnamon,
  cloves and nutmeg together. Sprinkle over coated pecans;
  toss to coat. Spread pecans on buttered baking sheet.
✦ Bake at 325 degrees for 30 minutes, stirring frequently
  and watching to be sure they do not burn. Chill for 1 to
  2 hours to avoid stickiness. Store in airtight container.

Preparation time: 8 minutes   10 servings

RANCH PRETZELS

1 envelope ranch salad dressing mix
1/2 teaspoon lemon pepper
1/2 teaspoon dried dill
1/2 teaspoon garlic powder
2 pounds pretzels
1 cup vegetable oil

✦ Mix salad dressing mix, lemon pepper, dill and garlic
  powder in bowl. Spread pretzels on baking sheet; sprinkle
  with mixture. Drizzle with oil, tossing to coat.
✦ Bake at 350 degrees for 15 minutes, turning several
  times and watching to ensure pretzels do not burn.
  Remove to paper towels to drain and cool. Store in
  airtight container.

Preparation time: 12 minutes   12 servings

GENERAL WAYNE INN

As the hard-working Welsh farmed the land, various
businesses grew up to support the growing population.
One of them was a way station with a full and rich history
now known as the General Wayne Inn.

Originally a one-acre plot in Merion, which William
Penn sold to Edward Rees in 1704, the site was later purchased
by Robert Jones for 20 shillings. Jones built a tavern and named
it the Wayside Inn. By 1709, traffic on the long and treacherous
Conestoga wagon trail heading west from Philadelphia to Ohio
had increased. Jones' Inn grew from a busy stagecoach stop to a
post office, a general store, and a tavern, eventually serving as the
center of a new town called Merioneth, derived from an ancient
Welsh war hero. The rich farm land around the Inn provided
many a dusty and tired traveler with a variety of inexpensive
locally grown produce and meats. A patron's full meal plus
housing for his horse cost as little as two shillings.

A few years later, the Wayside Inn was changed to
the William Penn Inn, to honor the man who had the vision to
settle this beautiful land. Many important people came to the
Inn, including Postmaster of the Colonies, Benjamin Franklin,
who in 1763 was exploring a better way to deliver the mail. It
was the first inn in the new charter and an outpost for British
soldiers in the Revolutionary War, which provided a wealthy
source of espionage for the Continental army. The William Penn
Inn witnessed many of the more colorful episodes of the era.

The Inn hosted its most notable reception in February
1795 to honor Major-General Anthony Wayne after his victory
over Indian tribes at the Battle of Fallen Timbers. Wayne,
brilliant and victorious in battle, but weary and ill in its
aftermath, was presented with a meal of such assortment that
his adoring officers and appreciative crowds would from then on
call the tavern the General Wayne Inn.

CREAMY ASPARAGUS SOUP

2^1/2 cups chicken broth
1 pound asparagus tips, cooked
Salt and pepper to taste
^{1}/2 cup whipping cream

✦ Blend broth, cooked asparagus, salt and pepper in blender.
✦ Combine with whipping cream in saucepan. Cook until heated through. Serve hot.
✦ May use fresh or frozen asparagus tips.

Preparation time: 20 minutes   4 servings

WHITE ASPARAGUS SOUP

2 pounds fresh white asparagus
5^1/2 cups chicken stock
^{1}/2 cup milk
2 cups whipping cream
1 cup minced onion
1 cup minced celery
1 cup butter
10 tablespoons flour
Salt and white pepper to taste
1 pound jumbo lump crab meat, picked

✦ Rinse and chop asparagus. Combine with chicken stock in saucepan. Cook until tender; drain and reserve cooking liquid. Purée asparagus in food processor.
✦ Heat mixture of milk and whipping cream in small saucepan; set aside and keep warm.
✦ Sauté onion and celery in butter in skillet. Stir in flour. Cook for 2 to 3 minutes or until tender. Add asparagus and reserved liquid. Cook until heated through, stirring until smooth. Stir in milk mixture. Season with salt and pepper. Stir in crab meat. Ladle into bowls. Garnish with parsley.

Preparation time: 20 minutes   8 to 10 servings

The General Wayne Inn near Montgomery Avenue and Meetinghouse Lane in Merion was a typical crossroads tavern that played many roles in the early 1700s. It served as a post office, and by 1746, had also expanded to a stagecoach stop, general store, hotel, restaurant and a provider of local news and lottery tickets. Edgar Allen Poe dined here in 1839 and scratched his initials in the windowsill as he worked on "The Raven."

SCALLOP AND CORN CHOWDER

2 slices bacon
1/2 cup chopped onion
2 1/2 cups peeled potatoes, cut into 1/2-inch pieces
1 (14-ounce) can chicken broth
1 (17-ounce) can cream-style corn
2 cups low-fat milk
8 ounces scallops
Salt and white pepper to taste
Chopped red and green bell peppers to taste

✦ Sauté bacon in saucepan until crisp. Drain, reserving
1/2 teaspoon drippings. Crumble bacon and set aside.
✦ Sauté onion in reserved drippings in saucepan for 5
minutes. Add potatoes and broth. Bring to a boil. Cook,
covered, over low heat for 20 minutes or until potatoes
are tender.
✦ Use slotted spoon to remove half the potato mixture to
food processor container fitted with metal blade. Add 1/2
cup of the broth. Process until smooth. Add processed
mixture to ingredients in saucepan. Stir in corn and
milk. Cook, covered, over low heat until hot, stirring
occasionally; do not boil.
✦ Stir in scallops, salt and white pepper. Cook, covered,
for 5 minutes. Ladle into bowls. Sprinkle with mixture of
bacon and peppers.

Preparation time: 1 hour   6 servings

SUMMER CUCUMBER SOUP

3 cucumbers, peeled, seeded, coarsely chopped
1 cup plain yogurt
2/3 cup sour cream
1/2 teaspoon English-style dry mustard
Salt and pepper to taste
1 cup finely chopped, seeded, peeled cucumber
1/4 cup chopped fresh mint leaves

✦ Purée coarsely chopped cucumbers, yogurt, sour cream,
mustard, salt and pepper in blender. Chill for 6 to 10
hours. Stir in finely chopped cucumber and mint.
✦ Ladle into bowls. Garnish with sprigs of mint.

Preparation time: 6 hours   6 servings

**Both Washington
and Lafayette lodged
at the General
Wayne Inn on many
occasions because of
its proximity to the
Paoli and Valley
Forge encampments.**

TOMATO CUCUMBER BISQUE

4 tablespoons butter
1 large onion, chopped
1/4 cup flour
4 cups chopped, seeded, peeled tomatoes
4 cups chopped, peeled, seedless cucumbers
4 cups chicken broth
Salt and freshly ground pepper to taste
1 cup chopped, peeled ripe avocado
1 cup whipping cream (optional)

✦ Melt butter in saucepan. Add onion. Cook until transparent, stirring constantly. Stir in flour until smooth.
✦ Add tomatoes and cucumbers. Whisk rapidly until well mixed. Add broth, salt and pepper. Simmer for 30 minutes. Cool slightly. Pour into blender container. Process until smooth.
✦ Strain soup if it is to be served cold. Return to heat and cook until heated through to serve warm.
✦ Stir in avocado and whipping cream.

Preparation time: 30 minutes   8 servings

CRAB BISQUE

6 scallions, finely chopped
1/4 cup unsalted butter, chopped
1/4 cup flour
3 cups milk
1 1/2 cups whipping cream
2 teaspoons salt
1 teaspoon Old Bay seasoning
1/2 teaspoon each ground mace and paprika
Tabasco sauce to taste
3/4 to 1 pound lump crab meat, picked

✦ Sauté scallions in butter in large, deep saucepan for 3 to 4 minutes or until softened. Add flour. Cook over low heat for 5 minutes.
✦ Add milk and whipping cream. Cook just until warm. Stir in seasonings and Tabasco sauce. Add crab meat; do not stir. Heat gently; do not boil.
✦ Ladle into bowls. Garnish with paprika.

Preparation time: 15 minutes   6 servings

LEMON CRAB SOUP

2 green onions
1 teaspoon minced garlic
4 cups chicken broth
1 cup cooked white rice
2 tablespoons fresh lemon juice
6 ounces lump crab meat, cleaned
1/8 teaspoon ground white pepper

✦ Chop white part and first 2 inches of green part of green onions. Mix garlic, green onions and 2 tablespoons of the chicken broth in 2 1/2-quart microwave-safe casserole. Microwave, covered, on High for 1 to 2 minutes or until green onions are soft.

✦ Stir in rice, lemon juice, crab meat, pepper and remaining broth. Microwave, tightly covered, on High for 3 to 4 minutes or until heated through.

Preparation time: 20 minutes   4 to 6 servings

LEMON EGGDROP SOUP

3 (14-ounce) cans chicken broth
1 onion, cut into quarters
1 clove of garlic, minced
2 carrots, sliced
1 stalk celery, chopped
1 sprig of fresh parsley, chopped
3 eggs
Juice of 2 lemons
1 1/2 cups cooked rice

✦ Combine broth, onion, garlic, carrots, celery and parsley in large saucepan. Simmer for 1 1/2 hours. Beat eggs with lemon juice in bowl. Add a small amount of hot mixture to egg mixture, stirring vigorously. Add egg mixture to hot mixture, stirring vigorously. Cook for several minutes. Stir in rice.

✦ Ladle into bowls. Garnish each serving with a thin slice of lemon.

Preparation time: 20 minutes   4 to 6 servings

The most common drink served in the early taverns was rum. Whiskey was not available until the early 1800s. Beer was a weak brew unrelished except to wash down a meal.

LENTIL SOUP AND SAGE FRAICHE

1 1/2 cups dried lentils
1/4 cup olive oil
1 carrot, peeled, finely chopped
White of 1 leek, finely chopped
2 stalks celery, finely chopped
1/2 cup chopped shallots
1 small head of garlic, peeled, crushed
1/4 cup chopped fresh Italian parsley
8 cups boiling water or chicken stock
Salt and freshly ground pepper to taste
2 tablespoons tarragon vinegar
8 to 10 fresh sage leaves or 1 teaspoon dried
1/2 cup crème fraîche or sour cream

✦ Soak lentils in cold water to cover for 2 to 3 hours.
✦ Heat olive oil in heavy casserole over medium heat. Add
  carrot, leek, celery, shallots, garlic and parsley. Sauté for
  5 minutes.
✦ Drain lentils and add to casserole. Add boiling water.
  Bring to a boil slowly; reduce heat. Simmer, covered,
  for 30 minutes or until lentils are tender, stirring
  frequently. Season with salt and pepper. Stir in vinegar.
  Ladle into bowls.
✦ Purée sage and crème fraîche in blender. Add dollop of
  mixture to each serving. Garnish with fresh sage.

Preparation time: 20 minutes   6 servings

MANHATTAN CHOWDER

4 cloves of garlic, minced
3/4 tablespoon olive oil
6 medium onions, chopped
3 green bell peppers, seeded, chopped
1 red bell pepper, seeded, chopped
9 medium potatoes, peeled, chopped
1 pound fresh mushrooms, sliced
8 carrots, peeled, sliced
9 stalks celery, chopped
1 (34-ounce) can chicken broth
2 (28-ounce) cans whole tomatoes, chopped
8 (7-ounce) cans minced clams
4 seafood bouillon cubes
8 cups water
1 tablespoon Old Bay seasoning
1 teaspoon dried thyme
1 teaspoon dried basil
1 1/2 teaspoons dried oregano
1 teaspoon pepper
3 dashes of Tabasco sauce

✦ Sauté garlic in olive oil in very large stockpot over medium heat. Add onions. Cook until opaque, stirring constantly. Add green peppers, red pepper, potatoes, mushrooms, carrots, celery, broth, undrained tomatoes, undrained clams, bouillon cubes, water, Old Bay seasoning, thyme, basil, oregano, pepper and Tabasco sauce in order given. Simmer, covered, for 1 hour or until flavors blend, adding more water if needed.

✦ May be frozen for up to 3 months. May be reheated on stove or in microwave.

Preparation time: 45 minutes   16 servings

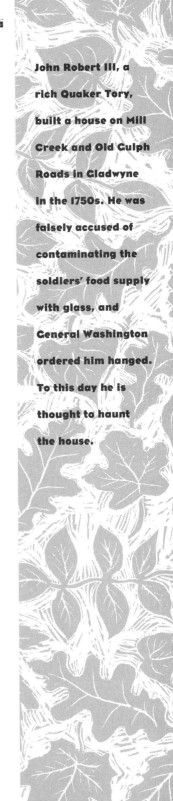

John Robert III, a rich Quaker Tory, built a house on Mill Creek and Old Gulph Roads in Gladwyne in the 1750s. He was falsely accused of contaminating the soldiers' food supply with glass, and General Washington ordered him hanged. To this day he is thought to haunt the house.

WILD MUSHROOM POTATO SOUP

2 tablespoons butter
1/4 pound fresh wild mushrooms, thinly sliced
2 tablespoons butter
3/4 pound fresh mushrooms, sliced
1 small onion, sliced
2 teaspoons fresh lemon juice
2 medium potatoes, peeled, sliced
2 (10-ounce) cans condensed chicken broth
1/3 cup flour
1/2 teaspoon salt
1/4 teaspoon pepper
3 cups half-and-half
1 1/2 tablespoons chopped fresh chives

✦ Melt 2 tablespoons butter in large saucepan. Add wild mushrooms. Sauté until tender. Remove wild mushrooms and set aside. Add remaining 2 tablespoons butter, uncooked mushrooms, onion and lemon juice to saucepan. Cook for 3 to 4 minutes or until tender, stirring constantly. Add potatoes and 1 can of the broth. Cook for 10 minutes or until potatoes are tender.
✦ Combine flour, remaining broth, salt and pepper in medium saucepan. Bring to a boil, stirring constantly, and cook until thickened. Cook over low heat for 5 minutes longer.
✦ Purée onion mixture 1/2 at a time in blender until smooth. Return to large saucepan. Stir in flour mixture. Add half-and-half; mix well. Cook until heated through; do not boil. Top with wild mushrooms and chives.

Preparation time: 45 minutes   6 servings

The first log cabin was built by the Swedes in Pennsylvania. English influence is seen in the Quaker meetinghouses, while many barns still standing throughout the area reflect German heritage.

MULLIGATAWNY SOUP

2 tablespoons chopped onion
1/4 cup each (1/2-inch) carrot and celery pieces
1 tablespoon chopped green bell pepper
1 large apple, peeled, cored, cut into 1/2-inch pieces
2 tablespoons butter
1/2 cup chicken broth
1/4 cup flour
3/4 cup chopped canned whole tomatoes
1/4 teaspoon each salt and curry powder
Pepper to taste
41/2 to 5 cups chicken broth
11/2 cups (1/2-inch) cooked chicken pieces

✦ Sauté first 4 ingredients in butter in heavy stockpot for 5 to 10 minutes or just until tender but not brown.
✦ Stir in mixture of 1/2 cup chicken broth and flour. Stir in remaining ingredients except chicken. Simmer for 1 hour. Stir in chicken.

Preparation time: 20 minutes   6 to 8 servings

SAUSAGE MINESTRONE SOUP

1 pound sweet Italian sausage, sliced
1 tablespoon vegetable oil
1 cup each chopped onion and carrots
1 teaspoon dried basil
2 small zucchini, chopped
1 (16-ounce) can Italian tomatoes
3 (10-ounce) cans beef broth
2 cups chopped green cabbage
1 large can white beans, drained
1/4 cup uncooked rice or barley
1/2 cup red wine
Freshly grated Parmesan cheese to taste

✦ Brown sausage in oil in 8-quart Dutch oven; drain. Add onion, carrots and basil. Cook for 5 minutes. Add zucchini, tomatoes, broth and cabbage. Simmer, covered, for 45 minutes. Add beans, rice and wine. Simmer for 10 to 15 minutes or until rice is tender.
✦ Ladle into bowls. Sprinkle with Parmesan cheese.

Preparation time: 25 minutes   8 servings

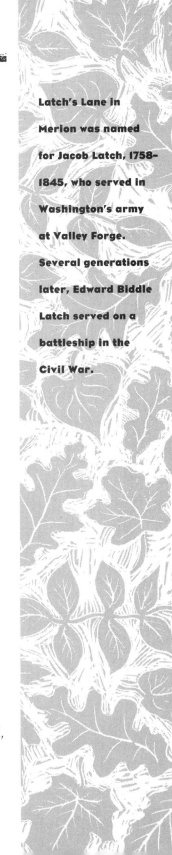

Latch's Lane in Merion was named for Jacob Latch, 1758-1845, who served in Washington's army at Valley Forge. Several generations later, Edward Biddle Latch served on a battleship in the Civil War.

The three-acre estate called "Lauraston" on Latch's Lane in Merion not only houses a famous Impressionist and Post-Impressionist art collection assembled by Dr. Albert Barnes, but also a beautiful garden planned by his wife, Laura Legget Barnes. A passionate gardener, she established a tuition-free three-year school of botany, horticulture and landscape architecture in 1940. Today there is a minimal charge to attend this exclusive school.

BASIL POTATO SOUP

1 large onion, finely chopped
1/2 cup sliced fresh mushrooms
2 teaspoons olive oil
3 to 4 potatoes, peeled, thinly sliced
1 (14-ounce) can beef broth
1 (14-ounce) can reduced-sodium chicken broth
1/2 cup buttermilk
1 tablespoon cornstarch
3 slices Canadian bacon, chopped
1 tablespoon fresh basil or 1 teaspoon dried
1/4 cup reduced-calorie sour cream

✦ Cook onion and mushrooms in hot oil in skillet over medium-high heat until onion is tender and lightly browned. Add potatoes and broths. Bring to a boil; reduce heat. Simmer, covered, for 30 minutes or until potatoes are tender.
✦ Mix buttermilk and cornstarch in small bowl. Stir into broth mixture. Stir in bacon and basil. Cook until thickened and bubbly, stirring frequently. Cook for 2 minutes longer, stirring constantly.
✦ Ladle into bowls. Top with sour cream.

Preparation time: 15 minutes   4 servings

WATERCRESS AND POTATO SOUP

1 small onion, finely chopped
2 bunches watercress, rinsed, finely chopped
8 ounces potatoes, peeled, chopped
1 tablespoon butter
1 cup half-and-half or milk
1 1/2 cups chicken stock
Salt and pepper to taste

✦ Cook onion, watercress and potatoes in butter in saucepan, covered, over low heat for 5 minutes, stirring occasionally. Stir in half-and-half, chicken stock, salt and pepper. Simmer, partially covered, for 30 minutes, stirring occasionally. Let stand until cool. Purée in blender.
✦ Heat to serving temperature; ladle into bowls. Garnish with additional watercress leaves.

Preparation time: 30 minutes   6 servings

SIMPLE SHRIMP BISQUE

1 large onion, chopped
1/2 cup finely chopped celery
2 cloves of garlic, minced
1/4 cup melted butter
2 tablespoons flour
2 tablespoons tomato paste
3 cups milk
2 cups chicken broth
1 bay leaf
1/4 teaspoon dried basil
1/2 teaspoon Tabasco sauce
1 1/2 pounds shrimp, peeled, deveined
1/4 cup chopped scallions

✦ Sauté onion, celery and garlic in butter in large stockpot.
Stir in flour and tomato paste. Add milk and chicken
broth gradually. Add bay leaf, basil and Tabasco sauce.
Bring to a boil; reduce heat. Add shrimp and scallions.
Cook for 5 minutes. Remove bay leaf and serve.

Preparation time: 40 minutes   6 to 8 servings

CHEESE TORTELLINI SOUP

1 tablespoon butter
4 cloves of garlic, minced
2 (14-ounce) cans chicken broth
9 ounces cheese tortellini
2 tablespoons freshly grated Parmesan cheese
Salt and pepper to taste
1 (14-ounce) can stewed tomatoes
1/2 bunch fresh spinach, stemmed, cleaned
6 fresh basil leaves, chopped, or 1 teaspoon
   crumbled dried
2 tablespoons freshly grated Parmesan cheese

✦ Melt butter in large heavy saucepan. Add garlic. Sauté
for 2 minutes. Stir in broth and tortellini. Bring to a
boil; reduce heat. Stir in 2 tablespoons cheese. Season
with salt and pepper. Stir in tomatoes, spinach and basil.
Simmer for 2 minutes.
✦ Ladle into bowls. Sprinkle with 2 tablespoons cheese.

Preparation time: 45 minutes   4 servings

In Pennsylvania,
it was customary
up to the early
1800s to charge
prisoners for the
food that they ate.
A long incarceration
could wipe out one's
entire savings and
property.

WHITE SAUCE

2 1/2 tablespoons butter

2 1/2 tablespoons flour

2 1/4 teaspoons salt

2 1/2 cups cold milk

✦

Melt butter in medium saucepan. Blend in flour and salt, stirring until smooth. Add milk gradually. Cook until mixture is thickened, stirring constantly.

FRESH TOMATO CREAM SOUP

3 1/2 to 4 cups fresh tomatoes, peeled, chopped
3 sprigs of fresh parsley
6 whole cloves
1/2 bay leaf
3/4 teaspoon whole black peppercorns
2 slices onion
2 teaspoons sugar
3/4 teaspoon salt
2 1/2 cups White Sauce (at left)

✦ Combine tomatoes, parsley, cloves, bay leaf, pepper, onion, sugar and salt in 3-quart saucepan. Bring to a boil; reduce heat. Simmer for 5 minutes. Remove bay leaf.

✦ Press through a food mill or sieve. Add enough boiling water to the purée if needed to measure approximately 2 cups. Stir the hot tomato purée gradually into the hot White Sauce; both must be at same temperature to prevent curdling. Serve immediately.

Preparation time: 30 minutes   6 to 8 servings

WINTER VEGETABLE SOUP

3 onions, coarsely chopped
2 tablespoons butter
1 pound lean ground beef
1 clove of garlic, minced
3 cups beef stock
2 (35-ounce) cans whole tomatoes
1 cup each chopped peeled potatoes, celery and carrots
1 cup dry red wine
1/2 teaspoon dried basil
1/4 teaspoon dried thyme
Salt and pepper to taste

✦ Cook onions in butter in large saucepan until translucent; set aside. Brown ground beef with garlic in skillet, stirring until crumbly; drain. Stir in onions. Add remaining ingredients. Bring to a boil; reduce heat. Simmer for 1 hour. Serve with crusty bread. Soup freezes well.

Preparation time: 30 minutes   8 servings

WEDDING SOUP

1 (5-pound) stewing chicken, cut into pieces
4 quarts chicken stock
1 (35-ounce) can plum tomatoes
4 stalks celery, chopped
2 tablespoons parsley flakes
2 large carrots, chopped
1 large onion, chopped
2 slices fresh ginger
1 teaspoon dried dill
1 (14-ounce) can chicken broth
Salt to taste
Meatballs (at right)
1/2 to 3/4 pound fresh spinach, chopped

✦ Place chicken and chicken stock in large stockpot. Bring
  to a boil over high heat. Reduce heat to medium; skim.
✦ Add tomatoes, celery, parsley flakes, carrots, onion,
  ginger, dill, chicken broth and salt. Simmer, covered,
  for 3 to 4 hours. Remove chicken, cool slightly, chop
  and return to stockpot. Chill for several hours; skim.
✦ Bring to a boil. Add Meatballs. Simmer for 10 minutes.
  Add spinach. Simmer for 5 minutes. Serve immediately.

Preparation time: 1 hour   12 to 16 servings

CURRIED ZUCCHINI SOUP

8 small zucchini, sliced 1 inch thick
3 cups chicken stock
1 cup chopped onion
1 clove of garlic, minced
1 teaspoon curry powder
1/2 cup each whipping cream and milk
Salt and pepper to taste

✦ Simmer zucchini with chicken stock, onion, garlic and
  curry powder in large saucepan until zucchini is tender
  when pricked with fork. Purée in blender. Pour into
  large bowl.
✦ Add cream, milk, salt and pepper. Chill for several hours.
✦ Ladle into bowls. Garnish each serving with 1 tablespoon
  sour cream and a sprig of parsley.

Preparation time: 20 minutes   6 servings

MEATBALLS

1/2 pound lean
ground veal

1/4 cup Italian
bread crumbs

1 egg, beaten

4 teaspoons
freshly grated
Parmesan cheese

1 teaspoon minced
fresh parsley

2 teaspoons
minced garlic

1/2 teaspoon
dried oregano

1/2 teaspoon
dried basil

1/4 teaspoon freshly
ground pepper

3 tablespoons
olive oil

✦

Mix veal, bread

crumbs, egg, cheese

and seasonings in

bowl. Shape into

3/4-inch meatballs.

Heat oil in large skillet

over medium heat.

Brown meatballs

in oil; drain on

paper towels.

CONESTOGA MILL TAVERN

The Lenni-Lenape Indians blazed many a trail
through the valley. The paths were circuitous and took strange
turns as they wound through the woods. The hills and valleys
dictated their irregular course and the unique locations of
the many homes and inns, such as the Conestoga
Mill Tavern, nearby. These dusty, worn trails
became the roads that carried settlers in loaded Conestoga
wagons to their new homes, their goods to markets, and vital
materials to the distant frontier forts. By 1791 traffic was so
heavy that the Pennsylvania Legislature authorized the
construction of the first turnpike in the country. Lancaster Pike
was completed by May, 1794, for $465,000. It skirted around
the Indian trails, which had to be maintained as working routes
while the turnpike was under construction. When complete, the
new road featured a regular stagecoach from Lancaster to
Philadelphia. The 66-mile trip took twelve hours.

The roads were mostly traveled by Conestoga wagons,
which were first developed in Pennsylvania in 1700. The wagon
drivers were a tough breed who smoked rank, pencil-thin cigars
called "stogies" and wielded huge, fourteen hundred-pound
horses to pull the wagons. It is believed that these men also
developed the American system of driving on the right side
of the road, since they were accustomed to walking alongside
the "wheelhorse," which was the rear horse on the
left-hand side. Conestoga wagons, with their team of four to six
horses, could move up to six tons of freight at a time, at a rate
of 12 miles a day. They made it possible for settlers to
conduct business in Philadelphia and for the wealthy to build
large homes on property far out of the city.

BLACK BEAN AND RICE SALAD

4 cups chicken stock
1 teaspoon salt
1 1/2 cups uncooked rice
8 ounces ham, chopped
1 cup each chopped green onions and fresh parsley
1/2 cup tiny peas, cooked
1/2 cup shredded carrot, blanched
1 cup cooked black beans
1/2 cup each chopped red and green bell pepper
1/2 cup chopped fresh basil
1/2 cup sliced olives
1/4 cup toasted pine nuts
1/4 cup capers
Salt and freshly ground pepper to taste
1 cup shredded Monterey Jack cheese
4 to 5 tablespoons olive oil
2 tablespoons red wine vinegar

✦ Bring chicken stock and 1 teaspoon salt to a boil in saucepan. Add rice; reduce heat. Cook for 15 minutes; drain well.

✦ Combine cooked rice, ham, green onions, parsley, peas, carrot, black beans, red pepper, green pepper, basil, olives, pine nuts, capers, salt to taste and pepper in bowl; mix well. Let stand until cool. Add cheese.

✦ Chill, covered, for 8 to 12 hours. Stir in mixture of oil and vinegar 4 hours before serving. Adjust seasonings if necessary. Serve at room temperature.

Preparation time: 40 minutes   12 to 16 servings

BLACK BEAN AND CORN SALAD

2 (16-ounce) cans black beans, rinsed, drained, or
   1 pound dried black beans, cooked, drained
1 1/2 cups fresh or frozen corn, cooked
1 1/2 cups chopped seeded tomatoes
1 large bunch scallions, thinly sliced
1/3 cup chopped fresh coriander
1/4 cup olive oil
1/4 cup fresh lemon juice
1/4 teaspoon fresh lime zest
1 to 2 teaspoons salt

✦ Combine beans, corn, tomatoes, scallions and coriander
in bowl. Whisk oil, lemon juice, lime zest and salt in
small bowl. Pour over bean mixture, tossing to coat.
✦ Chill, covered, until 1 hour before serving time. Serve at
room temperature or slightly chilled.

Preparation time: 1 hour   8 to 10 servings

COLD GREEN BEAN SALAD

2 cups water
Salt to taste
2 pounds fresh green beans, trimmed
3 shallots, minced
2 tablespoons balsamic vinegar
1/4 cup olive oil
3/4 cup chopped fresh basil leaves
2/3 cup freshly grated Romano cheese
Pepper to taste
2 tablespoons freshly grated Romano cheese

✦ Bring water and salt to a boil in large saucepan. Add
beans. Cook just until tender-crisp; drain. Rinse beans
with cold water; drain. Transfer to bowl.
✦ Combine shallots and vinegar in separate bowl. Whisk in
oil gradually. Stir in basil. Add enough basil mixture to
beans to coat. Add 2/3 cup Romano cheese just before
serving; toss gently. Season with salt and pepper. Place
beans on serving platter. Top with 2 tablespoons
Romano cheese.

Preparation time: 20 minutes   6 to 8 servings

Until about 1869, Bryn Mawr was called Humphreysville in honor of the Humphrey clan. It was renamed Bryn Mawr by the Pennsylvania Railroad because it sounded more distinguished. It means "high hill" in Welsh.

BALSAMIC DRESSING

Reserved liquid

3 tablespoons balsamic vinegar

1 tablespoon fresh lemon juice

1 teaspoon Dijon mustard

1 tablespoon minced onion

1 tablespoon minced fresh cilantro

1/2 teaspoon minced fresh tarragon

Salt and pepper to taste

✦

Pour reserved liquid into bowl. Whisk in vinegar, lemon juice, mustard, onion, cilantro, tarragon, salt and pepper.

SUMMER GARDEN MARINADE

1 pound fresh green beans, trimmed, cut into 3-inch
  pieces
1 pint cherry tomatoes
1/4 cup thinly sliced green onions
1 medium clove of garlic, minced
1/2 medium green bell pepper, chopped
1/2 cup extra-virgin olive oil
8 ounces small fresh mushrooms
Balsamic Dressing (at left)
Salt and pepper to taste

✦ Blanch green beans in boiling water for 4 minutes or until tender; drain. Rinse with cold water; drain. Place in large serving bowl. Add tomatoes and green onions.
✦ Sauté garlic and green pepper in olive oil in medium skillet over medium heat for 2 minutes. Add mushrooms. Cool. Drain, reserving liquid. Combine with beans and Balsamic Dressing. Season to taste.
✦ Chill, covered, for 5 hours or longer. Serve cold.

Preparation time: 45 minutes   6 to 8 servings

THREE-BEAN SALAD

1 (16-ounce) can black beans
1 (15-ounce) can pinto beans
1 (15-ounce) can cannellini or white kidney beans
1/2 red onion, finely chopped
1 stalk celery, sliced diagonally
3 tablespoons minced fresh parsley
3 ounces feta cheese, crumbled
1/3 cup red wine vinegar
1 clove of garlic, chopped
1/4 cup olive oil
Freshly ground pepper to taste

✦ Rinse and drain beans. Combine with onion, celery, parsley and cheese in serving bowl; toss gently.
✦ Whisk vinegar, garlic and olive oil together. Add to bean mixture; toss gently. Season with pepper. Let stand at room temperature for 30 minutes or chill for 8 to 12 hours before serving.

Preparation time: 15 to 20 minutes   8 servings

BROCCOLI CAULIFLOWER SALAD

1/2 cup mayonnaise
1/2 cup mayonnaise-type salad dressing
1/3 cup sugar
1 head fresh broccoli
1 head fresh cauliflower
1 small red onion, sliced
8 ounces bacon, crisp-fried, crumbled
1/2 cup shredded sharp Cheddar cheese

✦ Combine mayonnaise, mayonnaise-type salad dressing
  and sugar in bowl. Chill, covered, for 4 hours or longer.
✦ Break broccoli and cauliflower into bite-size pieces. Place
  in serving bowl. Add onion and bacon; toss gently. Add
  mayonnaise mixture, tossing to coat. Sprinkle with
  Cheddar cheese.

Preparation time: 30 minutes   6 to 8 servings

TWIGS SALAD

1 head fresh cauliflower
1 head fresh broccoli
1 medium red onion, minced
1 to 11/2 cups shredded sharp Cheddar cheese
1 cup raisins
1 cup unsalted peanuts
1 cup mayonnaise
1/4 cup white tarragon vinegar
1/4 cup sugar
1 pound bacon, crisp-fried, crumbled

✦ Break cauliflower and broccoli into bite-size pieces. Place
  in serving bowl. Stir in onion, cheese, raisins and
  peanuts.
✦ Whisk mayonnaise, vinegar and sugar in bowl. Add to
  broccoli mixture, tossing to coat.
✦ Chill, covered, for 1 to 2 hours. Add bacon just before
  serving; toss gently.

Preparation time: 30 minutes   8 servings

The first telephone rang in Lower Merion in the 1880s and the first switchboard was installed in Herman Stadelman's drugstore on Lancaster Pike and Anderson Avenue in Ardmore. By 1904, two hundred customers had telephones. The streets of Lower Merion were dark until 1880, when oil lamps were used to light the roads. Gas, and then electric, streetlights followed in 1901.

BALSAMIC VINEGAR DRESSING

6 tablespoons walnut oil or olive oil

3 tablespoons balsamic vinegar

1/3 clove of garlic, crushed

1/2 teaspoon coarse salt

Fresh pepper to taste

✦

Whisk oil, vinegar, garlic, salt and pepper in bowl.

FIELD GREENS WITH PEARS

1 head red leaf lettuce
2 to 3 bunches arugula
2 heads radicchio
Balsamic Vinegar Dressing (at left)
3 to 4 ripe pears, peeled, cored, sliced
3/4 cup walnuts, chopped, toasted

✦ Tear lettuce, arugula and radicchio into bite-size pieces.
✦ Mix with Balsamic Vinegar Dressing in bowl; toss to coat. Arrange on salad plates.
✦ Add pear slices and walnuts.

Preparation time: 20 minutes   6 to 8 servings

MANDARIN ORANGE SALAD

3 to 4 tablespoons butter
1 cup slivered almonds
1/4 to 1/2 cup sugar
1 head green leaf lettuce, torn into bite-size pieces
1 bunch green onions, chopped
1 (15-ounce) can mandarin oranges, drained
Poppy seed dressing (without honey)

✦ Melt butter in skillet over medium heat. Add almonds and sugar. Cook until almonds are golden brown, stirring constantly. Remove to baking sheet lined with waxed paper sprayed with nonstick cooking spray. Let stand until cool; crumble.
✦ Combine lettuce, green onions and mandarin oranges in serving bowl. Add poppy seed dressing and almonds just before serving.

Preparation time: 20 minutes   6 servings

RASPBERRY WALNUT SALAD

4 cups torn Boston lettuce
4 cups torn red leaf lettuce
3/4 cup walnuts, chopped, toasted
1 cup fresh raspberries
1 avocado, peeled, cubed
1 kiwifruit, peeled, sliced
Raspberry Salad Dressing (at right)

✦ Place Boston lettuce, red leaf lettuce, walnuts, raspberries, avocado and kiwifruit in serving bowl; toss gently. Serve with Raspberry Salad Dressing.

Preparation time: 15 minutes   6 servings

SEVEN-LAYER SPINACH SALAD

2 pounds fresh spinach, torn into bite-size pieces
10 hard-cooked eggs, sliced
1 pound bacon, crisp-fried, crumbled
1 head iceberg lettuce, shredded
1 cup chopped scallions
1 (16-ounce) package frozen peas, thawed
2 cups mayonnaise
2 cups sour cream
Juice of 1 lemon
1 tablespoon Worcestershire sauce
1 teaspoon dry mustard
1 tablespoon minced fresh dill
1 cup shredded Swiss cheese

✦ Layer spinach, eggs, bacon, lettuce, scallions and peas in large glass serving bowl.
✦ Blend mayonnaise, sour cream, lemon juice, Worcestershire sauce, mustard and dill in bowl. Spread over top of salad layers. Sprinkle with cheese.
✦ Chill, covered with plastic wrap, for 24 hours before serving.

Preparation time: 30 minutes   16 to 20 servings

RASPBERRY SALAD DRESSING

1/3 cup seedless raspberry jam

1/3 cup raspberry vinegar

1 cup vegetable oil

1 teaspoon poppy seeds

✦

Process jam and vinegar in blender at high speed for 20 seconds. Add oil gradually in a fine stream, processing until blended. Stir in poppy seeds.

HONEY-DIJON DRESSING

1/2 cup mayonnaise

1/2 cup sour cream

2 tablespoons honey

2 tablespoons Dijon mustard

✦

Blend mayonnaise, sour cream, honey and mustard in bowl. Chill, covered, until serving time.

ROMAINE CABBAGE SLAW

1 head romaine lettuce
1/2 head red cabbage
1/4 cup thinly sliced green onions
Honey-Dijon Dressing (at left)
1/2 cup broken pecans

✦ Cut romaine lettuce into 1/4-inch strips. Cut red cabbage into quarters; slice into thin strips. Combine lettuce, cabbage and green onions in large plastic container. Cover with paper towel. Close with sealable lid. Invert covered bowl in refrigerator. Remove lettuce mixture to serving bowl when ready to serve. Add Honey-Dijon Dressing; toss gently. Sprinkle pecans over top.

Preparation time: 15 minutes   8 servings

FRESH SPINACH AND FRUIT SALAD

8 cups torn fresh spinach or mixed baby greens
2 cups fresh cantaloupe balls
2 cups sliced fresh strawberries
1/4 cup seedless raspberry jam
1/4 cup raspberry white wine vinegar
2 tablespoons honey
1/4 cup olive oil
1/2 cup chopped macadamia nuts
Fresh raspberries to taste

✦ Place spinach on individual salad plates. Top with cantaloupe and strawberries. Combine jam, vinegar, honey and oil in bowl; mix well. Spoon jam dressing over top of cantaloupe and strawberries. Sprinkle with macadamia nuts. Top with fresh raspberries.

Preparation time: 30 minutes   6 to 8 servings

ITALIAN PASTA SALAD

16 ounces medium pasta noodles, cooked, rinsed
2 large tomatoes, seeded, chopped
2 (6-ounce) jars marinated artichokes, drained, chopped
1 green bell pepper, chopped
3/4 cup chopped red onion
5 ounces thinly sliced pepperoni (optional)
1 (6-ounce) can pitted small ripe olives, drained
8 ounces feta cheese, crumbled
Parsley and Basil Dressing (at right)

✦ Combine pasta, vegetables, pepperoni, olives and cheese in large serving bowl. Add dressing; toss to coat.
✦ Chill, covered, for 3 hours before serving.

Preparation time: 30 minutes   8 to 10 servings

ROASTED NEW POTATO SALAD

6 tablespoons olive oil
6 large cloves of garlic, chopped
1 teaspoon salt
1/2 teaspoon each ground pepper and crumbled dried thyme
1/4 teaspoon crumbled dried rosemary
2 1/2 pounds medium new red potatoes, scrubbed
5 tablespoons (about) olive oil
2 tablespoons white wine vinegar
2 teaspoons Dijon mustard
1/4 cup finely chopped shallots
Salt and pepper to taste

✦ Combine 6 tablespoons olive oil and seasonings in large bowl. Cut potatoes into eighths. Add to olive oil mixture; toss to coat. Spread in heavy broiler pan.
✦ Bake at 375 degrees for 55 minutes or until tender and golden brown, stirring occasionally. Cool; place in serving bowl.
✦ Scrape pan drippings into measuring cup. Add enough remaining olive oil to measure 6 tablespoons. Whisk vinegar and mustard in small bowl. Whisk in drippings mixture gradually. Stir in shallots.
✦ Pour over potatoes; toss to coat. Adjust seasonings. Let stand at room temperature for 1 hour before serving.

Preparation time: 1 hour and 20 minutes   8 servings

PARSLEY AND BASIL DRESSING

6 tablespoons olive oil

1 or 2 tablespoons red wine vinegar

1 clove of garlic, chopped

1/4 cup chopped fresh parsley

1 teaspoon dried basil

1/2 teaspoon dried oregano

2 teaspoons salt

1/2 teaspoon pepper

✦

Combine oil, vinegar, garlic, parsley, basil, oregano, salt and pepper in bowl; mix well.

Ardmore was

called Athensville

until 1873. The

community

renamed the town to

the Irish word

"Ardmore,"

meaning "high hill"

or "tract of wild

ground."

WARM RED POTATO SALAD

3 pounds small red potatoes, peeled
1/3 cup olive oil
3 tablespoons red wine vinegar
1 tablespoon Dijon mustard
1 teaspoon salt
1 teaspoon pepper
1/3 cup chopped green onions
1 tablespoon chopped fresh chives

✦ Cook potatoes in saucepan with enough water to cover until tender; drain.
✦ Whisk olive oil, vinegar, mustard, salt and pepper in bowl. Place warm potatoes in serving dish. Sprinkle with green onions and chives. Drizzle olive oil mixture over top, tossing gently to coat. Serve immediately.

Preparation time: 15 minutes   8 servings

ARTICHOKE AND RICE SALAD

1 (14-ounce) can artichoke hearts, drained, chopped
2/3 cup Italian salad dressing
1 (7-ounce) package chicken flavor rice mix
4 green onions, chopped
1/2 cup chopped green bell pepper
1 (3-ounce) jar pimento-stuffed olives, drained, sliced
3/4 teaspoon curry powder
1/2 cup mayonnaise

✦ Mix artichokes with Italian dressing in bowl. Chill, covered, for 3 hours. Drain, reserving marinade.
✦ Prepare rice mix using package directions. Chill, covered, in refrigerator.
✦ Add green onions, green pepper and olives; mix gently. Add drained artichokes.
✦ Combine curry powder and mayonnaise in bowl. Add reserved marinade. Pour over rice mixture; mix well. Chill until serving time.

Preparation time: 20 minutes   6 to 8 servings

WILD RICE WITH VINAIGRETTE

1 cup wild rice, cooked
1 cup orzo or tiny bow tie pasta, cooked
1/2 red or green bell pepper, cut into 1/2-inch pieces
1/2 cup sliced pitted olives
1/3 cup chopped sun-dried tomatoes
2 tablespoons drained capers
Balsamic Vinaigrette (at right)
1/4 cup pine nuts, toasted

✦ Combine rice, orzo, red pepper and olives in bowl. Blanch
tomatoes in boiling water for 2 minutes; drain. Add to
rice mixture. Stir in capers. Add vinaigrette; toss to coat.
Chill, covered, for 4 hours. Add pine nuts before serving.

Preparation time: 25 minutes   6 to 8 servings

WINTER FRUITS

1/4 cup vegetable oil
1/4 cup fresh orange juice
3 tablespoons balsamic vinegar
1 tablespoon honey
1/8 teaspoon cracked pepper
2 medium pears, cored, cut into wedges
1 medium apple, cored, cut into wedges
2 teaspoons fresh lemon juice
2 medium pink grapefruit, peeled, sectioned
1 medium orange, sliced into wedges
1 cup red or green seedless grapes
1 head red or green leaf lettuce

✦ Process oil, orange juice, vinegar, honey and pepper in
blender. Chill, covered, until serving time.
✦ Brush pear and apple wedges with lemon juice.
✦ Arrange grapefruit, orange, pears, apple and grapes
decoratively on lettuce-lined serving platter. Chill,
covered with plastic wrap, for up to 4 hours. Drizzle
with orange juice mixture before serving.

Preparation time: 30 minutes   6 to 8 servings

BALSAMIC VINAIGRETTE

1/3 cup olive oil

1/3 cup balsamic vinegar

2 tablespoons snipped fresh basil or 1 teaspoon crushed dried basil

1 tablespoon finely chopped shallots or green onions

2 cloves of garlic, chopped

1/2 teaspoon pepper

✦

Combine olive oil, vinegar, basil, shallots, garlic and pepper in glass jar with lid. Cover and shake until well blended.

GORGONZOLA CHEESE DRESSING

4 ounces Gorgonzola cheese, crumbled

6 tablespoons vegetable oil

2¹/₂ tablespoons red wine vinegar

1¹/₂ tablespoons coarse-grain mustard

2 large cloves of garlic, pressed

2 teaspoons dried basil, crumbled

Pepper to taste

✦

Process cheese, oil, vinegar, mustard, garlic and basil in blender until smooth. Season with pepper. Chill, covered, until serving time.

BLACKENED STEAK SALAD

8 large unpeeled cloves of garlic
1 tablespoon olive oil
1 large green bell pepper
8 teaspoons steak blackening mix
4 top sirloin steaks, 3/4 inch thick
6 cups torn mixed greens
1 small sweet onion, thinly sliced
1 large tomato, cut into wedges
Gorgonzola Cheese Dressing (at left)

✦ Mix garlic and olive oil and spread on baking sheet. Bake at 400 degrees for 10 minutes or until garlic is tender. Let stand until cool. Press garlic between fingers to release skins; slice.

✦ Broil green pepper until all sides are blackened. Place green pepper in paper bag made of non-recycled paper. Let stand for 10 minutes to steam. Peel and seed green pepper; cut into strips.

✦ Heat large cast-iron skillet over high heat for 10 minutes. Rub 1 teaspoon blackening mix on each side of the steaks. Cook steaks on both sides in heated skillet to desired doneness. Let stand for 5 minutes on cutting board. Cut diagonally into thin strips.

✦ Divide mixed greens on 4 salad plates. Top each with steak strips, green pepper, onion slices and tomato wedges. Spoon Gorgonzola Cheese Dressing over top. Sprinkle with roasted garlic.

Preparation time: 45 minutes   4 servings

STEAK NICOISE AND POTATO SALAD

Brandy-Wine Marinade (at right)
3 pounds lean sirloin steak
1 cup beef broth
2 pounds white potatoes, cooked, sliced
1 small green bell pepper, sliced
1 small red bell pepper, sliced
2 tablespoons capers
1 cup olive oil
2 teaspoons mustard
1/4 cup fresh lemon juice
2 tablespoons minced shallots
1/2 teaspoon celery salt
3/4 teaspoon dried thyme
1/2 teaspoon dried basil
1/2 teaspoon dried tarragon
1 tablespoon chopped fresh parsley
Salt and pepper to taste
4 cups torn lettuce
2 tomatoes, cut into wedges
4 hard-cooked eggs, cut into wedges

✦ Pour Brandy-Wine Marinade over steak in baking dish or
glass bowl. Chill, covered, for 8 to 12 hours. Simmer
steak in remaining marinade and beef broth in large
skillet until tender. Chill, covered, for 3 hours.
✦ Remove steak to cutting board, discarding marinade
mixture. Slice steak into thin strips; place in bowl. Add
potatoes, green pepper, red pepper and capers; mix well.
✦ Combine olive oil, mustard, lemon juice, shallots, celery
salt, thyme, basil, tarragon, parsley, salt and pepper in
small bowl; mix well. Pour over steak mixture, tossing to
coat. Chill, covered, for 2 to 3 hours.
✦ Arrange steak mixture on lettuce on salad plates. Top
with tomato and egg wedges.

Preparation time: 45 minutes   8 servings

BRANDY-WINE MARINADE

2 cups red wine

1/4 cup brandy

3 carrots, cut into
3/4-inch slices

2 stalks celery, cut
into 3/4-inch slices

5 or 6 whole
cloves of garlic

1/2 teaspoon
dried thyme

1/2 teaspoon
dried sage

1/2 teaspoon allspice

✦

Combine wine
and brandy in bowl.
Add carrots, celery
and garlic. Stir in
thyme, sage and
allspice; mix well.

CREAMY CURRY DRESSING

1 teaspoon minced garlic

2 teaspoons minced, peeled fresh gingerroot

2 tablespoons butter

1/2 cup whipping cream

2 tablespoons white wine vinegar

2 teaspoons curry powder

Dried hot red pepper flakes to taste

2 tablespoons mango chutney, drained, minced

✦

Sauté garlic and gingerroot in butter in skillet over low heat until garlic is tender; remove from heat. Add whipping cream and whisk until slightly thickened. Whisk in vinegar, curry powder, red pepper flakes and chutney.

CHICKEN CURRIED PASTA SALAD

2 whole boneless skinless chicken breasts
2 cups chicken stock
8 ounces rotelle pasta
10 cherry tomatoes, quartered
1 zucchini, cut into pieces, blanched
4 scallions, thinly sliced
2 tablespoons minced fresh basil leaves
Creamy Curry Dressing (at left)
Salt and pepper to taste

✦ Rinse chicken. Poach in chicken stock until tender; drain. Cut into bite-size pieces. Cook pasta in boiling water in saucepan for 10 minutes or until tender. Rinse with cold water; drain. Mix pasta, chicken, tomatoes, zucchini, scallions and basil leaves in large bowl. Add Creamy Curry Dressing, tossing to coat. Season with salt and pepper.

Preparation time: 25 minutes   4 servings

CHICKEN SPINACH SALAD

2 boneless chicken breasts, slightly flattened
6 tablespoons melted butter
3 tablespoons Worcestershire sauce
1/2 teaspoon paprika
1/2 cup red wine vinegar
4 teaspoons Dijon mustard
1 1/2 cups olive oil
6 tablespoons minced red onion
Salt and freshly ground pepper to taste
2 cups shredded fresh spinach leaves
2 cups thinly sliced red cabbage

✦ Rinse chicken; pat dry. Grill for 10 minutes on each side, brushing with mixture of butter, Worcestershire sauce and paprika. Cut chicken diagonally into thin slices.
✦ Combine vinegar and mustard in bowl. Whisk in olive oil slowly in a fine stream. Add red onion and season with salt and pepper.
✦ Combine spinach and cabbage in serving bowl. Arrange chicken over top. Add olive oil mixture.

Preparation time: 25 minutes   4 servings

CHICKEN PASTA SALAD

3 whole small chicken breasts
Salt and pepper to taste
16 ounces linguini, broken into 6-inch pieces
1 small green bell pepper, julienned
1 small red bell pepper, julienned
4 scallions, finely sliced
1 cup chopped salted roasted peanuts
Lemon-Ginger Vinaigrette (at right)
Peeled cucumber slices and watercress sprigs

✦ Rinse chicken; pat dry. Season with salt and pepper; place in baking dish. Bake at 375 degrees for 25 minutes. Cool. Slice thinly crossgrain.
✦ Cook linguini using package directions. Rinse with cold water; drain. Combine with chicken, bell peppers, scallions and peanuts in large bowl. Drizzle vinaigrette over salad; toss to mix. Top with cucumber slices and watercress.

Preparation time: 1 hour   8 to 10 servings

HONEY DIJON CHICKEN SALAD

3/4 cup mayonnaise
1/4 cup honey
1/4 cup Dijon mustard
1/2 teaspoon dried tarragon
4 boneless skinless chicken breast halves
6 cups torn assorted greens
1/2 cup thinly sliced red onion rings

✦ Blend mayonnaise, honey, mustard and tarragon in bowl. Reserve 1/2 cup. Rinse chicken; pat dry and place in shallow dish. Pour remaining mayonnaise mixture over chicken. Chill, covered, for 30 minutes to 8 hours.
✦ Grill chicken for about 10 minutes on each side or until tender. Slice into strips.
✦ Toss greens with onion rings. Arrange on serving platter. Top with chicken strips. Heat reserved mayonnaise mixture in saucepan over low heat. Drizzle over chicken.

Preparation time: 45 minutes   4 servings

LEMON-GINGER VINAIGRETTE

Juice of 1 lemon

1/4 to 1/3 cup red wine vinegar

1/3 cup sesame oil

1/3 cup vegetable oil

1/3 cup olive oil

2 tablespoons Dijon mustard

2 tablespoons brown sugar

2 cloves of garlic, minced

2 tablespoons finely chopped fresh gingerroot

Salt and pepper to taste

✦

Whisk lemon juice, vinegar, sesame oil, vegetable oil, olive oil, mustard, brown sugar, garlic, gingerroot, salt and pepper in bowl.

SOUTHWEST SPICE MIX

3 tablespoons chili powder

2 tablespoons ground cumin

1 tablespoon ground black pepper

1 tablespoon salt

1 tablespoon garlic powder

1¹⁄₂ teaspoons ground red pepper

◆

Combine chili powder, cumin, black pepper, salt, garlic powder and red pepper in small jar; mix well. Store for up to 3 months.

SOUTHWEST CHICKEN SALAD

4 medium boneless chicken breast halves
1 tablespoon Southwest Spice Mix (at left)
1 mango, chopped
1/2 medium green bell pepper, chopped
1/2 medium red bell pepper, chopped
3 scallions, thinly sliced
1 tablespoon chopped fresh cilantro or parsley
1/2 cup chopped jicama
Spicy Southwest Dressing (below)
4 (10-inch) flour tortillas
6 cups shredded Bibb lettuce

✦ Rinse chicken; pat dry. Coat chicken with Southwest Spice Mix in bowl. Chill, covered, for 4 hours.
✦ Cook chicken in large nonstick skillet sprayed with nonstick cooking spray over medium heat for 4 to 5 minutes on each side. Chill in bowl in refrigerator.
✦ Chop chicken. Return to bowl. Add mango, green pepper, red pepper, scallions, cilantro and jicama; mix well. Pour Spicy Southwest Dressing over top, tossing to coat.
✦ Press each tortilla into bottom of medium microwave-safe bowl. Microwave on High for 1¹⁄₂ minutes or until crisp. Remove bowl-shaped tortillas to individual serving plates. Spread lettuce inside each tortilla. Top with chicken mixture.
✦ May serve fajita-style or in pita bread halves with lettuce and chicken mixture inside.

Preparation time: 45 minutes   4 servings

SPICY SOUTHWEST DRESSING

2 teaspoons Southwest Spice Mix (at left)
2 tablespoons fresh lime or lemon juice
2 tablespoons vegetable oil
2 tablespoons water
1 teaspoon sugar

✦ Combine Southwest Spice Mix, lime juice, oil, water and sugar in bowl; mix well.

Preparation time: 5 minutes   4 servings

CHICKEN SALAD SANTA FE

3 pounds boneless skinless chicken breasts, cooked, cubed
1 (4-ounce) can green chiles, drained, chopped
1 small cucumber, peeled, cubed
2 stalks celery, sliced
1 red bell pepper, coarsely chopped
1 (16-ounce) can black beans, drained
1/2 cup fresh cilantro, coarsely chopped
1/2 cup each mayonnaise and sour cream
1/3 cup plus 1 tablespoon fresh lime juice
Tortilla chips, salsa and guacamole to taste

✦ Combine first 7 ingredients in large bowl. Add mixture
  of mayonnaise, sour cream and lime juice; toss to mix.
  Chill until serving time.
✦ Circle 4 dinner plates with tortilla chips. Spoon chicken
  mixture into center of each plate. Top with salsa and
  guacamole. Garnish with cilantro.

Preparation time: 45 to 60 minutes   4 servings

SHRIMP BASIL PASTA SALAD

1 pound large shrimp, peeled, deveined
1/2 cup olive oil
4 tablespoons fresh lemon juice
2 cups fresh basil leaves
1/8 teaspoon salt
Freshly ground pepper to taste
8 ounces fusilli or other twisted pasta, cooked, rinsed
1/2 cup each minced red bell pepper and purple onion
3/4 cup pitted kalamata olives, drained

✦ Cook shrimp in boiling water for 1 minute; drain.
✦ Process olive oil, lemon juice, basil leaves, salt and pepper
  in food processor container; process until blended.
✦ Combine pasta, shrimp, red pepper and onion in serving
  bowl. Pour basil mixture over top; toss to mix. Add
  olives. Serve at room temperature.

Preparation time: 30 minutes   4 to 6 servings

Bryn Mawr College was the first women's college on the Main Line. It was founded in 1885 by Dr. Joseph W. Taylor, a Quaker, who was also associated with the Haverford College for men. His goal was to establish a college for women that would equal the best male colleges in the country. Today, Bryn Mawr is one of the "Seven Sister" schools on the East Coast.

WYNNE WOOD

Thomas Wynne, a North Welshman, arrived with
William Penn in 1682 on the ship "Welcome." Wynne
eventually named his 442-acre holding "Wynne Wood."
He was prominent in the development of the area, serving as a
physician, a Quaker minister, and as a representative
and elected speaker of Philadelphia County's First Assembly.

Other famous original families who settled around
Wynne Wood bore the names of Jones, Wistar, Owen and Price.
In the late 1700s these families owned farms totaling over 600
acres of woodland, leaving only a small percentage for cultivation.
Most of the land was kept unplowed to supply firewood, fencing
and building materials for the owners.

Jonathan Jones built the mansion, "Wynne Wood,"
in 1818 using the vast supply of local materials. His son Owen,
who was born at Wynne Wood, became a congressman and
colonel in the Union Army. The magnificent house was
destroyed by fire in 1858, though most of its contents were
saved, and the mansion was rebuilt to its former elegance.
By the end of the 19th century, businessmen and their families
were moving in increasing numbers to Wynnewood,
Haverford and parts west of Philadelphia, staying close
enough to easily commute to the city.

ALMOND TEA BREAD

1/2 cup butter, softened
1 cup sugar
1 egg
1/2 cup evaporated milk
1/4 teaspoon almond extract
2 cups flour
1/4 teaspoon baking powder
1/4 teaspoon baking soda
1/4 teaspoon salt
1/2 cup slivered almonds

✦ Cream butter and sugar in mixing bowl until light and fluffy. Beat in egg. Stir in evaporated milk and flavoring.
✦ Mix flour, baking powder, baking soda and salt in bowl. Add to creamed mixture gradually, beating well after each addition. Stir in almonds. Pour into greased loaf pan.
✦ Bake at 350 degrees for 1 hour or until golden brown.

Preparation time: 25 minutes   8 servings

APPLE BREAD

1 1/2 cups flour
1 teaspoon cinnamon
1 teaspoon baking soda
3/4 teaspoon ground cloves
3/4 teaspoon salt
1/2 cup butter, softened
1 cup sugar
2 eggs
1/2 cup cold coffee
1 cup raisins
1/2 cup chopped pecans
2 large apples, peeled, chopped

✦ Sift flour, cinnamon, baking soda, cloves and salt into bowl. Cream butter, sugar and eggs in mixing bowl until light and fluffy. Add flour mixture gradually, beating well after each addition. Add coffee, raisins, pecans and apples; mix well. Pour into greased loaf pan.
✦ Bake at 350 degrees for 1 hour.

Preparation time: 30 minutes   8 servings

CARAMEL BANANA BREAD

2 cups unbleached flour
1 1/2 teaspoons baking soda
1 teaspoon salt
1 cup butter, softened
1 1/4 cups sugar
2 eggs, beaten
5 ripe bananas, mashed
1 teaspoon vanilla extract
1/4 cup buttermilk
Caramel Topping (at right)

✦ Sift flour, baking soda and salt together. Cream butter and sugar in mixing bowl until light and fluffy. Add eggs; mix well. Stir in bananas, vanilla and buttermilk. Add flour mixture gradually, beating well after each addition. Pour into 2 greased and floured 5x9-inch loaf pans.
✦ Bake at 350 degrees for 45 to 50 minutes or until loaves pull away from sides of pans. Cool completely.
✦ Pour Caramel Topping over bread. Broil for 5 minutes or until tops are bubbly.

Preparation time: 45 minutes   16 servings

BANANA-CHOCOLATE CHIP BREAD

2 cups flour
1 teaspoon baking soda
1/2 teaspoon salt
1/2 cup butter or margarine, softened
1 cup sugar
2 eggs
3 very ripe bananas, mashed
1 cup chopped pecans or walnuts (optional)
1 cup chocolate chips or carob chips

✦ Sift flour, baking soda and salt together. Cream butter, sugar and eggs in mixing bowl until light and fluffy. Add flour mixture gradually, beating well after each addition. Add bananas; mix well. Stir in pecans and chocolate chips. Pour into greased and floured loaf pan.
✦ Bake at 350 degrees for 45 to 60 minutes or until loaf tests done.

Preparation time: 15 minutes   8 servings

CARAMEL TOPPING

6 tablespoons butter

10 tablespoons packed brown sugar

5 tablespoons milk

✦

Melt butter in saucepan. Add brown sugar and milk. Cook until mixture is syrupy.

MACADAMIA NUT-BANANA BREAD

3/4 cup sweetened flaked coconut
2 1/4 cups flour
3/4 teaspoon baking powder
1/2 teaspoon baking soda
1 teaspoon salt
3/4 cup unsalted butter, softened
1 cup packed light brown sugar
1/2 cup sugar
1 1/2 teaspoons vanilla extract
3 eggs
1 tablespoon freshly grated lemon zest
1 1/3 cups mashed ripe bananas
3 tablespoons sour cream
3/4 cup chopped macadamia nuts

✦ Toast coconut lightly on baking sheet and set aside.
✦ Sift flour, baking powder, baking soda and salt together.
Cream butter, brown sugar and sugar in mixing bowl
until light and fluffy. Beat in vanilla. Add eggs 1 at a
time, beating well after each addition. Add lemon zest,
bananas and sour cream; mix until blended. Add flour
mixture; beat just until mixed. Stir in macadamia nuts
and toasted coconut. Pour into 2 buttered and floured
loaf pans.
✦ Bake at 350 degrees for 50 to 60 minutes or until
wooden pick comes out clean. Cool in pans for 15
minutes. Remove to wire racks to cool completely.

Preparation time: 40 minutes   16 servings

CARAMEL GINGERBREAD

1 cup molasses
2 teaspoons baking soda
1 teaspoon each cinnamon and ginger
1/4 teaspoon nutmeg
1/2 cup sugar
1/2 cup melted butter
2 cups flour
2 egg yolks, beaten
1 cup boiling water
2 egg whites, stiffly beaten
Caramel Sauce (at right)
Toasted pecans

✦ Mix molasses, baking soda and spices in bowl. Add sugar, butter, flour, egg yolks and water; mix well. Fold in egg whites. Pour into greased 8x8-inch square pan.
✦ Bake at 350 degrees for 35 to 40 minutes or until gingerbread tests done. Cool. Cut into squares. Serve with Caramel Sauce. Garnish with toasted pecans.

Preparation time: 30 minutes   12 servings

CRANBERRY NUT BREAD

2 cups sifted flour
1 cup sugar
1 1/2 teaspoons baking powder
1 teaspoon salt
1/2 teaspoon baking soda
1/4 cup shortening
3/4 cup fresh orange juice
1 teaspoon freshly grated orange peel
1 egg, beaten
1/2 cup chopped walnuts or pecans
1 cup coarsely chopped fresh cranberries

✦ Sift dry ingredients into bowl. Cut in shortening. Add mixture of orange juice, orange peel and egg; stir just until moistened. Fold in walnuts and cranberries. Spoon into greased and floured 5x9-inch loaf pan.
✦ Bake at 350 degrees for 1 hour. Cool in pan.

Preparation time: 20 minutes   8 servings

CARAMEL SAUCE

2 egg yolks

1 cup whipping cream

1 (1-pound) package light brown sugar

1 tablespoon butter

1 teaspoon vanilla extract

1/8 teaspoon salt

✦

Combine egg yolks, whipping cream and brown sugar in double boiler over hot water. Cook until creamy, stirring constantly. Stir in butter. Cool slightly. Beat in vanilla and salt.

LIME GLAZE

1/2 cup sugar

3 tablespoons fresh lime juice

Finely shredded fresh lime peel to taste

◆

Combine sugar, lime juice and lime peel in small saucepan. Cook over low heat until sugar dissolves, stirring constantly.

SWEET LIME BREAD

3 cups flour
2 teaspoons baking powder
1 teaspoon salt
1 cup butter or margarine, softened
2 cups sugar
2 tablespoons freshly grated lime peel
4 eggs, beaten
1 cup milk
Lime Glaze (at left)

◆ Sift dry ingredients together. Cream butter, sugar and grated lime peel in mixing bowl. Add dry ingredients and mixture of eggs and milk alternately, beating well after each addition. Pour into 2 lightly greased 4x8-inch or 5 miniature loaf pans.

◆ Bake at 350 degrees for 55 minutes or until golden brown. Pierce several holes in top of loaves. Drizzle with Lime Glaze.

Preparation time: 20 minutes   16 servings

ALMOND POPPY SEED BREAD

1 1/4 cups sugar
1 1/4 cups vegetable oil
1 cup evaporated milk
3 eggs
1/4 cup milk
2 1/2 cups flour
2 1/4 teaspoons baking powder
1/8 teaspoon salt
1/4 cup poppy seeds
1 1/4 teaspoons almond extract
1 egg white, beaten
2 tablespoons slivered almonds

◆ Mix sugar, oil, evaporated milk, eggs, and milk in bowl. Add mixture of dry ingredients; mix well. Stir in poppy seeds and flavoring. Pour into 2 greased loaf pans.

◆ Bake at 350 degrees for 40 minutes. Brush with egg white; sprinkle with almonds. Bake for 10 minutes longer. Remove to wire racks to cool.

Preparation time: 15 minutes   16 servings

RHUBARB BREAD

1 cup sour cream
1 teaspoon vanilla extract
1 teaspoon baking soda
1/4 teaspoon salt
1 1/2 cups packed light brown sugar
2/3 cup vegetable oil
1 egg
2 1/2 cups flour
1 1/2 cups chopped fresh rhubarb
1/2 cup chopped pecans
1/3 cup sugar
1 tablespoon melted butter
1 teaspoon cinnamon (optional)

✦ Mix sour cream, vanilla, baking soda and salt in small
  bowl. Mix brown sugar, oil and egg in large bowl. Add
  sour cream mixture and flour alternately, beating well
  after each addition. Fold in rhubarb and pecans. Pour
  into 2 greased and floured 4x8-inch loaf pans. Mix sugar,
  butter and cinnamon in bowl. Sprinkle over batter.
✦ Bake at 325 degrees for 45 minutes. Cool on wire rack.

Preparation time: 15 minutes   16 servings

STRAWBERRY BREAD

3 cups flour
1 teaspoon baking soda
1/2 teaspoon salt
1 tablespoon ground cinnamon
2 cups sugar
3 eggs, beaten
1 cup vegetable oil
1 (10-ounce) package frozen sliced strawberries (thawed)

✦ Combine flour, baking soda, salt, cinnamon and sugar in
  large bowl; mix well. Stir in mixture of eggs, oil and
  strawberries. Pour into 2 greased and floured 5x9-inch
  loaf pans.
✦ Bake at 350 degrees for 1 hour or until wooden pick
  comes out clean. Cool on wire rack.

Preparation time: 20 minutes   16 servings

Indian names,
identifying roads,
rivers and places,
are scattered
throughout Phila-
delphia and the Main
Line. They were not
introduced until the
19th century when it
became fashionable.

ZUCCHINI-SWEET POTATO BREAD

2 cups flour
2 teaspoons ground cinnamon
1 teaspoon baking soda
1/4 teaspoon baking powder
2 cups sugar
3/4 cup vegetable oil
3 eggs
1 teaspoon vanilla extract
2 cups each grated zucchini and peeled sweet potatoes
3/4 cup chopped pecans

✦ Sift flour, cinnamon, baking soda and baking powder together. Beat sugar, oil, eggs and vanilla in large bowl with wire whisk. Stir in zucchini and sweet potatoes. Add flour mixture and pecans; mix well. Pour into buttered and floured 5x9-inch loaf pan.

✦ Bake at 350 degrees for 1 hour and 20 minutes or until wooden pick comes out clean. Cool in pan on wire rack for 15 minutes. Remove to wire rack to cool completely.

Preparation time: 20 minutes   8 servings

APPLE-WALNUT MUFFINS

11/2 cups flour
1/2 teaspoon salt
1 teaspoon baking powder
1/4 cup butter or margarine, softened
1 cup packed brown sugar
1 teaspoon baking soda
1 egg
1/2 cup sour cream
1 teaspoon cinnamon
1 cup chopped walnuts
1 cup chopped tart apple

✦ Mix flour, salt and baking powder in small bowl with wire whisk. Cream butter, brown sugar and baking soda in bowl until light and fluffy. Add egg, sour cream and cinnamon; beat well. Add flour mixture; beat well. Fold in walnuts and apple. Spoon into greased muffin cups.

✦ Bake at 400 degrees for 20 minutes.

Preparation time: 20 minutes   12 servings

To this day, Wynnewood is a distinguished address. Walter Annenberg, a wealthy philanthropist, lives here. He built a communications empire of newspapers, magazines, radio stations and other enterprises. He also established the Annenberg Foundation and the Annenberg Fund, to support many cultural institutions in the area. Under President Nixon, Annenberg served as ambassador to the Court of St. James in England.

CARROT-FRUIT MUFFINS

2 cups flour
1 1/2 cups sugar
2 teaspoons baking soda
1 teaspoon ground cinnamon
1/2 teaspoon salt
2 cups grated carrots
1/2 cup raisins
1/2 cup coconut
1/2 cup chopped pecans
1 (8-ounce) can crushed pineapple, drained
1 cup vegetable oil
3 eggs, slightly beaten
2 teaspoons vanilla extract

✦ Mix flour, sugar, baking soda, cinnamon and salt in large bowl. Stir in carrots, raisins, coconut, pecans and pineapple. Make a well in center of mixture. Add mixture of oil, eggs and vanilla, stirring just until moistened. Fill paper-lined muffin cups 2/3 full.

✦ Bake at 350 degrees for 25 minutes or until golden brown. Remove from pans immediately.

Preparation time: 30 minutes   24 servings

Righters Mill Road, which passes from Penn Valley through Gladwyne, is rich in historic mills, once powered by rapid streams and now mostly in ruins from years of neglect. In its day, Robinson's Mill, which was rebuilt in 1882 for the manufacture of carpet yarn, turned out 7500 pounds of product a week.

MEAL-IN-A-MUFFIN

1 medium carrot
1 large Granny Smith apple
1/2 cup vegetable oil
2 eggs
1/3 cup sugar
2 teaspoons vanilla extract
1/2 cup shredded coconut
1/3 cup raisins
1/3 cup pecan halves
3/4 cup whole wheat flour
1/2 cup rolled oats
3 tablespoons wheat germ (optional)
1 teaspoon baking soda
1/2 teaspoon baking powder
1/4 teaspoon salt
3/4 teaspoon ground cinnamon
1/4 teaspoon ground ginger
1/8 teaspoon freshly grated nutmeg

✦ Peel carrot and cut apple into quarters. Shred in food processor container fitted with medium shredding blade; set aside. Combine oil, eggs, sugar and vanilla in food processor container fitted with metal blade. Process for 30 seconds or until blended. Add carrot, apple, coconut, raisins, pecans, whole wheat flour, oats, wheat germ, baking soda, baking powder, salt and spices. Process just until combined; do not over-process. Fill greased or paper-lined muffin cups 3/4 full.
✦ Bake at 375 degrees for 20 minutes or until wooden pick comes out clean.

Preparation time: 30 minutes   12 servings

The Pencoyd Ironworks in Lower Merion, founded in 1852 by Algernon and Percival Roberts (descendents of one of the original Welsh settlers, John Roberts), was a major source of locomotive axles. In 1859 wrought and cast-iron bridges were added to the line of manufacture, for which Pencoyd became famous. In 1900, the company merged with the American Bridge Company, which later became part of the U.S. Steel Corporation.

PEACH MUFFINS

1 1/2 cups flour
1/2 cup sugar
2 teaspoons baking powder
1/2 teaspoon each salt and cinnamon
1/2 cup milk
1/4 cup vegetable oil
1 egg
3/4 cup chopped fresh peaches

✦ Mix flour, sugar, baking powder, salt and cinnamon in bowl. Add milk, oil and egg; mix well. Stir in peaches. Fill greased or paper-lined muffin cups 2/3 full.
✦ Bake at 400 degrees for 20 minutes.

Preparation time: 10 minutes   12 servings

ZUCCHINI CORN MUFFINS

3 medium zucchini, shredded
1/2 teaspoon salt
1 1/4 cups flour
3/4 cup cornmeal
1 tablespoon baking powder
2 teaspoons sugar
3/4 teaspoon salt
Ground cayenne to taste
1/2 cup shredded sharp Cheddar cheese
1 large green onion, finely chopped
3/4 cup buttermilk
3 tablespoons vegetable oil
1 egg

✦ Place zucchini in colander over bowl. Sprinkle with salt and set aside. Combine flour, cornmeal, baking powder, sugar, salt and cayenne in medium bowl; mix well. Squeeze most of the moisture from the zucchini. Add zucchini, cheese and green onion to flour mixture; mix well. Add mixture of buttermilk, oil and egg, stirring just until evenly moistened. Spoon into muffin cups sprayed with nonstick cooking spray.
✦ Bake at 425 degrees for 20 to 25 minutes or until brown. Cool on wire rack.

Preparation time: 30 minutes   12 servings

Narberth, once known for its mills, introduced industry and employment to the Main Line. On the Old Gulph Road, just outside of Narberth, several ruins of mills that predated the Revolution can be found. At Dove Paper Mill, the paper for Continental Bank notes and government documents was made.

RHUBARB MUFFINS

1 1/4 cups flour
1/2 teaspoon baking soda
1/2 teaspoon baking powder
1/8 teaspoon salt
1/2 cup plus 2 tablespoons packed brown sugar
1 egg
1/4 cup melted butter
1/2 cup buttermilk
1 teaspoon vanilla extract
3/4 cup chopped fresh rhubarb
1/2 cup chopped walnuts
1/4 cup sugar
3/4 teaspoon cinnamon
1 tablespoon butter

✦ Mix flour, baking soda, baking powder, salt and brown sugar in large bowl. Mix egg, 1/4 cup butter, buttermilk and vanilla in small bowl. Stir into flour mixture. Fold in rhubarb and walnuts. Fill greased muffin cups 2/3 full. Sprinkle with mixture of sugar, cinnamon and 1 tablespoon butter.

✦ Bake at 400 degrees for 18 to 20 minutes or until brown.

Preparation time: 30 minutes   12 servings

BLUEBERRY COFFEE CAKE

1 cup sugar
1/3 cup butter, softened
1 egg, beaten
1 cup milk
2 cups flour
1 tablespoon baking powder
1 teaspoon salt
1 1/2 cups fresh blueberries
1 to 2 tablespoons fresh lemon juice
1 teaspoon freshly grated lemon peel
3/4 cup confectioners' sugar

✦ Cream sugar and butter in mixing bowl until light and fluffy. Beat egg with milk. Add mixture of flour, baking powder and salt alternately with milk mixture, beating well after each addition. Spread in greased 9x9-inch baking pan. Sprinkle with blueberries.
✦ Bake at 350 degrees for 40 minutes or until brown. Drizzle lemon juice over warm coffee cake. Sprinkle with lemon peel and confectioners' sugar.

Preparation time: 15 minutes   9 servings

FRUIT COBBLER CAKE

6 cups flour
2 teaspoons baking powder
1 teaspoon salt
2 cups sugar
3 eggs
1 pound butter, softened
3 (16-ounce) cans cherries, apples or blueberries
1/4 cup (or more) confectioners' sugar

✦ Sift dry ingredients together. Mix eggs and butter in large bowl. Mix in flour mixture. Divide dough into halves. Chill 1 portion for to 45 to 60 minutes. Spread remaining dough to cover large baking sheet. Spread with fruit. Crumble chilled dough over fruit.
✦ Bake at 400 degrees for 15 minutes. Reduce temperature to 325 degrees. Bake for 45 minutes longer. Sift confectioners' sugar over top.

Preparation time: 40 minutes   15 servings

The quaint village of Narberth was mistakenly named. It means "not" ("na") "beautiful" ("berth") in Welsh.

CINNAMON FRENCH TOAST

4 (³/4- to 1-inch) cinnamon bread slices
1 cup maple syrup
1 tablespoon butter
1 teaspoon cinnamon
3 eggs
1 cup whipping cream or half-and-half
2 teaspoons vanilla extract
1¹/2 teaspoons cinnamon
2 tablespoons butter

✦ Place bread in large baking dish. Bring syrup, 1
tablespoon butter and 1 teaspoon cinnamon to a boil in
heavy saucepan. Boil for 2 minutes.
✦ Whisk eggs, whipping cream, vanilla, 3 tablespoons syrup
mixture and 1¹/2 teaspoons cinnamon in bowl. Pour over
bread, turning slices to coat. Pierce bread several times
with fork. Let stand for 5 minutes.
✦ Melt half the remaining butter in large skillet over
medium-high heat. Add bread. Cook for 3 minutes or
until brown. Add remaining butter; turn bread. Cook for
3 minutes longer or until brown. Transfer to serving
plates. Serve with remaining syrup mixture.

Preparation time: 15 minutes   2 servings

NANTUCKET CINNAMON TOAST

6 (¹/2-inch) thick slices homemade-style bread
1 cup sugar
2 tablespoons cinnamon
10 tablespoons butter

✦ Remove crusts from bread; cut each slice into 4 strips.
Mix sugar and cinnamon in wide shallow bowl. Melt
butter in saucepan. Coat 1 strip of bread at a time with
butter, working quickly and letting excess drip off into
saucepan. Coat quickly with cinnamon-sugar. Place in
lightly buttered jelly roll pan.
✦ Bake at 350 degrees for 10 minutes. Turn strips. Bake
for 10 minutes longer. Remove to serving plate.

Preparation time: 20 minutes   6 servings

STUFFED FRENCH TOAST

4 (1-inch) slices diagonally cut French bread
1 tablespoon finely chopped dried apricots
1/2 cup nonfat ricotta cheese
2 tablespoons shredded part-skim mozzarella cheese
2 tablespoons sugar
1 teaspoon vanilla extract
2 tablespoons finely chopped, dried apricots
3/4 cup apricot nectar
1/2 cup sliced banana
1/2 cup skim milk
1/4 cup frozen egg substitute, thawed

✦ Cut slit in top of each bread slice to form a pocket. Mix 1 tablespoon apricots, ricotta cheese, mozzarella cheese, sugar and vanilla in bowl. Stuff 2 tablespoons mixture into each bread pocket; set aside.

✦ Combine remaining 2 tablespoons apricots and apricot nectar in small saucepan. Bring to a boil; reduce heat. Simmer for 1 minute; remove from heat. Stir in banana. Set aside and keep warm.

✦ Combine milk and egg substitute in large shallow dish; mix well. Add bread, turning to coat. Let stand until milk mixture is absorbed. Coat large nonstick skillet with nonstick cooking spray. Place over medium heat until hot. Add bread gently. Cook for 2 minutes on each side or until brown. Serve with warm apricot sauce.

Preparation time: 30 minutes   4 servings

Each wave of settlers to the Main Line left a legacy of descriptive place names. The Postmaster had the most influence in this matter and selected names to honor his family members, friends and sweethearts.

CHEDDAR CHEESE MUFFINS

2 cups flour
$2/3$ cup yellow cornmeal
4 teaspoons baking powder
1 teaspoon each red pepper flakes and salt
2 tablespoons sugar
8 ounces Cheddar cheese, shredded
2 scallions, minced
$1/2$ cup sour cream
$2/3$ cup vegetable oil
4 eggs
Dijon mustard to taste
20 thin slices of ham

✦ Combine flour, cornmeal, baking powder, pepper flakes, salt and sugar in bowl; mix well. Stir in cheese and scallions. Add mixture of sour cream, oil and eggs, stirring just until moistened; do not overmix. Fill greased muffin cups $2/3$ full.
✦ Bake at 375 degrees for 18 minutes. Cool on wire rack.
✦ Cut muffins into halves horizontally. Spread each half with a small amount of Dijon mustard. Place 1 folded ham slice between halves of each muffin.

Preparation time: 20 minutes   20 servings

PINEAPPLE SOUFFLE

1 (16-ounce) can crushed pineapple
$1/2$ cup (about) sugar
2 eggs, beaten
2 tablespoons flour
2 slices bread
2 to 4 tablespoons butter

✦ Combine undrained pineapple, sugar, eggs and flour in mixing bowl; mix well.
✦ Spread bread with a portion of the butter. Cut bread into 1x1-inch pieces.
✦ Pour pineapple mixture into buttered baking dish. Top with bread. Dot with remaining butter.
✦ Bake, covered, for 45 minutes. Bake, uncovered, for 15 minutes longer.

Preparation time: 10 minutes   Yield: 4 servings

GERMAN POPOVER PANCAKE

1/2 cup flour
1/2 cup milk
2 eggs
1/4 cup butter
2 tablespoons (or more) confectioners' sugar
Fresh juice of 1/2 lemon

✦ Mix flour, milk and eggs in bowl; batter should be slightly lumpy. Melt butter in au gratin dish or glass pie plate. Pour batter into very hot dish.
✦ Bake at 425 degrees for 20 minutes or until pancake is puffed and light brown.
✦ Remove pancake to plate. Sprinkle with confectioners' sugar and lemon juice. Return pancake to baking dish. Heat for 2 to 3 minutes or until pancake is glazed.
✦ Serve immediately. May serve with honey or jam.

Preparation time: 10 minutes   6 servings

ARTICHOKE FLAN

2 (14-ounce) cans artichoke hearts
1 medium onion, chopped
6 tablespoons unsalted butter
6 cups light cream
6 eggs, beaten
Salt and pepper to taste
1 cup shredded Gruyère cheese

✦ Rinse and drain artichoke hearts; cut into quarters. Sauté onion in butter in large skillet until soft. Add artichoke hearts. Cook until light brown. Let stand until cool. Mix cream with eggs in large bowl. Stir in sautéed mixture. Season with salt and pepper. Pour into 2-quart au gratin dish. Sprinkle with cheese.
✦ Bake at 350 degrees for 30 minutes or until golden brown. Serve at room temperature.

Preparation time: 15 minutes   16 servings

Down a winding lane off of Montgomery Avenue in Wynnewood is an English-style village designed by S. Arthur Love and built by his brother Donald Love in 1925. It was modeled after the quaint village of Cotswold, England. Starting at Loves Lane and turning down King Arthur's Round Table, you will feel that you have gone back in time.

BRUNCH SOUFFLE WITH SAUSAGE

8 slices white bread
$1^1/2$ pounds link sausage, cooked
12 ounces sharp Cheddar cheese, shredded
4 eggs
$2^1/2$ cups milk
$3/4$ teaspoon prepared mustard
$1/2$ teaspoon salt
1 cup mushroom soup
1 cup sliced fresh mushrooms
$1/2$ cup milk

✦ Remove crusts from bread; cut into cubes. Place in 9x13-inch baking dish. Top with sausage and cheese. Mix eggs, $2^1/2$ cups milk, mustard and salt in bowl. Pour over layers. Chill, covered, overnight. Mix soup, mushrooms and $1/2$ cup milk in bowl. Spread over top.
✦ Bake at 300 degrees for $1^1/2$ hours or until set.

Preparation time: 45 minutes   8 servings

FRENCH BREAD BRUNCH SOUFFLE

1 baguette French bread
6 large eggs
$1^1/2$ cups milk
1 cup half-and-half
1 teaspoon vanilla extract
$1/4$ teaspoon cinnamon
$1/4$ teaspoon ground nutmeg
$1/2$ cup packed light brown sugar
$1/4$ cup butter or margarine, softened
$1/2$ cup chopped walnuts
1 tablespoon light corn syrup

✦ Cut bread into 1-inch slices. Fill greased 9x9-inch baking pan with overlapping layer of bread slices. Combine eggs, milk, half-and-half, vanilla, cinnamon and nutmeg in bowl; mix well. Pour over bread. Chill, covered, overnight. Combine brown sugar, butter, walnuts and corn syrup in bowl. Spread over bread.
✦ Bake at 350 degrees for 40 minutes or until puffed and golden brown. Serve with maple syrup.

Preparation time: 20 minutes   9 servings

TARRAGON AND LEEK SOUFFLE

3 large leeks
1/4 cup unsalted butter
1 1/2 cups shredded Gruyère cheese
1/2 cup freshly grated Parmesan cheese
8 eggs, beaten
2 cups light cream
2 tablespoons chopped fresh tarragon
1/2 teaspoon salt
1/4 teaspoon ground pepper

✦ Chop white and pale green parts of leeks coarsely. Sauté
leeks in 3 tablespoons of the butter in heavy skillet over
medium-high heat for 5 minutes or until tender. Spread
in 9x13-inch glass baking dish coated with remaining 1
tablespoon butter. Mix cheeses in bowl; reserve 1/2 cup.
Spread remaining cheese over leeks. Whisk eggs with
remaining ingredients. Pour over leeks.
✦ Bake at 375 degrees for 30 minutes or until golden
brown and set. Sprinkle with reserved cheese. Bake for
5 minutes longer or until cheese is melted.

Preparation time: 30 minutes   8 servings

EGGS SUPREME

1 pound bulk sausage
4 ounces fresh mushrooms, chopped
1 medium onion, chopped
6 eggs
3 tablespoons sour cream
1/4 teaspoon each salt and pepper
1 (4-ounce) can Mexican green chiles
8 ounces each Cheddar, mozzarella and Monterey Jack
cheese, shredded

✦ Brown sausage with mushrooms and onion in large
skillet, stirring frequently; drain. Spoon into greased
9x13-inch baking dish. Process eggs, sour cream, salt
and pepper in blender for 1 minute. Pour over sausage
mixture. Top with chiles and cheese.
✦ Bake at 325 degrees for 30 minutes or until set.

Preparation time: 20 minutes   8 servings

SEAFOOD QUICHE

1 unbaked (9-inch) deep-dish pie shell
4 ounces shrimp, shelled, deveined
4 ounces scallops
2 tablespoons butter or margarine
1/4 cup chopped scallions
1/4 cup chopped fresh mushrooms
1 tablespoon butter or margarine
3 eggs
1 cup half-and-half
1 tablespoon dry sherry
1/2 teaspoon salt
1/4 teaspoon pepper
1/8 teaspoon ground nutmeg or to taste
1/2 cup shredded Swiss cheese

✦ Prick bottom and side of pie shell with fork. Bake at 350 degrees for 9 minutes.
✦ Rinse shrimp and scallops and cut into bite-size pieces. Melt 2 tablespoons butter in small skillet over medium heat. Add scallions. Sauté for 1 minute. Add mushrooms. Sauté for 2 minutes or until soft; remove to medium bowl and set aside.
✦ Melt remaining 1 tablespoon butter in skillet. Sauté seafood over medium heat until opaque, stirring frequently; drain. Stir into mushroom mixture.
✦ Beat eggs, half-and-half, sherry, salt, pepper and nutmeg in large bowl. Reserve 2 tablespoons of the cheese. Stir remaining cheese into egg mixture. Spread mushroom mixture in pie shell. Pour egg mixture over top. Sprinkle with reserved cheese.
✦ Bake at 350 degrees for 45 minutes or until center is set. Let stand for 10 minutes.

Preparation time: 30 minutes   6 to 8 servings

SHRIMP QUICHE

1 pound shrimp, shelled, deveined
4 ounces Swiss cheese, shredded
6 ounces Gruyère cheese, shredded
1 tablespoon flour
3 eggs
1 cup light cream
Salt, pepper, dry mustard, Worcestershire sauce and
　　Tabasco sauce to taste
1 unbaked (9-inch) pie shell

✦ Cut shrimp into bite-size pieces. Mix cheeses with flour in bowl. Spread 3/4 of the mixture in pie shell. Add shrimp. Mix eggs, cream, salt, pepper, mustard, Worcestershire sauce and Tabasco sauce in bowl. Pour over shrimp. Top with remaining cheese.
✦ Bake at 400 degrees for 15 minutes. Reduce oven temperature to 325 degrees. Bake for 40 minutes longer or until set. Let stand for 10 minutes.

Preparation time: 30 minutes　　　　　　6 servings

TORTILLA-BEAN CASSEROLE

2 cups chopped onions
1 1/2 cups chopped green peppers
1 (14-ounce) can whole tomatoes, chopped
3/4 cup picante sauce
2 teaspoons cumin
2 cloves of garlic, minced
2 1/2 (15-ounce) cans black beans, drained
12 (6-inch) flour tortillas
2 cups shredded Monterey Jack or Cheddar cheese
2 medium tomatoes, sliced
2 cups shredded lettuce
Green onions, sliced black olives and sour cream

✦ Bring first 6 ingredients to a simmer in skillet. Simmer for 10 minutes. Stir in black beans. Alternate layers of bean mixture, tortillas and cheese in baking dish.
✦ Bake, covered, at 350 degrees for 35 minutes. Let stand for 10 minutes. Top with sliced tomatoes and lettuce. Garnish with green onions, olives and sour cream.

Preparation time: 45 minutes　　　　　10 to 12 servings

MERION CRICKET CLUB

The Merion Cricket Club was founded in 1865 by William W. Montgomery, Maskell Ewing, and sixteen local young men in order to promote the English game of cricket. Archibald R. Montgomery was elected as its inaugural president. The first matches were played on the estate of Colonel Owen Jones in Wynnewood. Later, members searched for a more permanent home, leading to purchase in 1892 of the club's current site in Haverford. The two large fieldstone houses on the parcel were moved closer together and joined with a wide hall to create the current clubhouse. Unfortunately, the edifice was destroyed twice by fire in 1896, and was twice rebuilt in the same year.

The homes surrounding the club were owned by families that summered away from the city heat, including the family of Alexander Cassatt, Superintendent of the Pennsylvania Railroad and brother of the artist Mary Cassatt. Alexander Cassatt encouraged many of his fellow businessmen to establish their estates on the Main Line, which in turn spurred growth of the local railroad. The easy commute between city and country brought spectators to the popular cricket matches on the great lawn at Merion.

Cricket was introduced to America by British settlers, and is believed to be the second-oldest sport in the United States, after boating. It was a gentleman's game, full of detailed rules, including one which stated that no game could end before its time. Some games would play out over ten hours. Cricket eventually became dominated by the faster American games of baseball and tennis. Tennis became more popular in 1876 when visiting British officers brought out their rackets after a cricket match and began to teach the Merion cricket players and spectators how to play. Tennis became very popular with women, who were no longer relegated to the sidelines.

CREAM SAUCE

3 tablespoons butter

2 tablespoons flour

1 cup milk

1 cup shredded
Cheddar cheese

Tabasco sauce
to taste

1/4 teaspoon salt

Melt butter in

saucepan. Stir in

flour gradually. Cook

until thickened and

bubbly, stirring

constantly. Add milk

gradually, stirring

constantly until

mixture is smooth.

Add cheese, Tabasco

sauce and salt. Cook

until heated through,

stirring until blended

and smooth.

ASPARAGUS SUPREME

2 pounds fresh asparagus
Salt to taste
3 hard-cooked eggs, sliced
Cream Sauce (at left)
1/2 cup chopped toasted almonds
Buttered bread crumbs to taste

✦ Trim hard ends from asparagus. Peel stalks lightly and
rinse. Soak tips for several minutes; drain. Combine
asparagus with salted water to cover in large saucepan.
Bring to a boil over medium-high heat. Simmer, covered,
for 5 to 10 minutes or until stalks are tender but do not
fall apart when pierced with a fork. Layer asparagus, egg
slices, Cream Sauce and almonds 1/2 at a time in greased
casserole dish. Top with bread crumbs.

✦ Bake at 350 degrees for 30 to 40 minutes or until bubbly
and heated through.

Preparation time: 30 minutes   6 to 8 servings

ASPARAGUS WITH CAPERS

4 pounds fresh asparagus
1/2 cup fresh lemon juice
1/2 cup cider vinegar
4 cloves of garlic, minced
1 tablespoon salt
1/2 teaspoon freshly ground pepper
1/4 cup sugar
3 cups safflower oil
2 tablespoons finely chopped green bell pepper
2 tablespoons finely chopped red bell pepper
1/4 cup chopped fresh parsley
1/4 cup capers

✦ Steam asparagus until tender-crisp. Immerse immediately
in bowl of cold water; drain and pat dry. Combine
remaining ingredients in large bowl; mix well. Pour over
asparagus. Chill for 30 minutes or longer. Remove
asparagus to serving plate; discard vinaigrette. Serve cold.

Preparation time: 15 minutes   12 servings

COLD ASPARAGUS VINAIGRETTE

1 pound fresh asparagus
1 medium leek
1 tablespoon each white wine vinegar and fresh lemon juice
1 small clove of garlic, minced
1/2 teaspoon Dijon mustard
1/4 cup each vegetable oil and olive oil
Freshly ground black pepper
2 hard-cooked eggs, finely chopped (optional)
1 tablespoon chopped fresh parsley

✦ Steam asparagus in saucepan for 4 to 5 minutes or until tender-crisp; drain, reserving cooking liquid. Place asparagus on serving plate. Split and rinse leek. Cut into 1/2-inch pieces. Blanch leek in reserved cooking liquid in saucepan; drain. Sprinkle leek over asparagus. Combine vinegar, lemon juice, garlic, mustard, oils and pepper in sealable jar. Shake jar vigorously for 30 seconds. Pour over asparagus. Chill, covered, for 2 hours. Sprinkle eggs and parsley over top. Serve at room temperature.

Preparation time: 20 minutes   4 servings

ASPARAGUS WITH TOMATO

1 pound large fresh asparagus spears, trimmed
1/3 cup plus 2 tablespoons olive oil
1/3 cup red wine vinegar
1 tomato, peeled, seeded, finely chopped
1 green bell pepper, finely chopped
1 green onion, finely chopped
1 tablespoon chopped fresh parsley
Salt and pepper to taste

✦ Cook asparagus in boiling water in large saucepan for 5 minutes or until tender-crisp; drain. Blanch under cold water; drain. Arrange on large platter. Chill, covered. Whisk oil with vinegar in bowl. Add tomato, green pepper, green onion, parsley, salt and pepper; mix well. Spoon half the vinaigrette over asparagus. Serve with remaining vinaigrette.

Preparation time: 10 minutes   4 servings

PENCIL ASPARAGUS WITH HERBS

1/2 pound fresh pencil asparagus
1 tablespoon unsalted butter, softened
1/4 teaspoon freshly ground pepper
1 1/2 teaspoons chopped fresh dill
1 teaspoon chopped fresh rosemary
1 1/2 teaspoons each chopped fresh chives and
    Italian parsley
1 tablespoon freshly grated Parmesan cheese

✦ Trim ends of asparagus. Steam in saucepan until tender-crisp; rinse and pat dry. Combine butter, pepper, dill, rosemary, chives and parsley in skillet. Add asparagus. Cook until heated through, stirring occasionally. Remove to serving bowl. Sprinkle with cheese. Serve immediately.

Preparation time: 20 minutes   2 servings

GREEN BEAN BUNDLES

2 pounds small fresh green beans, trimmed
1 quart water
2 to 3 small red or yellow sweet peppers
1/2 cup coarsely chopped cashews
1/2 cup melted butter
1/2 teaspoon freshly grated lemon peel
2 teaspoons fresh lemon juice
2 tablespoons sliced green onions
2 tablespoons chopped fresh parsley

✦ Blanch beans in boiling water for 4 to 5 minutes or until tender-crisp; drain. Plunge into cold water; drain. Divide beans into 8 bundles. Slice peppers into eight 1/4-inch rings. Secure each bundle with pepper ring. Arrange on baking sheet. Chill, covered, overnight.
✦ Sauté cashews in butter in skillet until lightly browned; remove from heat. Add lemon peel, lemon juice, green onions and parsley. May chill, covered, for up to 24 hours.
✦ Let cashew butter and beans stand for 30 minutes. Spoon butter over beans. Bake, covered, at 350 degrees for 10 minutes or until heated through. Baste with pan juices. Garnish with whole cashews.

Preparation time: 30 minutes   8 servings

LEMON WALNUT GREEN BEANS

1 1/2 pounds fresh green beans
2 tablespoons butter
1/4 cup chopped walnuts
1/4 teaspoon salt
1 teaspoon freshly ground pepper
2 tablespoons fresh lemon juice

✦ Steam green beans until tender-crisp. Heat butter in large skillet. Add walnuts, salt and pepper. Cook until lightly browned. Add green beans and lemon juice, stirring to toss. Pour into serving dish. Garnish with strips of lemon peel and red pepper.

Preparation time: 15 minutes   4 servings

THREE-CHEESE BROCCOLI BAKE

1 1/2 to 2 bunches fresh broccoli
1/4 cup freshly grated Parmesan cheese
1 cup shredded Monterey Jack cheese
8 ounces cottage cheese
4 eggs, beaten
3 tablespoons minced fresh parsley
1 teaspoon salt
1/4 teaspoon pepper
Fresh bread crumbs to taste
1 tablespoon butter

✦ Cook broccoli in water to cover in saucepan until tender-crisp; drain and chop. Combine cheeses, eggs, parsley, salt and pepper in bowl; mix well. Stir in broccoli. Spoon into buttered 2-quart baking dish. Top with bread crumbs. Dot with butter.
✦ Bake, uncovered, at 375 degrees for 30 minutes.

Preparation time: 20 minutes   6 to 8 servings

The Grange of Haverford, near City Line Avenue and Haverford Road, is the ancient seat of grandeur and elegance of the Lewis family. The estate was settled in 1682 by Henry Lewis, a Welsh Quaker. In the late 1700s this celebrated colonial home, still "in the depths of the wilderness," was visited by General Washington.

BROCCOLI WITH LEMON GARLIC

Florets of 1 large bunch broccoli
Salt to taste
6 tablespoons unsalted butter
1 tablespoon minced lemon peel
1 medium clove of garlic, minced
1 1/2 cups soft white bread crumbs
Pepper to taste

+ Blanch broccoli in salted water to cover in large saucepan for 4 minutes or until tender-crisp; drain. Plunge broccoli into bowl of ice water; drain and pat dry. Broccoli may be prepared up to 8 hours ahead and stored, tightly covered, in refrigerator.
+ Melt half the butter in large heavy skillet over medium heat. Add broccoli. Sauté for 1 minute or until heated through. Remove to serving plate and keep warm.
+ Combine remaining butter, lemon peel and garlic in skillet. Cook for 1 minute or until butter begins to brown. Add bread crumbs. Cook for 3 minutes or until golden brown. Sprinkle over broccoli. Season with salt and pepper.

Preparation time: 15 minutes   4 servings

BOURBON CARROTS

5 tablespoons unsalted butter
5 medium carrots, peeled, diagonally sliced
1 medium onion, thinly sliced
2 tablespoons bourbon
1 teaspoon (or more) light brown sugar
Salt to taste

+ Melt butter in large saucepan. Add carrots and onion; mix well. Stir in bourbon, brown sugar and salt. Cook, covered, for 5 minutes or until carrots are tender.

Preparation time: 15 minutes   4 servings

SUPER CARROT BAKE

4 cups cooked sliced carrots
1 1/2 cups croutons
1 1/4 cups shredded sharp Cheddar cheese
2 eggs, beaten
1/4 cup half-and-half
1/4 cup melted margarine
1 teaspoon Worcestershire sauce
1 teaspoon salt

✦ Place carrots in buttered 1 1/2-quart casserole. Stir in croutons and cheese. Mix eggs, half-and-half, margarine, Worcestershire sauce and salt in bowl. Pour over carrots.
✦ Bake at 400 degrees for 20 minutes or until browned. Mixture may be prepared ahead and chilled until baking time.

Preparation time: 25 minutes   6 to 8 servings

CAULIFLOWER-TOMATO AU GRATIN

1 head cauliflower
1/4 cup melted butter
1 teaspoon sugar
1/2 cup chopped green bell pepper
3/4 cup cracker crumbs
1 1/4 cups shredded sharp Cheddar cheese
1 medium onion, chopped
4 to 6 large ripe tomatoes, chopped
Salt and pepper to taste
1/4 cup shredded sharp Cheddar cheese

✦ Combine cauliflower with water to cover in saucepan. Bring to a boil. Simmer for 5 minutes; drain. Cut cauliflower into florets. Place in lightly buttered 9x13-inch baking dish. Mix butter, sugar, green pepper, cracker crumbs, 1 1/4 cups cheese, onion, tomatoes, salt and pepper in bowl. Pour over cauliflower.
✦ Bake at 350 degrees for 1 hour. Sprinkle with 1/4 cup cheese. Return to oven and bake until cheese is melted.

Preparation time: 30 minutes   10 to 12 servings

Haverford College was founded in 1833, exclusively for male students, by prominent members of the Quaker sect. In 1980 the college became coeducational. Stone gates and vast playing fields along Lancaster Avenue announce the extensive 200-acre campus, which lies in Haverford.

BAKED CHILI CHEESE CORN

4 cups corn kernels, drained
1 cup shredded sharp Cheddar cheese
8 ounces cream cheese, softened
1 (7-ounce) can chopped green chiles
2 teaspoons chili powder, or to taste
2 teaspoons ground cumin

✦ Mix all ingredients in bowl. Spoon into buttered
1¹/2-quart baking dish or cast-iron skillet.
✦ Bake at 350 degrees for 30 minutes or until bubbly and
heated through.

Preparation time: 10 minutes   8 servings

SILKY CORN CASSEROLE

1 tablespoon margarine
¹/2 cup sliced green onions
2¹/4 cups low-fat milk
4 teaspoons sugar
¹/2 teaspoon salt
¹/4 teaspoon ground red pepper
¹/3 cup plus 1 tablespoon flour
2 eggs, lightly beaten
3 egg whites, lightly beaten
3¹/2 cups fresh corn kernels

✦ Melt margarine in saucepan over medium heat. Add
green onions. Sauté for 1 minute. Add milk, sugar, salt
and pepper. Cook for 3 minutes or until heated through;
do not boil. Set aside and keep warm.
✦ Combine flour, eggs and egg whites in mixing bowl. Beat
at medium speed until blended. Add ¹/2 cup of the hot
milk mixture gradually. Stir in remaining milk mixture
gradually. Stir in corn. Pour into lightly greased shallow
2-quart baking dish.
✦ Bake at 350 degrees for 1 hour and 20 minutes or until
knife inserted near center comes out clean.

Preparation time: 20 minutes   6 servings

EGGPLANT MAURICE

1 tablespoon sugar
1 teaspoon salt
1/4 teaspoon pepper
1/2 teaspoon garlic salt
1 small eggplant, peeled, chopped
1 (16-ounce) can tomatoes, drained, chopped
1 green bell pepper, chopped
1 medium onion, thinly sliced
8 ounces sharp Cheddar cheese, shredded

+ Mix sugar, salt, pepper and garlic salt in bowl. Alternate layers of eggplant, tomatoes, green pepper, onion, sugar mixture and cheese in greased casserole until all ingredients are used, ending with cheese. Force cover down over the high mound of vegetables, since casserole will shrink quite a bit.
+ Bake, covered, at 400 degrees for 20 minutes. Reduce oven temperature to 350 degrees. Bake, uncovered, for 30 minutes longer.

Preparation time: 15 minutes   6 servings

ELEGANT MUSHROOMS

6 tablespoons margarine
3 tablespoons flour
1 cup sour cream
1/4 cup each chopped onion and fresh parsley
2 teaspoons salt
2 teaspoons Dijon mustard
1/2 teaspoon fresh lemon juice
1/2 teaspoon ground nutmeg
1/4 teaspoon pepper
3 pounds fresh mushrooms, sliced

+ Melt margarine in large saucepan. Add flour. Cook over medium heat for 1 minute, stirring constantly. Add sour cream, onion, parsley, salt, mustard, lemon juice, nutmeg and pepper; mix well. Cook until heated through, stirring constantly; remove from heat. Stir in mushrooms. Spoon into greased 2 1/2-quart casserole.
+ Bake at 350 degrees for 1 hour.

Preparation time: 25 minutes   8 to 10 servings

VIDALIA ONION CASSEROLE

1/4 cup unsalted butter
7 medium Vidalia onions, sliced
1/2 cup white rice
5 cups boiling water
1 teaspoon salt
1 cup shredded Jarlsburg or Swiss cheese
2/3 cup half-and-half
1/8 teaspoon ground nutmeg, or to taste
Salt and pepper to taste

✦ Melt butter in heavy skillet. Sauté onions in butter until soft and transparent, stirring frequently.
✦ Cook rice in boiling salted water in saucepan for 5 minutes; drain.
✦ Combine rice, onions, cheese, half-and-half, nutmeg, salt and pepper in bowl; mix well. Spoon into greased shallow baking dish.
✦ Bake at 325 degrees for 1 hour.

Preparation time: 15 minutes   8 servings

ROSEMARY GARLIC POTATOES

3 tablespoons olive oil
12 cloves of garlic
3 large sprigs of fresh rosemary
1 1/2 pounds new potatoes
1/2 teaspoon coarse (kosher) salt

✦ Pour oil into 9x13-inch baking pan. Add garlic, stirring to coat. Heat at 450 degrees for 5 minutes. Chop rosemary; if potatoes are large, cut into halves or quarters. Add rosemary and potatoes to baking pan.
✦ Bake at 450 degrees for 30 to 40 minutes or until potatoes are tender and browned, shaking pan every 5 minutes.
✦ Remove potatoes to serving platter. Sprinkle with salt. Serve garlic cloves with potatoes. Squeeze cloves according to individual preference.

Preparation time: 5 minutes   4 to 6 servings

GARLIC CHEESE POTATOES

1 1/2 pounds potatoes
12 ounces sharp Cheddar cheese, shredded
2/3 cup whipping cream
Salt and pepper to taste
6 cloves of garlic, minced

✦ Boil potatoes with water to cover in large saucepan. Simmer for 20 minutes or until tender; drain. Let cool. Cut into slices.
✦ Reserve 1/4 of the cheese. Layer potatoes, remaining cheese, whipping cream, salt and pepper 1/3 at a time in buttered shallow baking dish. Top with reserved cheese. Sprinkle with garlic.
✦ Bake at 350 degrees for 40 minutes or until browned.

Preparation time: 45 minutes   4 to 6 servings

OVEN FRIES

2 large baking potatoes
1 tablespoon vegetable oil
1/4 teaspoon salt
Onion powder to taste
Garlic powder to taste
Chili powder to taste
Paprika to taste

✦ Cut potatoes into 1/4-inch sticks. Toss with oil in bowl. Arrange in single layer on baking sheet sprayed with nonstick cooking spray.
✦ Bake at 500 degrees for 15 to 20 minutes or until potatoes are done, tossing occasionally.
✦ Mix salt, onion powder, garlic powder, chili powder and paprika in bowl. Sprinkle over potatoes.

Preparation time: 10 minutes   4 servings

Castle Bith, 530 Ardmore Avenue, was the homestead of Morris Llewellyn, a pioneer settler of Haverford in the 1690s. Originally a four-room structure, the house has been expanded to ten rooms, partly through the inclusion of a neighboring slaughterhouse. Many homes evolved in this manner, incorporating other structures and businesses as the need for more space dictated.

JAZZY MASHED POTATOES

4 large russet potatoes, peeled
1/2 cup milk
3 tablespoons unsalted butter, softened
1 bunch green onions, chopped
1 tablespoon unsalted butter
1 1/2 cups freshly grated Parmesan cheese
Salt and pepper to taste

✦ Cut potatoes into large chunks. Boil in water to cover in saucepan until tender; drain. Mash potatoes until smooth. Stir in milk and 3 tablespoons butter.
✦ Sauté green onions in 1 tablespoon butter until wilted. Combine green onions, potatoes and cheese in bowl; mix gently. Season with salt and pepper. Spoon into buttered baking dish.
✦ Bake, covered, at 350 degrees for 15 minutes or until heated through.

Preparation time: 30 minutes   4 servings

SPECIAL MASHED POTATOES

3 pounds potatoes, peeled
8 ounces cream cheese, softened
1/2 cup butter or margarine, softened
1/4 cup sour cream
1/4 cup milk
1 egg, lightly beaten
1/4 cup finely chopped onion
1 teaspoon salt
1/8 teaspoon pepper, or to taste
Shredded sharp white Cheddar cheese to taste (optional)

✦ Cook potatoes in water to cover in saucepan; drain. Mash hot potatoes until smooth. Add cream cheese gradually. Beat in butter until cream cheese and butter are completely mixed.
✦ Combine sour cream, milk, egg, onion, salt and pepper in bowl. Add to potato mixture, beating until light and fluffy. Spoon into greased casserole. Sprinkle with cheese.
✦ Bake at 350 degrees for 45 minutes or until light brown.

Preparation time: 30 minutes   8 to 10 servings

TANGY NEW POTATOES

18 new potatoes
2 small onions, finely chopped
3 tablespoons butter
2 tablespoons sugar
1 tablespoon salt
2 tablespoons flour
1 1/2 cups milk
1 cup sour cream
2 tablespoons white vinegar

✦ Cut potatoes into quarters. Cook with water to cover in saucepan until tender; drain and set aside.

✦ Sauté onions in butter in medium saucepan until transparent. Stir in sugar, salt and flour. Add milk gradually, mixing well after each addition. Simmer until thickened, stirring constantly. Add sour cream and vinegar. Cook until bubbly.

✦ Combine sauce with potatoes in bowl. Serve hot.

Preparation time: 30 minutes   10 servings

SPINACH WITH PINE NUTS

2 pounds fresh spinach
2 tablespoons light or extra-virgin olive oil
1 clove of garlic, minced
Salt and white pepper to taste
1/4 cup toasted pine nuts

✦ Rinse and trim spinach; tear large leaves into halves. Heat oil in large sauté pan over low heat. Add garlic. Cook for 1 minute, stirring constantly; do not brown. Add spinach gradually. Cook until spinach is coated and wilted. Sprinkle with salt and pepper.

✦ Stir in pine nuts at serving time.

Preparation time: 15 minutes   6 servings

The Shipley School, founded in 1894 across the street from Bryn Mawr College, is the former farmstead of "Indian Nelly." She was one of the first settlers to associate with the Lenni-Lenape Indians.

In 1832 the Philadel-

phia and Columbia

Railroad was

completed to serve

the suburbs west of

the city. It was part

of the state system

of canals and rail-

roads called the

Main Line of Public

Works. Eventually

the "Main Line"

came to refer to the

stretch between

Overbrook and Paoli.

SPINACH MADELEINE

2 (10-ounce) packages frozen chopped spinach
2 tablespoons chopped onion
1/4 cup melted butter
2 tablespoons flour
1/2 cup evaporated milk
3/4 teaspoon garlic salt
3/4 teaspoon salt
1/2 teaspoon pepper
1 teaspoon Worcestershire sauce
8 ounces jalapeño cheese, shredded

✦ Cook spinach using package directions; drain, reserving
1/2 cup cooking liquid. Sauté onion in butter in saucepan
until tender. Add flour, stirring until blended. Add
reserved liquid and evaporated milk. Cook until thickened,
stirring constantly. Add garlic salt, salt, pepper and
Worcestershire sauce. Stir in cheese. Cook until cheese is
melted, stirring frequently. Stir in spinach. Spoon into
2-quart casserole.
✦ Bake at 350 degrees for 30 minutes.

Preparation time: 30 minutes   6 to 8 servings

SPINACH ARTICHOKE CASSEROLE

4 (10-ounce) packages frozen spinach
1 (9-ounce) can artichoke hearts
1 (8-ounce) can water chestnuts
11 ounces cream cheese
1/2 cup butter
1 cup buttered bread crumbs

✦ Cook spinach using package directions; drain well. Cut
artichoke hearts into halves. Cut water chestnuts into
thin slices.
✦ Heat cream cheese with butter in saucepan until melted.
✦ Arrange artichoke hearts in buttered 10x15-inch baking
dish. Layer spinach, cream cheese mixture and water
chestnuts 1/2 at a time over artichoke hearts. Top with
bread crumbs.
✦ Bake at 350 degrees for 45 minutes.

Preparation time: 25 minutes   12 to 16 servings

SPINACH BACON AU GRATIN

2 (10-ounce) packages frozen chopped spinach
1 cup cooked sliced fresh mushrooms
6 slices bacon, crisp-fried, crumbled
1/4 teaspoon crushed marjoram
Salt and pepper to taste
1 cup sour cream
1/2 cup shredded sharp Cheddar cheese

✦ Cook spinach using package directions; drain well. Arrange in 8x12-inch baking dish. Top with mushrooms and 2/3 of the bacon. Sprinkle with marjoram, salt and pepper.
✦ Bake at 325 degrees for 15 minutes. Remove from oven. Top with sour cream and cheese. Sprinkle with remaining bacon. Bake for 5 minutes longer or until cheese is melted.

Preparation time: 30 minutes   4 servings

SPICED BUTTERNUT SQUASH

1 (4-pound) butternut squash
3 tablespoons unsalted butter
1/4 cup maple syrup
1/2 teaspoon salt
1/2 teaspoon nutmeg
1/2 teaspoon freshly ground pepper

✦ Peel squash; cut into large pieces. Cook in boiling water in large saucepan for 25 minutes or until tender; drain. Mash coarsely with potato masher.
✦ Cut butter into small pieces. Combine squash, butter, syrup, salt, nutmeg and pepper in saucepan. Cook over low heat until heated through, stirring frequently. Adjust seasonings.

Preparation time: 15 minutes   6 servings

The Pennsylvania Railroad, or "Pennsy," replaced the Pennsylvania and Columbia Railroad in the 1800s, and began to exert tremendous influence on the development of the Main Line. The railroad bought property, renamed villages, and unsuccessfully tried to eliminate competition from trolleys. In 1876, A. J. Cassatt, railroad president, actually purchased Lancaster Pike from 52nd Street to Paoli to prevent streetcars from being tracked. Tolls were levied to raise money for the railroad.

SPAGHETTI SQUASH MEDLEY

1 medium spaghetti squash
1 onion, chopped
2 tablespoons melted butter or margarine
2 zucchini, sliced
1/2 cup grated carrot
1/2 cup chopped green bell pepper
2 tomatoes, coarsely chopped
2 tablespoons chopped fresh parsley
Salt and pepper to taste
Grated Parmesan cheese to taste

✦ Rinse squash; cut into halves lengthwise and remove seeds. Place squash cut side down in Dutch oven. Add 2 inches of water. Bring to a boil. Cook, covered, for 30 to 35 minutes or until squash is tender; drain and cool. Use fork to remove enough spaghetti-like strands to measure 3 cups; set aside.

✦ Sauté onion in butter in large skillet for 2 minutes. Add zucchini, carrot and green pepper. Sauté for 5 minutes. Stir in tomatoes, parsley, salt and pepper. Cook over low heat for 5 minutes. Combine with squash in large bowl, stirring to toss gently. Sprinkle with cheese.

Preparation time: 20 minutes   8 servings

BAKED SWEET POTATO ROUNDS

2 pounds sweet potatoes, peeled
1/4 cup melted butter
2 teaspoons dried rubbed sage
Coarse salt to taste
Pepper to taste

✦ Cut sweet potatoes into 1/4-inch rounds. Arrange on 2 foil-covered baking sheets. Brush both sides of rounds with melted butter. Sprinkle with sage, salt and pepper.

✦ Bake at 450 degrees for 15 minutes or until golden brown and tender, turning once.

Preparation time: 15 minutes   6 servings

EASY SWEET POTATO CASSEROLE

1 large can sweet potatoes
2 eggs
1/2 cup sugar
1 cup evaporated milk
1/2 teaspoon each cinnamon and cardamom
5 tablespoons butter, softened
1 cup crushed cornflakes
1/2 cup packed brown sugar
5 tablespoons melted butter
1/2 cup chopped walnuts

✦ Beat sweet potatoes, eggs, sugar, evaporated milk,
   cinnamon, cardamom and softened butter in bowl.
   Spread in greased large quiche pan.
✦ Bake at 400 degrees for 15 minutes.
✦ Mix cornflakes, brown sugar, butter and walnuts in bowl.
   Spread over casserole. Bake for 15 minutes longer.

Preparation time: 15 minutes   8 servings

SWEET POTATO CASSEROLE

6 fresh yams
4 tablespoons butter or margarine
1/4 cup each packed brown sugar and sugar
1 1/2 teaspoons cinnamon
Salt and pepper to taste
1/2 to 1 cup warm milk
1/2 to 3/4 cup walnut pieces

✦ Boil yams in water to cover in saucepan until tender;
   drain and cool. Peel by slitting warm yams down one
   side. Mash with 2 to 3 tablespoons butter. Add sugar,
   brown sugar, cinnamon, salt and pepper; mix well with
   wire whisk or electric mixer. Whip in enough warm milk
   to make of desired consistency. Spoon into 1 1/2-quart
   baking dish. Dot with remaining 1 tablespoon butter.
   Top with walnuts. Sprinkle with additional cinnamon
   and brown sugar to taste.
✦ Bake at 325 degrees for 30 minutes.

Preparation time: 20 minutes   8 to 10 servings

PLUM TOMATOES AND ARTICHOKES

1 (2-pound) can whole plum tomatoes
1 (14-ounce) can artichoke hearts
1/2 cup finely chopped onion
2 tablespoons finely chopped shallots
1/2 cup butter
1/2 teaspoon dried basil
2 tablespoons sugar, or to taste

✦ Drain tomatoes and artichoke hearts. Rinse artichoke hearts and cut into quarters. Sauté onion and shallots in butter in sauté pan. Add tomatoes, artichokes and basil. Cook for 2 to 3 minutes. Sprinkle with sugar. Spoon into greased shallow baking dish.

✦ Bake at 325 degrees for 10 to 15 minutes or until heated through.

Preparation time: 15 minutes   4 servings

ZUCCHINI MUSHROOM CASSEROLE

1 pound zucchini
1/8 teaspoon fresh dill, or to taste
1 clove of garlic
Salt to taste
8 ounces fresh mushrooms, sliced
3 tablespoons butter
2 tablespoons flour
1 cup sour cream
Buttered bread crumbs

✦ Cut zucchini crosswise into 1-inch slices. Combine with dill, garlic and boiling salted water to cover in saucepan. Return to a boil; reduce heat. Simmer until tender; do not overcook. Drain, reserving 2 tablespoons cooking liquid and discarding garlic.

✦ Sauté mushrooms in butter in sauté pan. Stir in flour. Cook for 2 minutes. Add sour cream, zucchini and reserved liquid. Cook until heated through, stirring constantly; do not boil. Spoon into baking dish. Top with bread crumbs. Brown quickly under broiler.

Preparation time: 30 minutes   5 to 6 servings

SQUASH AND TOMATO GRATIN

2 small zucchini and 2 small yellow squash
1/2 cup finely chopped onion
2 teaspoons finely chopped garlic
2 sprigs of fresh thyme, chopped, or 1/2 teaspoon dried
2 tablespoons olive oil
Salt and freshly ground pepper to taste
3 medium tomatoes, thinly sliced
1/2 cup fresh basil leaves, cut into thin strips
1/2 to 1 cup freshly grated Parmesan cheese

✦ Rinse zucchini and squash; pat dry. Trim ends but do not peel. Slice very thin. Stir-fry zucchini, squash, onion, garlic and thyme in 1 tablespoon olive oil in skillet. Add salt and pepper. Cook for 5 minutes. Spoon into square baking dish. Top with sliced tomatoes, salt, pepper, basil strips and cheese. Drizzle with 1 tablespoon oil.
✦ Broil for 4 minutes or until golden brown. May serve cold.

Preparation time: 20 minutes   6 servings

TINKA'S ZUCCHINI CLIPPERS

2 medium zucchini, ends trimmed
1/4 cup finely chopped onion
2 tablespoons chopped fresh parsley
1 tablespoon chopped fresh basil
1 teaspoon each salt and pepper
1 egg, beaten
1/4 cup melted butter
1 1/2 cups crushed corn flakes
1/2 cup each bread crumbs and grated Parmesan cheese

✦ Cook zucchini in boiling salted water to cover in saucepan for 5 minutes or until tender-crisp. Cut into halves lengthwise; remove and chop pulp, keeping shells intact. Mix pulp with onion, parsley, basil, salt, pepper and egg in bowl. Spoon into reserved shells. Mix butter, corn flakes, bread crumbs and cheese in bowl. Spread over zucchini mixture. Place on baking sheet.
✦ Bake at 350 degrees for 30 minutes or until browned.

Preparation time: 30 minutes   4 servings

1704

HARRITON HOUSE

The original Harriton estate was founded in 1704 by
Rowland Ellis, a Welsh Quaker, who called his land "Bryn
Mawr," or "High Hill," after his ancestral farm in Wales.
The house is historically notable for the materials that were
brought by horse over nearly impassable roads through a
690-acre property of wilderness. Richard Harrison purchased
the estate in 1719 and renamed it "Harriton" to reflect his
own family name as well as his wife's nearby home town,
Norriton. In 1774, Charles Thomson acquired the property
through marriage to his wife Hannah, 42-year-old heiress
and only daughter of Richard Harrison.

Thomson was one of this nation's earliest and most
dedicated public servants. He had a fifteen-year career as the
first and only secretary to the Continental and Confederation
Congress; he was the historical archivist of Congress, a signer of
the Declaration of Independence, and the primary force
behind the Great Seal of the United States. He counted
Benjamin Franklin as a close and dear friend. After retiring from
public life to his successful tobacco farm, Thomson abolished
slavery and encouraged other farmers to do the same.
Indians who were still part of the community gave him the
name, "the man who always speaks truth."

CELEBRATION PASTA

1 1/4 cups sliced fresh mushrooms
1 tablespoon extra-virgin olive oil
1 pound large shrimp, peeled
1 1/2 cups Champagne
1/4 teaspoon salt
2 tablespoons minced shallots
3 plum tomatoes, chopped
1 cup whipping cream
Salt and pepper to taste
8 ounces angel hair pasta, cooked, drained
3 tablespoons chopped fresh parsley

✦ Sauté mushrooms in olive oil in skillet over medium-high
heat until juices evaporate. Remove mushrooms with
slotted spoon to bowl. Stir shrimp, Champagne and 1/4
teaspoon salt into pan drippings.
✦ Bring just to a boil over high heat; remove shrimp. Add
shallots and tomatoes. Boil for 8 minutes or until liquid
is reduced to 1/2 cup, stirring frequently. Add 3/4 cup of
the whipping cream; mix well. Boil for 1 to 2 minutes or
until slightly thickened and reduced in volume. Stir in
shrimp and mushrooms. Cook until heated through,
stirring occasionally. Season with salt and pepper to taste.
✦ Mix hot pasta with remaining 1/4 cup cream and parsley.
Spoon onto serving platter. Top with shrimp and sauce.

Preparation time: 30 minutes   4 servings

MCCARTHY'S SHRIMP AND PASTA

1 pound large shrimp, peeled, deveined
1 cup Italian-seasoned bread crumbs
1 teaspoon garlic powder
1/4 cup each olive oil and butter
4 ounces angel hair or lemon pasta, cooked, drained
Parsley flakes and olive oil to taste
Freshly grated Romano cheese to taste

+ Cut 1/2 inch split in end of each shrimp tail. Coat with mixture of bread crumbs and garlic powder.
+ Sauté shrimp in mixture of 1/4 cup olive oil and butter in skillet until cooked through and light brown. Remove shrimp with slotted spoon to bowl. Remove any breading from pan drippings with slotted spoon; reserve.
+ Mix hot pasta with reserved breading, parsley flakes and olive oil to taste in bowl. Spoon onto individual plates. Arrange shrimp over pasta. Sprinkle with Romano cheese. Garnish with chopped fresh parsley and lemon zest.

Preparation time: 20 minutes   2 servings

CREAMY BRIE AND BASIL PASTA

4 large tomatoes, chopped
1 cup fresh basil, cut into strips
1 clove of garlic, crushed
3/4 cup olive oil
1 teaspoon salt
1/2 teaspoon freshly ground pepper
1 (1-pound) wheel Brie cheese
12 ounces bow tie pasta, cooked, drained
1/4 cup freshly grated Parmesan cheese
Freshly ground pepper to taste

+ Combine first 6 ingredients in bowl; mix gently. Let stand at room temperature for 1 hour.
+ Remove rind from Brie cheese; cut into chunks. Let stand at room temperature for 1 hour.
+ Mix Brie cheese with hot pasta in bowl. Add tomato mixture and mix gently. Sprinkle with Parmesan cheese and pepper to taste. Serve immediately.

Preparation time: 30 minutes   6 to 8 servings

Harriton House was built in 1704 by Rowland Ellis, a Welsh Quaker, and was originally called "Bryn Mawr" for his family estate in Wales. The house is noteworthy because glass panes, sand, stone and other construction materials were painstakenly transported by horse through the wooded valley because there were no roads.

Richard Harrison,
a tobacco farmer,
bought the "Bryn
Mawr" estate in 1719
and renamed it
Harriton. Unfortu-
nately on his moving
day, his possessions
were stolen by river
pirates as he tried
to transport them
up the Schuylkill
River.

PASTA WITH SUGAR SNAP PEAS

1 pound asparagus, trimmed, cut into 1 1/2-inch pieces
Salt to taste
8 ounces bow tie pasta
8 ounces fresh sugar snap peas
3 tablespoons olive oil
2/3 cup freshly grated Parmesan cheese
Pepper to taste

✦ Cook asparagus in salted boiling water in saucepan just
until tender. Remove asparagus with slotted spoon to
bowl of cold water; reserve boiling water. Cool asparagus
slightly; drain.

✦ Boil pasta in reserved water until tender-crisp; remove
pasta with slotted spoon to bowl. Add sugar snap peas to
same water. Boil for 2 minutes. Add asparagus. Cook just
until heated through; drain.

✦ Combine pasta, asparagus mixture and olive oil in bowl,
tossing gently until coated. Stir in Parmesan cheese.
Season with salt and pepper. Garnish with additional
Parmesan cheese. Serve immediately.

Preparation time: 10 minutes   4 servings

PASTA WITH RED PEPPER SAUCE

1 (7-ounce) jar roasted red peppers, drained
3/4 cup half-and-half
1/3 cup freshly grated Parmesan cheese
1/4 cup finely chopped fresh basil
1 clove of garlic, minced
1 teaspoon salt
Red pepper flakes to taste
12 ounces bow tie pasta, cooked, drained

✦ Process roasted red peppers, half-and-half, cheese, basil,
garlic, salt and red pepper flakes in blender until smooth.
Combine with hot pasta in bowl, mixing gently until
coated. Garnish with additional Parmesan cheese and
additional chopped fresh basil.

✦ Serve warm or chill until serving time. May add grilled
chicken or sausage.

Preparation time: 10 minutes   4 servings

FUSILLI WITH ARTICHOKES

1 (8-ounce) jar artichoke hearts, chopped
2 large tomatoes, peeled, seeded, chopped
5 scallions with tops, thinly sliced
2 or 3 cloves of garlic, minced
1/4 cup white wine
5 tablespoons olive oil
8 ounces fresh fusilli, cooked, drained
Salt and pepper to taste
Freshly grated Parmesan cheese to taste

✦ Sauté artichokes, tomatoes, scallions and garlic in white wine and olive oil in large skillet for 5 minutes or until scallions are tender. Add fusilli and mix gently.
✦ Spoon into serving bowl. Season with salt and pepper. Serve with Parmesan cheese. May omit white wine. May add grilled chicken to pasta mixture.

Preparation time: 10 minutes   4 servings

FETTUCCINI WITH PROSCIUTTO

6 ounces thinly sliced prosciutto, cut into thin strips
3 shallots, minced
1 red bell pepper, chopped
2 large cloves of garlic, minced
3 tablespoons butter
1/2 cup dry white wine
1 cup whipping cream
1/2 cup pesto sauce
Salt and pepper to taste
16 ounces fettuccini
1/3 cup pine nuts, toasted

✦ Sauté prosciutto, shallots, red pepper and garlic in butter in saucepan over medium-low heat for 5 minutes or until red pepper is tender. Stir in wine.
✦ Bring to a boil. Boil until slightly reduced in volume, stirring frequently. Stir in whipping cream and pesto sauce. Season with salt and pepper.
✦ Cook pasta in salted boiling water in saucepan until tender; drain. Mix with prosciutto mixture in bowl. Sprinkle with pine nuts.

Preparation time: 20 minutes   4 servings

The village of Rosemont was named for the 625-acre Rosemont farm, settled by Rees Thomas in 1683. Ashbridge House was built in 1769 by one of Thomas' sons in the northern section of the property, and now contains the library of the Lower Merion Historical Society. Approximately 30 acres was bequeathed to the community in the 1940s for recreation, and is known as Ashbridge Memorial Park.

GARLIC SAUCE

1/2 cup whipping
cream

4 cloves of garlic,
crushed

1/4 cup fresh
lemon juice

3/4 cup extra-virgin
olive oil

1 1/2 tablespoons
minced fresh dill

2 tablespoons
minced fresh
parsley

Salt and pepper
to taste

✦

Bring cream to a boil

in saucepan. Stir in

garlic. Simmer for

15 minutes or until

reduced to 1/4 cup.

Purée in blender. Add

lemon juice and olive

oil in a fine stream,

processing constantly

until smooth. Add

remaining ingredients.

Process until blended.

FETTUCCINI AND SMOKED SALMON

16 ounces fettuccini
Salt to taste
6 ounces thinly sliced smoked salmon, cut into
  1/3x2-inch strips
1 red bell pepper, cut into 2-inch strips
1 small red onion, thinly sliced
Garlic Sauce (at left)

✦ Cook fettuccini in salted boiling water using package
  directions; drain.
✦ Reserve several strips of salmon. Combine remaining
  salmon, hot fettuccini, red pepper, red onion and Garlic
  Sauce in bowl and mix gently. Spoon onto serving
  platter. Top with reserved salmon; garnish with sprigs of
  fresh dill. Serve warm or at room temperature.

Preparation time: 30 minutes   4 servings

CHICKEN FETTUCCINI

1 pound boneless skinless chicken breasts
1 tablespoon chopped onion
2 tablespoons butter
Salt and pepper to taste
Florets of 1 bunch broccoli
12 ounces fettuccini, cooked, drained
1/2 cup butter
1 cup half-and-half
3/4 cup plus 2 tablespoons freshly grated Parmesan cheese

✦ Rinse chicken and pat dry. Cut into 1-inch pieces. Sauté
  chicken and onion in 2 tablespoons butter in skillet until
  chicken is cooked through. Season with salt and pepper.
  Keep warm.
✦ Cook broccoli in boiling water in saucepan for 2 minutes;
  drain. Keep warm.
✦ Combine pasta, chicken and broccoli in bowl and mix
  gently. Add 1/2 cup butter, half-and-half and cheese,
  tossing until coated. Serve immediately.
✦ May substitute shrimp or scallops for chicken, snow peas
  for broccoli and whipping cream for half-and-half.

Preparation time: 10 minutes   4 to 6 servings

SPINACH PASTA WITH TUNA

2 tablespoons olive oil
1 (28-ounce) can crushed tomatoes
1 (15-ounce) can diced tomatoes, drained
1 clove of garlic, finely chopped
1/4 teaspoon red pepper
1/4 teaspoon salt
1/4 teaspoon ground black pepper
1 (16-ounce) tuna steak, cut into 3/4-inch pieces
1/4 teaspoon vegetable oil
1 (14-ounce) can artichoke hearts, drained, cut into
    quarters
1 tablespoon capers, rinsed
1 tablespoon slivered fresh basil leaves
12 ounces fresh spinach fettuccini, cooked, drained

◆ Heat olive oil in 3-quart saucepan. Add undrained
  crushed tomatoes, diced tomatoes, garlic, red pepper, salt
  and black pepper; mix well. Bring to a boil. Cook for 25
  minutes, stirring occasionally.

◆ Sauté tuna in vegetable oil in skillet until tuna is no
  longer pink inside and light brown on both sides. Fold
  tuna, artichoke hearts, capers and basil into tomato
  mixture. Cook just until heated through.

◆ Spoon hot fettuccini onto serving platter. Top with tuna
  mixture. Garnish with additional fresh basil leaves. May
  substitute frozen artichoke hearts for canned artichoke
  hearts and nonstick cooking spray for vegetable oil.

Preparation time: 40 minutes   4 servings

The Octagonal School House at Diamond Rock and Yellow Springs Road was built in 1818. The eight-sided form was introduced so that all could benefit from a central stove. The standing joke is that it was designed as a square school, but that the money ran out, and corners were cut to complete the building.

SPINACH FETTUCCINI

16 ounces spinach fettuccini
Salt to taste
1 pound fresh mushrooms, sliced
3 large cloves of garlic, crushed
1 teaspoon fresh thyme
3 tablespoons olive oil
1 large red bell pepper, coarsely chopped
1 (14-ounce) can artichoke hearts, drained
1 cup whipping cream
1/2 cup chicken stock
1/2 cup freshly grated Parmesan cheese
Pepper to taste
1 tablespoon olive oil
Freshly grated Parmesan cheese to taste

✦ Combine fettuccini and salt with just enough water to cover in saucepan. Cook just until pasta is tender but firm; drain. Keep warm.

✦ Sauté mushrooms, garlic and thyme in 3 tablespoons olive oil in skillet for 6 minutes or until mushrooms are brown. Stir in red pepper. Sauté for 3 minutes. Stir in artichoke hearts, cream, stock and 1/2 cup cheese. Simmer for 3 minutes, stirring occasionally. Season with salt and pepper.

✦ Toss hot pasta with 1 tablespoon olive oil in bowl. Add mushroom mixture and mix gently. Sprinkle with Parmesan cheese to taste. Serve immediately. May add cooked shrimp to pasta mixture.

Preparation time: 15 minutes   4 to 6 servings

FETTUCCINI WITH BRIE CHEESE

8 ounces bacon, chopped
1/2 cup half-and-half
1/2 cup reduced-sodium chicken broth
1 cup freshly grated Parmesan cheese
1 teaspoon cracked pepper
3 ounces Brie cheese, thinly sliced
16 ounces fresh fettuccini, cooked, drained

✦ Cook bacon in skillet over medium heat for 6 minutes or until bacon begins to brown. Remove bacon with slotted spoon to bowl. Discard bacon drippings from skillet.

✦ Bring half-and-half and chicken broth to a boil over medium heat in same skillet, stirring occasionally. Add Parmesan cheese gradually, stirring until melted. Stir in pepper and bacon. Reduce heat to low. Add Brie cheese gradually, stirring until melted.

✦ Combine hot pasta with bacon mixture in bowl and mix gently. Spoon onto serving platter. Garnish with fresh parsley. Serve immediately.

Preparation time: 10 minutes   6 servings

FETTUCCINI WITH GORGONZOLA

6 ounces Gorgonzola cheese, cut into pieces
1 clove of garlic, thinly sliced
2 tablespoons unsalted butter, cut into pieces
Salt to taste
8 ounces fresh fettuccini
Freshly ground pepper to taste

✦ Bring enough water to cover fettuccini to a boil in saucepan. Cover with heatproof bowl.

✦ Combine cheese, garlic and butter in the heatproof bowl. Cook over boiling water until the cheese and butter melt, stirring constantly. Remove bowl. Add salt and pasta to boiling water.

✦ Cook pasta al dente; drain. Toss with Gorgonzola sauce. Season with salt and pepper. Serve with Caesar salad.

Preparation time: 5 minutes   2 servings

In 1908, Joseph Newton Pew, founder of the Sun Company and president of the Peoples Natural Gas Company, purchased Glenmede, a 15-acre estate in Bryn Mawr at Old Gulph and Morris Roads. This vast Victorian Gothic mansion was one of the first brick houses in the area. His daughter, Miss Ethel Pew, bequeathed it to Bryn Mawr College in 1980, for use as the Glenmede Graduate Center.

WHITE WINE SAUCE

2 tablespoons butter

2 tablespoons flour

2 tablespoons dry white wine

3/4 cup milk

1/2 cup shredded sharp Cheddar cheese

✦

Heat butter in saucepan until melted. Stir in flour. Cook for 1 minute, stirring constantly. Add wine and milk gradually. Cook until thickened, stirring constantly. Add cheese, stirring until melted.

CHEESY VEGETABLE LASAGNA

12 fresh spinach leaves, chopped
1 clove of garlic, crushed
2 scallions, chopped
1 tablespoon vegetable oil
1 3/4 cups ricotta cheese
1/2 cup freshly grated Parmesan cheese
2 eggs
1 onion, chopped
8 ounces fresh mushrooms, sliced
1 small green bell pepper, chopped
1 tablespoon vegetable oil
1 (14-ounce) can peeled, whole tomatoes
2 tomatoes, peeled, chopped
1 (6-ounce) can tomato paste
1 teaspoon dried basil
1/2 teaspoon dried oregano
1/2 teaspoon sugar
8 ounces lasagna noodles
White Wine Sauce (at left)

✦ Sauté spinach, garlic and scallions in 1 tablespoon oil in skillet over high heat for 3 minutes or until spinach wilts; drain. Combine ricotta cheese, Parmesan cheese and eggs in bowl; mix well.

✦ Sauté onion, mushrooms and green pepper in 1 tablespoon oil in skillet for 3 minutes or until onion is tender. Add undrained tomatoes, fresh tomatoes, tomato paste, basil, oregano and sugar; mix well. Bring to a boil; reduce heat. Simmer for 30 minutes, stirring occasionally.

✦ Pour 1/2 of the tomato mixture into 6x10-inch baking pan. Layer with 1/2 of the noodles, spinach mixture, ricotta cheese mixture, remaining noodles and remaining tomato mixture. Pour White Wine Sauce over prepared layers.

✦ Bake at 425 degrees for 30 minutes or until light brown and bubbly. Let stand for 10 minutes before serving. Serve with a spinach or Caesar salad and a glass of white wine. Flavor is enhanced if prepared, chilled for 8 to 10 hours and baked on the day of serving.

Preparation time: 1 hour   6 servings

LASAGNA WITH SMOKED HAM

2 pounds fresh spinach, trimmed
3 cups ricotta cheese
1 egg yolk, beaten
1/2 teaspoon nutmeg
1/4 cup chopped fresh parsley
1/4 cup chopped fresh basil
1/4 cup chopped fresh oregano
1 1/2 pounds mozzarella cheese, shredded
3/4 cup freshly grated Parmesan cheese
4 cups spaghetti sauce
2 pounds fresh pasta, cut into 3-inch wide strips
12 ounces smoked ham, thinly sliced
Salt and pepper to taste

✦ Steam spinach in steamer for 1 minute; drain.
Combine ricotta cheese, egg yolk and nutmeg in bowl;
mix well. Mix parsley, basil and oregano in bowl.
✦ Reserve enough mozzarella cheese and Parmesan cheese
to sprinkle on top.
✦ Spread a thin layer of spaghetti sauce over bottom of
lasagna pan. Sprinkle with 1/3 of the herb mixture. Layer
pasta, ricotta cheese mixture, remaining mozzarella and
Parmesan cheese, ham, spinach, salt and pepper in
prepared pan, spreading some of the remaining spaghetti
sauce and sprinkling some of the herb mixture between
each layer. Top with reserved mozzarella cheese and
Parmesan cheese.
✦ Bake at 350 degrees for 40 to 60 minutes or until brown
and bubbly.

Preparation time: 50 minutes   12 servings

To control density and development on the Main Line, the Pennsylvania Railroad bought all the remaining land between Haverford and Rosemont in the late 1800s and parceled it into large lots. Although deed restrictions dictated the use, placement and value of potential buildings, buyers were attracted nevertheless.

ORIENTAL SESAME NOODLES

16 ounces linguini
Peanut Butter Dressing (at left)
4 or 5 scallions, chopped
1/4 cup sesame seeds, toasted

✦ Cook linguini using package directions. Drain well.
Combine with Peanut Butter Dressing, scallions and
sesame seeds in large bowl; toss to mix.
✦ Chill for 30 minutes or longer before serving.

Preparation time: 20 minutes   Yield: 8 servings

PEANUT BUTTER DRESSING

1/4 cup peanut butter

6 tablespoons rice vinegar

2 tablespoons honey mustard

1/4 cup soy sauce

1 1/2 tablespoons chili oil

1/2 cup sesame oil

1/3 cup vegetable oil

1/4 cup fresh orange juice

Salt and pepper to taste

✦

Blend peanut butter, vinegar, mustard and soy sauce in bowl. Whisk oils together. Whisk into peanut butter mixture. Whisk in orange juice, salt and pepper.

LINGUINI WITH MACADAMIA NUTS

3/4 cup olive oil
1 small bunch fresh basil, chopped
1 1/2 tablespoons minced garlic
1 cup finely chopped salted macadamia nuts, lightly
   toasted
1/4 cup freshly grated Parmesan cheese
Salt and freshly ground white pepper to taste
1 pound linguini

✦ Process 1/4 cup of the olive oil, basil and garlic in blender
until blended. Add macadamia nuts and cheese. Process
until blended. Add remaining 1/2 cup olive oil gradually,
processing constantly until blended. Season with salt and
white pepper. Cook in saucepan just until heated
through, stirring frequently.
✦ Cook pasta in boiling salted water just until tender but
firm; drain. Combine macadamia nut mixture and hot
pasta in bowl and mix gently. Spoon onto serving platter.
Garnish with chopped fresh basil and freshly grated
Parmesan cheese. Serve immediately.
✦ May prepare up to 1 week in advance and store in airtight
container in refrigerator.

Preparation time: 15 minutes   2 to 4 servings

LINGUINI WITH CLAMS

1 (7-ounce) can minced clams
3 cloves of garlic, minced
1/4 cup olive oil
1 small onion, chopped
8 ounces fresh mushrooms
6 tablespoons minced fresh parsley
1 teaspoon salt
1/4 teaspoon dried oregano
1/4 teaspoon dried red pepper flakes
1/4 cup dry white wine or white vermouth
6 ounces linguini, cooked, drained
Freshly grated Parmesan cheese to taste

✦ Drain clams, reserving liquid.
✦ Sauté garlic in olive oil in skillet just until garlic begins
  to turn golden brown; do not burn. Add onion and
  mushrooms. Sauté until onion is tender. Stir in clams.
  Cook over medium heat for 5 minutes. Stir in parsley,
  salt, oregano and red pepper flakes. Cook over low heat
  for 2 minutes, stirring frequently. Add reserved clam
  liquid and white wine. Cook over low heat for 15 to 20
  minutes or until of the desired consistency, stirring
  occasionally.
✦ Spoon hot linguini onto 2 dinner plates. Top with clam
  mixture; sprinkle with Parmesan cheese. Garnish with
  fresh parsley.

Preparation time: 20 minutes   2 servings

In 1871 the Pennsyl-
vania Railroad built
the Bryn Mawr Hotel
at Morris and Mont-
gomery Avenues to
encourage summer
visitors to use the
train. The hotel
burned in the winter
of 1889 and was
replaced in the
1890s. Today it is
the Baldwin School,
a college prepara-
tory school for girls.

SHRIMP WITH LINGUINI

3/4 cup clarified butter

1/4 cup virgin olive oil

3 tablespoons minced garlic

2 tablespoons chopped fresh parsley

2 tablespoons fresh lemon juice

1 tablespoon Worcestershire sauce

1 teaspoon minced fresh oregano or 1/2 teaspoon dried

1 teaspoon minced fresh basil or 1/2 teaspoon dried

1 teaspoon minced fresh tarragon or 1/2 teaspoon dried

1/2 teaspoon dried red pepper flakes

1/2 teaspoon dry mustard

1/4 teaspoon salt

2 pounds uncooked jumbo shrimp with tails, peeled, deveined and butterflied

1/2 cup white wine

1 pound spinach linguini, cooked, drained

1/2 cup freshly grated Parmesan cheese

2 tablespoons chopped fresh parsley

✦ Combine butter, olive oil, garlic, 2 tablespoons parsley, lemon juice, Worcestershire sauce, oregano, basil, tarragon, red pepper flakes, dry mustard and salt in saucepan; mix well. Cook until garlic is tender, stirring occasionally. Dip shrimp in butter mixture. Arrange shrimp on foil-lined baking sheet. Bake at 400 degrees until shrimp turn pink.

✦ Stir wine into remaining butter mixture. Cook until reduced by 1/4, stirring occasionally.

✦ Spoon hot linguini onto dinner plates. Arrange shrimp with tails pointed outward around perimeter of plate. Drizzle remaining butter mixture over shrimp and pasta. Sprinkle with cheese and 2 tablespoons parsley. May substitute 1 1/2 tablespoons dried parsley flakes for fresh parsley.

Preparation time: 40 minutes   4 to 6 servings

PENNE WITH MUSHROOMS

1 pound penne pasta
2 cups finely chopped onions
2 cloves of garlic, minced
1 teaspoon dried basil
1/2 teaspoon dried oregano
1/4 teaspoon dried red pepper flakes
2 tablespoons olive oil
1 pound (or less) fresh shiitake mushrooms, sliced
4 tablespoons unsalted butter
3 tablespoons flour
2 cups milk
2 (28-ounce) cans Italian tomatoes, drained, chopped
4 ounces thinly sliced prosciutto, cut into strips
1 cup shredded Italian fontina cheese
1 cup crumbled Gorgonzola cheese
1 1/2 cups freshly grated Parmesan cheese
1/2 cup minced fresh parsley
Salt and pepper to taste

✦ Cook pasta in boiling water in saucepan for 5 minutes; drain.

✦ Sauté onions, garlic, basil, oregano and red pepper flakes in olive oil in skillet over medium-low heat until onions are tender. Add mushrooms. Cook over medium heat for 10 to 15 minutes or until mushrooms are tender, stirring frequently. Remove mushroom mixture to bowl.

✦ Heat 3 tablespoons of the butter in saucepan over medium-low heat until melted. Whisk in flour. Cook for 3 minutes, stirring constantly. Add milk in fine stream, whisking constantly. Cook for 2 minutes or until thickened, whisking constantly. Pour over mushroom mixture; mix well. Stir in tomatoes, prosciutto, fontina cheese, Gorgonzola cheese, 1 1/4 cups of the Parmesan cheese and parsley. Add pasta, salt and pepper to mixture and mix gently. Spoon into buttered 3- or 4-quart baking dish. Sprinkle with remaining Parmesan cheese; dot with remaining 1 tablespoon butter.

✦ Bake at 450 degrees for 25 to 30 minutes or until golden brown and pasta is tender. Garnish with sprigs of Italian parsley.

Preparation time: 45 minutes   8 servings

Gertrude Ely, a famous resident of Bryn Mawr from 1876 to 1970, was the state director of women's projects in Roosevelt's 1935–37 Works Progress Administration (WPA). She helped establish the United Service Organization (USO) in World War II, was very active in the National Association of American Indian Affairs, organized areawide UNICEF, and ran twice for the Senate on the Democratic ticket. Her family owned Wyndham House, which is now part of Bryn Mawr College.

PASTA WITH CHICKEN DIJON

1/2 cup chopped green onions
1/4 cup chopped fresh basil
2 large cloves of garlic, minced
1/4 cup butter
1 1/2 pounds poached chicken, chopped
1 pound fresh mushrooms, sliced
3/4 cup white wine
Salt and pepper to taste
1 cup nonfat sour cream
1 tablespoon Dijon mustard
1 pound pasta, cooked, drained

✦ Sauté green onions, basil and garlic in butter in skillet until green onions and garlic are tender. Add chicken, mushrooms and white wine; mix well. Simmer for 20 minutes, stirring occasionally. Season with salt and pepper. Stir in mixture of sour cream and Dijon mustard.
✦ Combine chicken mixture with hot pasta in bowl and mix gently. Serve with freshly grated Parmesan cheese.

Preparation time: 30 minutes   4 to 6 servings

PASTA WITH TOMATOES

4 medium fresh tomatoes, seeded, chopped
4 to 6 oil-pack sun-dried tomatoes, drained, chopped
1 clove of garlic, chopped
1/4 cup extra-virgin olive oil
Salt and pepper to taste
8 ounces penne pasta
3/4 cup coarsely chopped fresh basil
Freshly grated Parmesan cheese to taste

✦ Combine fresh tomatoes, sun-dried tomatoes, garlic, olive oil, salt and pepper in bowl; mix well. Marinate at room temperature for 1 hour, stirring occasionally.
✦ Cook pasta using package directions; drain. Toss hot pasta with tomato mixture in bowl. Stir in basil. Serve hot or at room temperature with grated Parmesan cheese.

Preparation time: 20 minutes   6 to 8 servings

PASTA WITH SHRIMP AND ARUGULA

2 tablespoons olive oil
1/4 teaspoon dried red pepper flakes
1 1/2 pounds uncooked medium or large shrimp,
    peeled, deveined
1/4 teaspoon salt
12 sun-dried tomatoes, cut into strips
2 medium tomatoes, seeded, chopped
3 cloves of garlic, minced
2 medium shallots, finely chopped
1/2 cup chopped fresh basil
1 teaspoon dried oregano
6 tablespoons olive oil
1/4 cup toasted pine nuts
1 1/2 tablespoons fresh lemon juice
2 bunches arugula, trimmed, coarsely chopped
16 ounces penne or fusilli, cooked al dente, drained
Salt and freshly ground black pepper to taste
Freshly grated Parmesan cheese to taste

+ Heat 2 tablespoons olive oil and red pepper in skillet over
medium heat. Sprinkle shrimp with 1/4 teaspoon salt; add
to skillet. Cook for 2 minutes or just until shrimp turn
pink, stirring occasionally. Stir in sun-dried tomatoes,
fresh tomatoes, garlic, shallots, basil and oregano. Cook
until the shallots are tender and shrimp are cooked
through, stirring occasionally.
+ Combine 6 tablespoons olive oil, pine nuts and lemon
juice in bowl; mix well. Add arugula and toss to coat. Add
the shrimp mixture and mix gently. Add hot pasta and
mix well. Season with salt and black pepper; sprinkle with
Parmesan cheese. Serve immediately.

Preparation time: 45 minutes   4 to 6 servings

**The Shipley School
was founded in 1894
by three Quaker sis-
ters named Shipley.
It was intended as
a preparatory
school for Bryn
Mawr College.**

PASTA WITH FRESH SALMON

2 scallions, chopped
1 clove of garlic, minced
1/2 teaspoon minced fresh gingerroot
1 tablespoon olive oil
1 tablespoon melted butter
1/2 (16-ounce) can water-pack artichokes, quartered
1/2 cup chicken broth
2 tablespoons fresh lemon juice
11/2 cups (1-inch pieces) fresh asparagus
1 (8-ounce) salmon steak, grilled, boned, cut into
   bite-size pieces
Freshly ground pepper to taste
8 ounces thin spaghetti, cooked, drained

✦ Sauté scallions, garlic and gingerroot in mixture of olive
  oil and butter in skillet for 1 minute. Add artichokes,
  broth and 1 tablespoon lemon juice. Simmer for 1
  minute, stirring frequently. Stir in asparagus. Cook for 2
  to 4 minutes or until asparagus is tender-crisp. Add
  salmon and mix gently. Season with pepper.
✦ Toss hot pasta with 1 tablespoon lemon juice in bowl.
  Place on serving platter; top with salmon mixture.

Preparation time: 20 minutes   4 servings

VERMICELLI WITH SUMMER HERBS

1/2 cup fresh bread crumbs
3 tablespoons extra-virgin olive oil
1 cup any combination chopped fresh herbs
1 or 2 small shallots, finely chopped
2 tablespoons unsalted butter, chopped
8 ounces vermicelli, cooked al dente
Salt and freshly ground pepper to taste

✦ Sauté bread crumbs in 1 tablespoon olive oil in skillet
  over medium heat until brown and crisp.
✦ Combine herbs, shallots, 2 tablespoons olive oil and
  butter in bowl; mix well. Add hot pasta and mix gently.
  Season with salt and pepper. Spoon onto serving platter;
  top with bread crumbs.

Preparation time: 10 minutes   2 to 3 servings

PESTO AL BURRO

1 cup packed chopped fresh parsley
3 tablespoons chopped fresh basil
1 clove of garlic
1 tablespoon pine nuts
6 whole almonds, blanched
1/2 teaspoon salt
6 tablespoons melted butter, cooled
3/4 cup freshly grated Parmesan cheese
10 ounces spaghetti or linguini, cooked, drained

✦ Process parsley, basil, garlic, pine nuts, almonds and salt
in blender at high speed until finely chopped. Add butter.
Process at high speed until blended. Pour into bowl; stir
in cheese. Combine hot spaghetti and parsley mixture in
bowl and mix gently.

Preparation time: 15 minutes   4 to 6 servings

LIGHT TOMATO SAUCE

2 tablespoons olive oil
1/3 cup finely minced red onion
11/2 teaspoons minced garlic
1 (28-ounce) can Italian plum tomatoes, coarsely chopped
3 tablespoons minced fresh basil
1 teaspoon sugar
1/2 teaspoon coarse salt
1/2 teaspoon freshly ground pepper

✦ Heat olive oil in 12-inch skillet over medium heat;
reduce heat to low. Add onion to skillet. Cook for 4
minutes or until onion is tender but not brown, stirring
constantly. Stir in garlic. Cook for 1 minute, stirring
frequently. Add undrained tomatoes, basil, sugar, salt and
pepper. Bring to a boil over high heat; reduce heat to
medium.
✦ Cook for 25 minutes or until slightly thickened, stirring
frequently. Remove from heat. Let stand at room
temperature for 1 hour or longer before serving.

Preparation time: 15 minutes   2 servings

Cabrini College sits on a 230-acre estate which has passed through several families. The Lewises first purchased the land in the 1800s. Around 1900, "Woodcrest Farms" was acquired by James W. Paul, a wealthy Philadelphia banker. He hired the renowned architect Horace Trumbauer to design an Elizabethan-styled mansion, which was the scene of many gala affairs on the Main Line.

MARINATED TOMATO SAUCE

2 pounds very ripe tomatoes, chopped
6 medium cloves of garlic, crushed
30 large fresh basil leaves, torn into thirds
2/3 cup olive oil
Salt and freshly ground pepper to taste
1 pound pasta, cooked, drained

✦ Combine tomatoes, garlic and basil in bowl; mix well. Add olive oil, salt and pepper and mix gently.
✦ Marinate, covered, at room temperature for up to 2 hours or in refrigerator for 2 hours or longer.
✦ Pour marinated tomato mixture over hot pasta in bowl and mix gently. Serve hot or cold.

Preparation time: 30 minutes   6 servings

FRESH CORN RISOTTO

2 medium shallots, chopped
1/3 cup butter
1/2 cup arborio rice
1/3 cup dry white wine
3 cups chicken stock
2 cups fresh corn, puréed
1 cup fresh corn
1/3 cup freshly grated Parmesan cheese
Salt and pepper to taste

✦ Sauté shallots in butter in saucepan over medium heat for 5 minutes or until tender. Stir in rice. Cook for 1 minute, stirring constantly. Add white wine; mix well. Cook for 5 minutes or until liquid evaporates. Add stock. Cook for 10 minutes, stirring frequently; increase heat to high. Bring to a boil. Boil for 18 minutes or until thickened, stirring frequently.
✦ Add puréed corn, fresh corn and cheese; mix well. Cook for 3 minutes, stirring occasionally. Season with salt and pepper. Add additional chicken stock if desired for thinner consistency. Garnish with fresh parsley. May substitute thawed frozen corn for fresh corn.

Preparation time: 15 minutes   4 servings

HARVEST RICE

1 medium onion, chopped
2 cups shredded carrots
1/2 cup chopped pecans
1/4 cup butter
1 tablespoon olive oil
1 cup orzo
2 cups long grain rice
1/4 cup butter
1 tablespoon olive oil
4 cloves of garlic, minced
1/4 cup butter
1 tablespoon olive oil
1 pound fresh mushrooms, sliced
1 cup chopped fresh parsley
Salt and pepper to taste
4 cups chicken broth
1/2 cup white wine
1 cup freshly grated Parmesan cheese or Romano cheese

✦ Sauté onion, carrots and pecans in skillet in mixture of 1/4 cup butter and 1 tablespoon olive oil until brown. Spoon into bowl.

✦ Brown orzo and rice in mixture of 1/4 cup butter and 1 tablespoon olive oil in same skillet, stirring occasionally. Stir into onion mixture.

✦ Sauté garlic in mixture of 1/4 cup butter and 1 tablespoon olive oil in same skillet. Stir in mushrooms, parsley, salt and pepper. Stir into rice mixture. Add broth and wine; mix well. Spoon into large saucepan.

✦ Simmer, covered, over low heat for 25 minutes. Spoon 1/2 of the mixture into buttered 2-quart baking dish; sprinkle with cheese. Top with remaining rice mixture. Bake at 350 degrees for 25 minutes.

Preparation time: 45 minutes   10 to 12 servings

The Black Rock Farmhouse on Black Rock Road in Bryn Mawr, built around 1780, is a fine example of an early Pennsylvania stone farmhouse. It was sited near a great mountain ash known as the Indian Council Tree. The last resident Indians of Montgomery County used to meet under its branches.

SAFFRON AND PARMESAN RICE

1 1/2 cups water
1 1/2 cups chicken broth
1 teaspoon salt
15 saffron threads
1 cup short grain brown rice
2 tablespoons unsalted butter
2 tablespoons freshly grated Parmesan cheese

✦ Bring water, broth, salt and saffron to a boil in saucepan. Stir in brown rice; reduce heat.

✦ Cook, covered, for 35 minutes or until liquid evaporates. Stir in butter and cheese. Let stand, covered, for 10 minutes before serving.

Preparation time: 5 minutes   4 servings

RICE WITH WATER CHESTNUTS

1/2 cup chopped scallions
1 (3-ounce) can sliced mushrooms, drained
2 tablespoons olive oil
1 (5-ounce) can water chestnuts, drained, chopped
2 tablespoons light soy sauce
1 (6-ounce) package long grain and wild rice with seasoning envelope
2 cups nonfat chicken broth

✦ Sauté scallions and mushrooms in olive oil in saucepan. Add water chestnuts and soy sauce; mix well. Stir in rice, seasoning envelope and broth. Spoon into baking pan.

✦ Bake, covered, at 350 degrees for 45 minutes; remove cover. Bake for 15 minutes longer. May assemble in advance, chill and bake just before serving time.

Preparation time: 15 minutes   4 servings

SHRIMP PILAF

2 pounds shrimp with heads and tails
1 large onion, finely chopped
1 carrot, peeled, chopped
2 bay leaves
Salt and pepper to taste
1 quart water
10 slices bacon, chopped
1 large green bell pepper, finely chopped
1 large onion, finely chopped
1^1/2 cups long grain rice
3 large tomatoes, peeled, chopped
^{1}/3 cup chopped fresh parsley

✦ Remove heads and peel shrimp, reserving heads and shells. Store shrimp, covered, in refrigerator. Combine reserved shrimp heads, shells, 1 onion, carrot, bay leaves, salt and pepper in roasting pan. Roast at 375 degrees for 20 minutes. Spoon into stockpot. Add water. Bring to a boil over medium heat; reduce heat. Simmer, covered, for 30 minutes, stirring occasionally. Strain, reserving broth.

✦ Fry bacon in skillet until crisp. Drain, reserving pan drippings. Crumble bacon.

✦ Sauté green pepper and 1 onion in reserved pan drippings in skillet for 10 minutes. Add rice. Cook for 7 minutes or until tender, stirring occasionally.

✦ Add tomatoes, parsley and 2^1/2 cups of the reserved broth. Bring to a boil; reduce heat. Simmer, covered, for 20 minutes, stirring occasionally.

✦ May add additional broth at this time for desired consistency. Add shrimp. Cook for 10 minutes longer, stirring occasionally. Stir in bacon. Season with salt and pepper. Serve immediately.

Preparation time: 1 hour   6 servings

ST. THOMAS OF VILLANOVA

Villanova College was founded in 1842 by members
of the oldest religious teaching order of the Roman Catholic
Church, the Order of St. Augustine, who came to this country
in search of religious freedom. They were a dedicated
group of scholars who were committed to their religion, to
teaching, and to the dream of being able to found
an institution of learning that aspired to the noblest ideals
of academic and spiritual integrity.

In the early 1800s, the Augustines purchased 222
acres of land from the Belle-Air estate of the late John
Rudolph, built in 1806. Classes commenced in September,
1843, with just seven students, all of whom lived
with their faculty and priests in the estate mansion. Little is
known of the original curriculum except that it probably
included the traditional collegiate subjects of the time: Greek,
Latin, math, and philosophy.

Students could easily reach the college by railroad or
by the Lancaster Pike, which passed through the north
side of the property. Only Catholics were admitted to the school
in the first years, but this rule was relaxed by the 1850s, and a
few Protestant boys were invited to attend. Tuition for a religious
education of this quality amidst the beautiful surroundings of the
Main Line was $125 per year.

BAKED FLOUNDER

1/4 cup finely chopped onion
1/4 cup butter
1 (3-ounce) can chopped broiled mushrooms
7 ounces fresh lump crab meat, picked
1/2 cup coarsely crumbled saltines
2 tablespoons snipped fresh parsley
1/2 teaspoon salt
Dash of pepper
2 pounds fresh flounder fillets
White Wine Sauce (below)
1 cup shredded Swiss cheese
1/2 teaspoon paprika

✦ Sauté onion in butter in skillet until tender but not brown. Drain mushrooms, reserving liquid. Add mushrooms, crab meat, cracker crumbs, parsley, salt and pepper to onion in skillet; mix well. Spread crab meat mixture over flounder fillets.
✦ Roll fillets; place seam side down in nonstick baking dish. Pour White Wine Sauce over top.
✦ Bake at 400 degrees for 25 minutes. Sprinkle with cheese and paprika. Bake for 10 minutes longer or until fish flakes easily.

Preparation time: 15 minutes   8 servings

WHITE WINE SAUCE

3 tablespoons butter
3 tablespoons flour
1/4 teaspoon salt
Milk
Reserved mushroom liquid
1/3 cup dry white wine

✦ Melt butter in saucepan. Blend in flour and salt. Add enough milk to reserved mushroom liquid to measure 1 1/2 cups. Add to butter mixture. Stir in wine.
✦ Cook over low heat until mixture thickens and bubbles.

Preparation time: 5 minutes   8 servings

SOUTHWESTERN HALIBUT

$^1/_4$ cup fresh lemon juice
1 tablespoon fresh lime juice
1 tablespoon olive oil
1 clove of garlic, crushed
$^1/_4$ cup minced onion
1 tablespoon grated fresh ginger
1 jalapeño, seeded, minced
$^1/_2$ teaspoon cumin
$^1/_4$ teaspoon salt
$^1/_8$ teaspoon cayenne pepper
$1^1/_2$ pounds halibut or swordfish
Lemon and lime slices to taste

✦ Pour mixture of lemon juice, lime juice, olive oil, garlic, onion, ginger, jalapeño, cumin, salt and cayenne over fish in dish.
✦ Chill, covered, for 1 to 2 hours.
✦ Brush grill rack with oil. Remove fish from marinade, reserving marinade. Grill fish for 4 minutes per side, basting with reserved marinade. Top with lemon and lime slices.

Preparation time: 10 minutes   4 servings

CHIVE SAUCE

1/2 cup sour cream

1/4 cup mayonnaise

1/3 cup chopped
fresh chives

1 1/2 tablespoons
fresh lime juice

Salt and pepper
to taste

✦

Blend sour cream,

mayonnaise, chives,

lime juice, salt

and pepper in bowl;

mix well.

BAKED SALMON AND CHIVE SAUCE

Butter to taste
1 to 1 1/4 pounds salmon fillets
Salt and pepper to taste
1/2 cup packed fresh parsley
1 large clove of garlic
5 ounces French bread, crusts trimmed, torn into
    bite-size pieces
1/4 cup butter
1 1/2 tablespoons fresh lime juice
1 tablespoon freshly grated lime peel
Chive Sauce (at left)

✦ Line baking sheet with foil. Butter foil. Arrange salmon
  on foil. Season with salt and pepper.
✦ Chop parsley and garlic in food processor. Add bread
  pieces. Process until mixture forms coarse crumbs.
✦ Melt 1/4 cup butter in large heavy skillet over
  medium-high heat. Add lime juice, lime peel and bread
  crumb mixture. Cook for 8 minutes or until crumbs
  begin to crisp, stirring constantly. Press crumb mixture
  over salmon, covering completely.
✦ Bake at 400 degrees for 15 minutes or just until
  cooked through. Remove to serving platter. Serve with
  Chive Sauce.

Preparation time: 30 minutes   4 servings

SALMON FILLETS

1/4 cup balsamic vinegar
2 tablespoons olive oil
4 (4-ounce) fresh salmon fillets
Salt and pepper to taste
3 tablespoons chopped fresh mint
Lime wedges to taste

✦ Brush mixture of vinegar and olive oil on salmon fillets.
  Sprinkle with salt and pepper.
✦ Broil or grill fillets 6 inches from heat source for 8
  minutes or until fish flakes easily. Sprinkle immediately
  with mint. Top with lime wedges.

Preparation time: 5 to 10 minutes   4 servings

SALMON WITH CHAMPAGNE SAUCE

1/2 cup toasted pine nuts
1/2 cup packed fresh basil leaves
1 tablespoon olive oil
Salt and pepper to taste
4 (3/4-inch thick) salmon fillets
Olive oil to taste
Champagne Cream Sauce (at right)

+ Process pine nuts, basil leaves and olive oil in food
  processor until nuts are finely chopped. Season with salt
  and pepper.
+ Brush salmon with olive oil. Season with salt and pepper.
  Broil for 3 minutes on both sides or until salmon is
  cooked through.
+ Sprinkle pine nut mixture over salmon; press pine nut
  mixture gently into salmon.
+ Spoon warm Champagne Cream Sauce onto serving
  plates. Top with salmon.

Preparation time: 30 minutes   8 servings

SALMON WITH MINT PUREE

1 cup firmly packed fresh mint leaves
1 cup firmly packed fresh parsley tops
4 shallots, quartered
1/2 cup white wine
1 cup olive oil
1 tablespoon salt, or to taste
1 teaspoon pepper
Seasonings to taste
1 large salmon fillet
3 lemon slices

+ Combine mint leaves, parsley tops, shallots, wine, olive
  oil, salt and pepper in food processor container. Purée
  into paste.
+ Season salmon. Coat gently with mint purée. Arrange
  fan of 3 lemon slices on top. Bake in parchment at 350
  degrees for 30 minutes.

Preparation time: 15 to 30 minutes   2 to 4 servings

CHAMPAGNE CREAM SAUCE

1/4 cup chopped
shallots

2 tablespoons butter

2 cups dry
Champagne

2 cups whipping
cream

Salt and pepper
to taste

1/2 cup chopped
chives

+

Sauté shallots in
butter in large heavy
skillet over medium
heat for 3 minutes.
Increase heat to high.
Add Champagne.
Boil for 10 minutes
or until reduced to
1/2 cup, stirring
frequently. Add cream
and boil for 8 minutes
or until thickened,
stirring occasionally.
Stir in salt, pepper
and chives.

LEMON-MUSTARD MAYONNAISE

3 egg yolks

1 teaspoon fresh lemon juice

2 teaspoons Dijon mustard

1/2 cup olive oil or sunflower oil

✦

Whisk egg yolks, lemon juice and mustard in small bowl for 2 minutes. Add olive oil gradually in a fine stream, whisking constantly until of desired consistency.

MARINATED SALMON STEAKS

2 tablespoons thinly sliced fresh basil
1 teaspoon fresh thyme leaves
4 salmon steaks or fillets
Milk to taste
Lemon-Mustard Mayonnaise (at left)

✦ Sprinkle mixture of basil and thyme over salmon in shallow dish. Pour in enough milk to cover salmon. Marinate, covered, in refrigerator for 4 hours or longer; drain.
✦ Coat salmon on both sides with Lemon-Mustard Mayonnaise. Spray grill with nonstick cooking spray. Grill for 5 minutes. Remove to serving platter. Spoon remaining Lemon-Mustard Mayonnaise over top. Garnish with additional basil and parsley. Serve immediately.

Preparation time: 15 minutes   4 servings

BASIL ORANGE SALMON

1/2 cup packed thinly sliced fresh basil leaves
1/4 cup fresh orange juice
2 1/2 tablespoons fresh lemon juice
2 tablespoons olive oil
2 teaspoons freshly grated orange peel
2 salmon steaks

✦ Combine basil leaves, orange juice, lemon juice, olive oil and orange peel in large shallow dish. Add salmon, turning to coat. Chill, covered, for 30 to 60 minutes.
✦ Grill over medium-high heat for about 3 minutes on each side or until cooked through. Remove to serving plate. Serve immediately.

Preparation time: 10 minutes   2 servings

SALMON WITH SALSA

4 (6-ounce) salmon steaks
Olive oil to taste
Salt and pepper to taste
Arugula, Tomato and Caper Salsa (at right)
Lemon wedges to taste

✦ Brush both sides of salmon with olive oil. Season with salt and pepper. Grill over medium heat for 5 minutes on each side or just until cooked through.
✦ Remove to serving plates. Spoon Arugula, Tomato and Caper Salsa over top. Top with lemon wedges.

Preparation time: 15 minutes   4 servings

SALMON AND LEMON DIJON SAUCE

1/4 cup sour cream
2 tablespoons Dijon mustard
1/2 tablespoon fresh lemon juice
2 tablespoons melted butter or margarine
1 clove of garlic, crushed
3/4 teaspoon chopped fresh dill
4 salmon steaks
1 tablespoon melted butter or margarine
Fresh parsley to taste

✦ Blend sour cream, mustard, lemon juice and 2 tablespoons melted butter in bowl. Stir in garlic and dill. Chill, covered, until serving time.
✦ Brush salmon with remaining 1 tablespoon melted butter. Grill for 10 to 12 minutes, turning once. Remove to serving plate. Serve with lemon Dijon sauce. Top with parsley. May bake at 425 degrees until cooked through, turning once.

Preparation time: 5 minutes   4 servings

ARUGULA, TOMATO AND CAPER SALSA

1 pound fresh, ripe plum tomatoes, seeded, chopped

2/3 cup lightly packed chopped fresh arugula or basil

1 shallot, chopped

1 1/2 tablespoons drained capers

1/2 cup olive oil

2 tablespoons fresh lemon juice

✦

Combine tomatoes, arugula, shallot and capers in bowl. Add mixture of olive oil and lemon juice; mix well.

RED SNAPPER IN PARCHMENT

8 ounces cooked peeled shrimp, chopped
8 ounces cooked lobster, chopped
White Wine Cream Sauce (below)
Butter to taste
1 pound red snapper fillets

✦ Add shrimp and lobster to White Wine Cream Sauce in skillet; mix gently.
✦ Butter 4 one-foot lengths of parchment. Spread 1/4 cup White Wine Cream Sauce in center of each parchment sheet. Top with snapper fillet. Spread White Wine Cream Sauce over top. Fold parchment to form bag with crimped edges. Bake at 350 degrees for 30 minutes.

Preparation time: 1 hour   4 servings

WHITE WINE CREAM SAUCE

1 onion, finely chopped
1/4 cup butter
1/4 cup flour
1 cup light cream
1 cup milk
1 egg
1/8 teaspoon nutmeg
8 dashes of Tabasco sauce
1/2 cup white wine
Salt to taste

✦ Sauté onion in butter in skillet for 5 minutes or until tender. Add flour gradually to form paste, stirring well after each addition. Cook over low heat until liquid is absorbed, stirring constantly and being careful not to burn. Add light cream and milk. Cook over medium heat until thickened, stirring constantly.
✦ Beat egg and nutmeg in small mixing bowl. Fold mixture of Tabasco sauce and white wine into cream sauce. Stir a small amount of hot mixture into egg mixture; stir egg mixture into hot mixture. Season with salt.

Preparation time: 10 minutes   2 1/2 cups

BROILED RED SNAPPER

4 (6-ounce) red snapper fillets
Olive oil and fresh lime juice to taste
Salt and pepper to taste
Chopped fresh cilantro to taste
Black Bean Salsa (at right)

✦ Brush snapper fillets with olive oil. Sprinkle with lime
juice, salt and pepper. Broil without turning just until
cooked through or for about 9 minutes per inch of
thickness.
✦ Transfer snapper to serving plates. Sprinkle with cilantro.
Spoon Black Bean Salsa over top.

Preparation time: 15 minutes   4 servings

FILLET OF SOLE WITH CRAB

3 pounds sole fillets
3 cups milk
2 tablespoons minced onion
6 tablespoons butter
1 1/2 teaspoons dry mustard
5 tablespoons flour
1 tablespoon fresh lemon juice
3 tablespoons sherry
1 1/2 pounds fresh crab meat or lobster
1 cup shredded sharp Cheddar cheese

✦ Roll sole fillets and place in skillet. Pour milk over top.
Simmer for 5 to 10 minutes. Drain sole; reserving milk.
Place sole in shallow baking dish.
✦ Sauté onion in butter in skillet until tender. Stir in
mustard, flour and reserved milk. Cook over low heat
until thickened, stirring constantly. Add lemon juice,
sherry and crab meat. Pour crab meat mixture over sole.
Sprinkle with cheese.
✦ Bake at 350 degrees for 30 to 40 minutes or until hot
and bubbly. Increase oven temperature and broil until
light brown.
✦ May be frozen before baking; thaw for 4 hours
before baking.

Preparation time: 1 hour   6 to 8 servings

BLACK BEAN SALSA

1 (16-ounce)
can black beans,
rinsed, drained

2 oranges, peeled,
seeded, chopped

1 ripe tomato, seeded,
chopped

3/4 cup chopped
fresh cilantro

1 large jalapeño,
seeded, minced

2 tablespoons fresh
lime juice

1 tablespoon olive oil

1 avocado, peeled,
chopped

Salt and pepper
to taste

✦

Combine first 8

ingredients in bowl.

Season with salt and

pepper. Chill, covered,

until serving time or

for up to 24 hours.

MARINATED SWORDFISH

1/3 cup soy sauce
1/4 cup dry white wine
3/4 cup melted butter, divided
2 tablespoons sugar
3/4 tablespoon grated fresh ginger
1 clove of garlic, minced
4 swordfish steaks
6 tablespoons fresh lemon juice
1/4 cup dry sherry

✦ Mix soy sauce, wine, 1/4 cup melted butter, sugar,
ginger and garlic in bowl. Place swordfish steaks in
shallow glass dish. Pour 1/2 cup marinade over swordfish.
Marinate, covered, in refrigerator for 1 hour or longer.

✦ Mix remaining 1/2 cup melted butter, remaining
marinade, lemon juice and sherry in bowl. Arrange
swordfish in grilling basket; baste with sherry mixture.
Grill until done to taste, turning and basting with
sherry mixture.

Preparation time: 10 minutes   4 servings

SWORDFISH WITH HORSERADISH

1 pound (1-inch thick) swordfish steak
1/3 cup milk
2 1/2 tablespoons unsalted butter
1 1/2 tablespoons prepared white horseradish
1 tablespoon fresh lemon juice
2 sprigs of fresh thyme or 1/4 teaspoon dried thyme

✦ Soak swordfish in milk in baking dish for 1 hour; drain.

✦ Melt butter over medium heat in small saucepan. Add
horseradish, lemon juice and thyme. Cook for 3 minutes
or until slightly thickened, stirring constantly. Spoon
horseradish mixture over swordfish.

✦ Bake at 350 degrees for 15 minutes or until fish is
tender and flakes easily.

✦ Broil for 5 minutes or until golden brown and bubbling.
Garnish with lemon wedges. May grill for 10 to 12
minutes on each side.

Preparation time: 10 minutes   1 to 2 servings

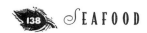
SWORDFISH WITH LEMON BASIL

2¹/2 tablespoons fresh lemon juice
2 tablespoons olive oil
2 cloves of garlic, crushed
¹/2 teaspoon grated lemon peel
3 tablespoons thinly sliced fresh basil or 1 tablespoon
    dried basil
2 teaspoons drained capers
Salt and pepper to taste
4 swordfish fillets

✦ Whisk lemon juice, olive oil, garlic and lemon peel in
    small bowl. Add 2 tablespoons of the basil, capers, salt
    and pepper. Let stand for 1 hour or longer.
✦ Season swordfish with salt and pepper. Brush with small
    amount of vinaigrette.
✦ Grill swordfish for about 4 minutes on each side. Remove
    to serving plate. Whisk vinaigrette. Pour over swordfish.
    Top with remaining 1 tablespoon basil.

Preparation time: 1¹/2 hours   4 servings

MARINATED TUNA STEAKS

1 teaspoon white pepper
1 teaspoon grated fresh ginger
4 sprigs of fresh thyme, coarsely chopped, or 1 teaspoon
    dried thyme
1 clove of garlic, minced
2 tablespoons light soy sauce
1 tablespoon fresh lemon juice
2 tablespoons virgin olive oil
4 (8-ounce) tuna steaks

✦ Combine white pepper, ginger, thyme, garlic, soy sauce,
    lemon juice and olive oil in bowl; mix well. Place tuna in
    shallow dish. Brush tuna on both sides with marinade.
    Pour remaining marinade over top. Let stand, covered,
    for 1 hour or longer before grilling.
✦ Grill tuna steaks for 3 to 6 minutes on each side; do not
    overcook. May serve with tomato salsa.

Preparation time: 10 minutes   4 servings

The furnishings
and layout of the
Assembly Room at
Agnes Irwin School
are copied from an
English mansion.
Several interesting
fireplaces with iron
fire backs include
one dated 1765 from
a local foundry,
Warwick Furnace.
The oldest fireplace
is lined with Delft
tiles painted with
Biblical scenes.

EASTERN-SHORE CRAB CAKES

3 1/2 tablespoons flour
1/4 teaspoon baking powder
4 to 5 dashes of Worcestershire sauce
1 tablespoon sherry
1 egg
1 tablespoon chopped fresh parsley
1 tablespoon prepared Dijon mustard
2 tablespoons mayonnaise
1 pound lump or back-fin crab meat
3/4 cup vegetable oil or butter, or mix

✦ Mix flour, baking powder, Worcestershire sauce, sherry, egg, parsley, mustard and mayonnaise in bowl.
✦ Fold crab meat into flour mixture gently. Chill, covered, for 1 hour or longer.
✦ Shape crab meat mixture into 4 or 5 patties; flatten slightly. Cook in hot oil in skillet over medium heat for 5 to 7 minutes on each side or until light brown.

Preparation time: 15 to 30 minutes   4 to 5 servings

VIRGINIA TIDEWATER CRAB CAKES

2 cups or 1 pound lump crab meat
1 cup fresh bread crumbs
Salt and pepper to taste
2 large eggs
1/2 cup whipping cream
Dash of hot sauce
2 teaspoons Worcestershire sauce
2 tablespoons chopped fresh parsley
2 teaspoons grated onion
2 teaspoons unsalted butter

✦ Mix crab meat, bread crumbs, salt and pepper in bowl.
✦ Whisk eggs in small bowl. Whisk in whipping cream. Add hot sauce, Worcestershire sauce, parsley and onion; mix well. Combine with crab meat mixture. Shape into 4 large patties or 24 appetizer-size balls.
✦ Sauté in butter in skillet over medium heat until brown.

Preparation time: 15 minutes   4 servings

CRAB MEAT ASPARAGUS CREPES

32 stalks asparagus, trimmed to 3 1/2 inches, peeled
Salt to taste
2 tablespoons unsalted butter
2 tablespoons flour
1 cup milk
1 teaspoon dry cooking sherry
1/3 cup freshly grated Parmesan cheese
1/2 cup shredded Gruyère cheese
8 ounces fresh lump crab meat
1 teaspoon fresh nutmeg
Pepper to taste
8 Crepes (page 141)
Béchamel Sauce (page 141)

✦ Cook asparagus in boiling salted water in saucepan just until tender. Place asparagus in ice water in bowl for 1 minute; drain.

✦ Melt butter in saucepan over low heat. Add flour. Cook for 3 minutes, stirring constantly. Add milk gradually in a fine stream, whisking constantly. Simmer for 5 minutes, stirring constantly. Add sherry, Parmesan cheese and Gruyère cheese. Simmer until cheese is melted. Combine cheese mixture with crab meat in bowl. Add nutmeg, salt and pepper.

✦ Place Crepes on work surface. Mound 1/8 of crab meat mixture on each crepe. Arrange 4 asparagus spears on top of crab meat mixture. Roll up as for jelly roll, with asparagus tips extending beyond edge of crepe. Place seam side down in buttered shallow baking dish. Bake at 400 degrees for 10 minutes. Spoon warm Béchamel Sauce over top.

Preparation time: 45 minutes   8 servings

Historically, Villanova was a crossroads on the Main Line, and it continues to be a hub of activity. In the 1700s, farmers busily took produce and herds through the gulph to Philadelphia on Old Gulph and New Gulph Roads, while Spring Mill Road, running north-south, served as another busy route to the ferry on the Schuylkill River.

CREPES

1 cup flour
1/2 cup plus 2 tablespoons water
1/2 cup milk
3 eggs
2 tablespoons melted unsalted butter
1/2 teaspoon salt

✦ Process flour, water, milk, eggs, butter and salt in blender for 5 seconds. Shake, covered, in blender container. Process for 20 seconds longer. Remove batter to bowl. Let stand, covered, for 1 hour.

✦ Brush 6- or 7-inch nonstick skillet lightly with butter. Pour a small amount of batter into skillet. Swirl until batter covers bottom of skillet. Cook over low heat, loosening edge of crepe with spatula. Cook until underside of crepe is light brown. Turn crepe; cook until underside is light brown. Repeat process until all batter is used.

Preparation time: 20 minutes   20 crepes

BECHAMEL SAUCE

1/4 cup butter
1/4 cup flour
2 cups cold milk
Dash of nutmeg
1/2 teaspoon salt
1/8 teaspoon white pepper
1 teaspoon sugar

✦ Melt butter in skillet. Add flour. Cook over low heat for 3 minutes, stirring constantly; do not brown. Add milk, nutmeg, salt, white pepper and sugar. Cook over low heat until thickened, stirring constantly.

Preparation time: 10 minutes   2 cups

MARYLAND SOFT-SHELL CRABS

1 cup vegetable oil
2 tablespoons white vinegar
1 teaspoon salt
1/4 teaspoon dried tarragon
1 teaspoon lemon pepper seasoning
1 teaspoon fresh lemon juice
1/8 teaspoon garlic powder
12 live Maryland soft crabs, cleaned

✦ Whisk oil, vinegar, salt, tarragon, lemon pepper seasoning, lemon juice and garlic powder in bowl. Let stand at room temperature for several hours.
✦ Baste bottom side of crabs liberally with marinade. Place crabs bottom side down on grill rack. Grill over low heat for 5 minutes. Baste top side of crabs liberally with marinade. Turn carefully. Grill for 5 minutes longer. Transfer to serving plate.

Preparation time: 10 minutes   4 to 6 servings

ZESTY GARDEN CRAB BAKE

2 medium zucchini, sliced
1/2 cup chopped onion
2 cloves of garlic, crushed
1/2 cup butter
1 teaspoon dried basil
1/2 teaspoon salt
1/8 teaspoon pepper
1 (15-ounce) package snow crab meat
1 1/2 cups shredded Swiss cheese
1 cup soft bread crumbs
3 medium tomatoes, seeded, chopped

✦ Sauté zucchini, onion and garlic in butter in skillet for 5 minutes or until tender. Stir in basil, salt and pepper. Add crab meat, cheese and bread crumbs; mix well. Add tomatoes; toss lightly.
✦ Spoon into buttered 2-quart casserole. Bake at 375 degrees for 30 to 35 minutes.

Preparation time: 20 minutes   4 to 5 servings

COUSIN JULIA'S COQUILLES

1 1/2 pounds bay scallops
1 1/2 cups dry white wine
3/4 cup chopped fresh mushrooms
1/4 cup chopped onion
5 tablespoons butter
1 tablespoon chopped fresh parsley
1/4 teaspoon fresh thyme
1/8 teaspoon fresh marjoram
1/4 cup flour
1 cup cream
Juice of 1/2 lemon
Bread crumbs to taste
Chopped fresh parsley to taste

✦ Shell scallops, reserving several shells. Bring wine to a boil in saucepan. Add scallops. Cook over medium heat for 5 minutes. Drain, reserving scallops and 1 cup of liquid.

✦ Sauté mushrooms and onion in butter in skillet for 10 minutes. Sprinkle with 1 tablespoon parsley, thyme and marjoram. Stir in flour. Cook until bubbly, stirring constantly. Add cream; mix well. Stir in reserved liquid. Add scallops and lemon juice.

✦ Cook over medium to high heat for 3 to 5 minutes or until of desired consistency, stirring frequently. Spoon into reserved scallop shells; sprinkle with bread crumbs and parsley to taste.

✦ Bake at 350 degrees for 25 to 30 minutes or until brown and bubbly.

Preparation time: 45 minutes   4 to 6 servings

William Goldman (1888–1974), head of a multimillion dollar chain of movie companies, lived on an 18-acre estate in Villanova near Spring Mill and Old Gulph Roads. He was a well-known philanthropist who promoted better education for children. He is credited with making WHYY (Channel 12) an educational TV station.

SCALLOPS AND SPINACH

20 large sea scallops, shelled
Olive oil to taste
Salt and pepper to taste
1 teaspoon chopped garlic
3 tablespoons butter
1 1/2 pounds fresh spinach, thinly sliced
3 tablespoons fresh lemon juice
1 tablespoon water
5 tablespoons chilled butter

✦ Brush both sides of scallops with olive oil; season with salt and pepper. Arrange in baking pan. Bake at 400 degrees for 10 minutes or until tender.

✦ Sauté garlic in 3 tablespoons butter in skillet over medium heat for 1 minute. Add spinach. Sauté for 6 minutes or until spinach wilts. Stir in 1 1/2 tablespoons of the lemon juice. Season with salt and pepper. Remove from heat and cover. Keep warm.

✦ Boil remaining lemon juice and water in saucepan for 2 minutes or until most of the liquid evaporates. Remove from heat. Whisk in 2 tablespoons of the chilled butter. Place pan over low heat. Whisk in remaining butter 1 tablespoon at a time, removing pan from heat if drops of melted butter appear. (If sauce breaks down at any time, remove from heat and whisk in 2 tablespoons cold butter.)

✦ Arrange wilted spinach on 4 plates. Top with scallops; drizzle with lemon butter sauce.

Preparation time: 20 minutes   4 servings

Appleford, west of Spring Mill Road, dates from the period 1705 to 1728 and was the home of Moro Phillips, a wealthy chemical manufacturer and real estate investor from Poland. He and his sons amassed 800 acres of farms, including Appleford, to create a beautiful retreat from the city.

SHRIMP AND ARTICHOKE MEDLEY

1 (16-ounce) can artichoke hearts, drained, chopped
1 pound shrimp, cooked, peeled, deveined
8 ounces fresh mushrooms, sliced
6 1/2 tablespoons butter
4 1/2 tablespoons flour
3/4 cup each milk and whipping cream
Salt and pepper to taste
1/4 cup sherry
1 tablespoon Worcestershire sauce
1/4 cup freshly grated Parmesan cheese

✦ Layer artichokes and shrimp in buttered baking dish.
Sauté mushrooms in 2 tablespoons of the butter in
skillet for 5 minutes. Spoon over shrimp.
✦ Melt remaining butter in saucepan. Stir in flour. Stir in
milk and cream gradually. Cook until thickened, stirring
constantly. Stir in salt, pepper, sherry and Worcestershire
sauce. Pour over layers; sprinkle with cheese.
✦ Bake at 375 degrees for 30 minutes or until bubbly.
Serve with wild rice.

Preparation time: 30 minutes   4 servings

SIMPLY DELICIOUS SHRIMP

1 cup unsalted butter
1/4 cup fresh lemon juice
1 clove of garlic, minced
1 teaspoon each parsley flakes, Worcestershire sauce
   and soy sauce
1/2 teaspoon pepper
1/4 teaspoon each salt and garlic salt
2 pounds large shrimp, peeled, deveined

✦ Melt butter in large skillet. Add mixture of lemon juice,
garlic, parsley flakes, Worcestershire sauce, soy sauce,
pepper, salt and garlic salt; mix well. Add shrimp.
✦ Cook over medium heat for 5 minutes or until shrimp
turn pink, stirring occasionally. Serve over rice or angel
hair pasta. Garnish with chopped fresh parsley.

Preparation time: 30 minutes   6 servings

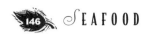

MEDITERRANEAN SHRIMP

1 1/2 pounds shrimp, peeled, deveined
Juice of 1/2 lemon
6 scallions, trimmed, chopped
1/3 cup olive oil
4 cups chopped Italian plum tomatoes with purée
1/4 cup chopped fresh parsley
1 large clove of garlic, minced
1/8 teaspoon sugar
Salt and pepper to taste
1/2 cup dry vermouth
1/4 cup unsalted butter
1 teaspoon dried oregano
8 ounces feta cheese, crumbled

✦ Place shrimp in dish; drizzle with lemon juice. Marinate
  in refrigerator.
✦ Sauté scallions in olive oil in skillet. Stir in tomatoes,
  parsley, garlic, sugar, salt and pepper. Simmer for 20 to
  25 minutes or until of the desired consistency, stirring
  occasionally. Stir in vermouth. Simmer for 10 minutes,
  stirring frequently.
✦ Melt butter in skillet. Add shrimp. Sauté just until
  shrimp turn pink; do not overcook. Add sautéed shrimp
  to the tomato mixture. Add oregano and feta cheese; mix
  well. Cook, covered, over low heat until feta cheese melts,
  stirring frequently.
✦ Serve shrimp mixture over rice, flavored fettuccini or
  orzo. Garnish with chopped fresh parsley.

Preparation time: 25 minutes   6 to 8 servings

BARBECUED SHRIMP SCAMPI

1/4 cup olive oil
1/4 cup fresh lemon juice
3 tablespoons each chopped fresh parsley and garlic
1 tablespoon lemon zest
36 fresh large peeled shrimp with tails, deveined
1 1/2 lemons, cut into 6 wedges

✦ Soak six 8-inch wooden skewers in water for 1 hour.
✦ Whisk olive oil, lemon juice, parsley, garlic and lemon
  zest in large bowl.
✦ Rinse shrimp in cold water; drain. Add to lemon juice
  mixture in bowl. Marinate for 15 to 30 minutes.
✦ Drain shrimp, reserving marinade. Thread 6 shrimp on
  each skewer. Strain reserved marinade and brush on
  shrimp. Place on grill rack.
✦ Grill 4 to 5 inches from medium-hot coals for 2 minutes
  on each side. Serve with lemons.

Preparation time: 15 to 20 minutes   4 servings

GARLIC SHRIMP FETTUCCINI

18 peeled jumbo shrimp, deveined
Salt to taste
3/4 cup butter, softened
1 cup fine dry bread crumbs
1/3 cup minced fresh parsley leaves
1/2 cup dry sherry
1 to 5 cloves of garlic, minced
1 teaspoon salt
Cayenne pepper and paprika to taste
8 ounces fettuccini or favorite pasta, cooked, drained

✦ Cook shrimp in salted boiling water in saucepan for 2
  minutes or until barely pink; drain. Let stand until cool.
✦ Mix next 8 ingredients in bowl. Spoon over shrimp in
  buttered shallow casserole.
✦ Bake at 375 degrees for 30 to 35 minutes or until
  crumbs are golden brown. Serve over fettuccini.
✦ May freeze, covered, before baking. Let stand until room
  temperature before baking.

Preparation time: 40 to 45 minutes   4 servings

SHRIMP AND TOMATO STRATA

4 green onions, chopped
1 large Italian frying pepper, chopped
2 teaspoons fresh basil
1/4 cup chopped fresh parsley
1 1/2 teaspoons fresh chives, chopped
2 cloves of garlic, chopped
Salt and pepper to taste
1/4 cup butter
1 egg, slightly beaten
1 egg yolk, slightly beaten
1/2 cup mayonnaise
3/4 pound Jarlsburg cheese or Cheddar cheese, shredded
2 tomatoes, seeded, chopped
1 pound shrimp, peeled, cooked and deveined
1 unbaked (9-inch) pie shell
Dash of paprika

✦ Sauté green onions, Italian pepper, basil, parsley, chives, garlic, salt and pepper in butter in skillet until vegetables are tender.

✦ Mix egg, egg yolk, mayonnaise and cheese in bowl. Add tomatoes; toss until well mixed. Add shrimp and sautéed mixture; mix well. Pour into pie shell. Sprinkle paprika on top.

✦ Bake at 350 degrees for 45 minutes. Chill, covered, for 24 hours. Let stand until room temperature. Bake at 350 degrees for 15 minutes or until heated through.

Preparation time: 45 minutes   6 to 8 servings

When the railroad was established on the Main Line in the late 1800s, many executives working in Philadelphia were encouraged to build large summer homes in the area, away from the dust and heat of the city. The railroad became the lifeline of the community, transporting household supplies to the suburbs and, on the return trip, carrying locally grown fruits and vegetables back to the city.

SHRIMP THERMIDOR

1 1/2 pounds medium shrimp, peeled
1 cup thinly sliced celery
6 tablespoons butter or margarine
1/4 cup flour
1 cup half-and-half
Sherry to taste (optional)
1 teaspoon seasoned salt
Dash of seasoned pepper
1 cup long grain rice, cooked
1/2 cup (or more) shredded sharp Cheddar cheese

✦ Sauté shrimp and celery in butter in skillet over medium-high heat for 10 minutes or until shrimp turn pink, stirring occasionally. Remove 6 shrimp with slotted spoon; set aside for topping.

✦ Reduce heat to medium. Stir flour into remaining shrimp mixture. Stir in half-and-half and sherry gradually. Sprinkle with seasoned salt and seasoned pepper. Cook over medium heat until mixture thickens and shrimp are tender, stirring frequently.

✦ Place cooked rice in 1 1/2-quart casserole. Top with shrimp mixture. Sprinkle with cheese. Top with reserved sautéed shrimp. Bake at 450 degrees for 5 minutes or until cheese is melted.

Preparation time: 15 to 20 minutes   6 servings

SEAFOOD CASSEROLE

1 pound fresh special or back-fin crab
1/2 cup butter
1 (10-ounce) package frozen chopped spinach
1/2 cup fresh sliced mushrooms
1/2 cup dry red wine
2 teaspoons tarragon vinegar
2 cloves of garlic, chopped
Juice of 1 lemon
1 cup (or less) butter
1 egg
1/2 cup milk
1 pound fresh flounder fillets or any other mild white fish
Italian-style bread crumbs

✦ Sauté crab in 1/2 cup butter in skillet. Cook spinach
  in a small amount of water in saucepan until heated
  through; drain. Add sliced mushrooms. Combine with
  crab in skillet.
✦ Cook wine, vinegar and garlic in small skillet until liquid
  evaporates. Add lemon juice and 1 cup butter, stirring
  until butter melts; keep warm.
✦ Mix egg and milk in large bowl. Dip flounder fillets in
  egg mixture, then in bread crumbs, coating both sides.
  Alternate layers of flounder and crab mixture in buttered
  casserole, ending with flounder.
✦ Bake, covered, at 350 degrees for 10 to 15 minutes.
  Spread wine sauce over top. Broil until sizzling.
  Serve immediately.

Preparation time: 30 minutes   4 to 6 servings

The first regular postal services by railroad from Philadelphia to Ohio began in 1843. Mailbags were hung on hooks outside the local train stations and grabbed as the train rolled by. Men sorted the mail in baggage cars while the train was moving and slung the pouches back onto waiting hooks at different stations.

SEAFOOD MELANGE

1 1/2 cups cooked rice
8 ounces fresh deveined peeled shrimp
8 ounces sea scallops
8 ounces fresh crab meat
1/2 cup finely chopped red bell pepper
1/2 cup finely chopped onion
1/2 cup finely chopped celery
1 cup sliced fresh mushrooms
1/2 teaspoon salt
1 cup mayonnaise
1 cup light cream
1 1/2 cups shredded sharp white Cheddar cheese

✦ Spoon cooked rice into greased 9x13-inch baking pan.
✦ Combine shrimp, scallops, crab meat, red pepper, onion, celery and mushrooms in bowl. Stir in mixture of salt, mayonnaise and light cream; mix gently. Spoon over rice.
✦ Bake, covered, at 375 degrees for 30 minutes.
✦ Sprinkle with Cheddar cheese. Bake, uncovered, for 15 minutes longer.

Preparation time: 30 minutes   4 to 6 servings

SEAFOOD MARINADE

1/4 cup soy sauce
2 tablespoons dark sesame oil
2 tablespoons rice vinegar
1 tablespoon minced garlic
1 tablespoon minced fresh ginger
1/2 teaspoon freshly ground pepper
Fish or shrimp

✦ Whisk soy sauce, sesame oil, vinegar, garlic, ginger and pepper in bowl. Pour over fish or shrimp in shallow dish. Marinate, covered, in refrigerator for 30 minutes before grilling.

Preparation time: 10 minutes   6 servings

SUMMER MANGO SALSA

1 or 2 ripe mangoes, peeled, cubed
2 ripe tomatoes, peeled, cubed (optional)
3 scallions, chopped
Peel of 1 lime, minced
2 cloves of garlic, minced
1 teaspoon chopped fresh jalapeño
Juice of 1/2 lemon or 1/2 lime

✦ Combine mangoes, tomatoes, scallions, lime peel, garlic
  and jalapeño in bowl. Add lemon juice. Chill, covered, for
  several hours. Serve with fish or chicken.

Preparation time: 20 minutes   6 servings

MUSTARD GRILLING SAUCE

1/2 cup melted margarine
3 tablespoons Dijon mustard
1 tablespoon fresh lemon juice
2 tablespoons chopped fresh parsley
Pepper to taste
1 clove of garlic, crushed (optional)

✦ Blend margarine, mustard and lemon juice in bowl.
  Add parsley, pepper and garlic; mix well. Brush on fish
  or chicken before grilling or broiling. May marinate
  chicken in mustard mixture in refrigerator for 1 to
  2 hours before cooking.

Preparation time: 5 minutes   4 servings

OLD EAGLE SCHOOL

The Old Eagle School began in 1739 when a German Lutheran immigrant, Jacob Sharraden, purchased 150 acres to build a church and a schoolhouse. When the cornerstone was laid at the school's dedication, only eleven states had adopted the U.S. Constitution and George Washington had not yet served as President. Several years later, in the cemetery adjoining the school, markers were placed over many graves of local men killed in the Battle at Valley Forge.

Subjects at the Old Eagle School were taught in both English and German. Parents paid three cents a day for their children to attend, providing them with their own goose-quilled pens. Classes gathered in the one-room log building on benches made of harshly cut wood timber, which were arranged in double rows around the open fire. This arrangement allowed the schoolmaster to have complete control of the room, since discipline in those days was meted out at the firm end of a birch stick.

Jacob Sharraden had had the foresight to deed the school to notable community individuals who formed its board of trustees, committing the school to public use in a contract that would extend over many future generations. In 1842, the Old Eagle School was enlarged by about one-third when it became part of the Tredyffrin Township School District.

HORSERADISH AND WALNUT SAUCE

1¹/₂ cups whipping cream, chilled

¹/₃ cup cream-style white horseradish

2 teaspoons fresh lemon juice

¹/₂ teaspoon sugar

Salt and pepper to taste

1 cup chopped walnuts, toasted

✦

Beat cream in mixing bowl until soft peaks form. Add horseradish, lemon juice and sugar gradually, beating until stiff peaks form. Add salt and pepper. Fold in walnuts. Chill, covered, until serving time.

RIB ROAST OF BEEF

1 (8- to 9-pound) beef rib roast with bones
3 tablespoons prepared hot English mustard
Horseradish and Walnut Sauce (at left)

✦ Place beef roast in roasting pan; spread with mustard.
✦ Roast at 425 degrees for 45 minutes. Cover loosely with foil. Roast for 1 hour longer or to 125 degrees for rare on meat thermometer inserted straight down from top into center. Remove from oven. Let stand at room temperature, loosely covered with foil, for 30 minutes. Remove to serving platter. Serve with Horseradish and Walnut Sauce and hot English mustard.

Preparation time: 2 to 4 hours   16 servings

LOBSTER BEEF TENDERLOIN

3 (4-ounce) lobster tails
Salt to taste
1 (4- to 6-pound) beef tenderloin
1 tablespoon melted butter
1¹/₂ teaspoons fresh lemon juice
Garlic and freshly ground pepper to taste
6 slices bacon, partially cooked
¹/₂ cup sliced green onions
¹/₂ cup each melted butter and dry white wine

✦ Cook lobster in boiling salted water in saucepan for 5 minutes; drain and remove from shell in 1 piece. Trim fat from beef; remove small end and discard. Cut slit down center, leaving both ends intact. Place lobsters tails end to end in cavity. Drizzle with mixture of 1 tablespoon butter and lemon juice. Tie with heavy string; rub with garlic. Sprinkle with pepper. Place on rack in roasting pan.
✦ Roast at 425 degrees for 35 to 40 minutes or until done to taste. Arrange bacon crosswise on top. Roast for 4 minutes longer or until bacon is crisp.
✦ Sauté green onions in ¹/₂ cup butter in small saucepan. Add wine and garlic. Heat to serving temperature. Serve over sliced tenderloin.

Preparation time: 30 minutes   12 servings

TENDERLOIN OF BEEF

1 (6- to 7-pound) tenderloin of beef
Mustard Caper Sauce (at right)

✦ Arrange beef tenderloin on rack in roasting pan.
Place in 500-degree oven for 10 minutes. Reduce
oven temperature to 325 degrees. Bake for 45 minutes
or until meat thermometer registers 150 degrees
for medium.
✦ Let cool to room temperature; cut cross grain into
1/3-inch slices.
✦ May be cooked and kept for 2 days in refrigerator. Bring
to room temperature before slicing. Serve with Mustard
Caper Sauce.

Preparation time: 25 minutes   12 servings

ROQUEFORT LONDON BROIL

1/2 cup olive oil
1 clove of garlic, minced
1 teaspoon salt
1/2 teaspoon pepper
1/2 teaspoon dry mustard
1 1/2 tablespoons Roquefort cheese, crumbled
2 teaspoons instant coffee powder
2 tablespoons dry vermouth
1 (2-pound) London broil, 1 1/2 inches thick

✦ Combine olive oil, garlic, salt, pepper, dry mustard,
cheese, instant coffee and vermouth in bowl to make a
thick mixture. Pierce beef with fork. Rub olive oil
mixture into beef. Marinate, covered, in refrigerator for
4 hours or longer.
✦ Cook beef on hot grill for 15 to 20 minutes for rare or
about 30 minutes for well done. Cut cross grain into
diagonal slices.

Preparation time: 20 minutes   8 servings

MUSTARD CAPER SAUCE

1 tablespoon
egg yolk

6 tablespoons each
whipping cream and
white vinegar

1 tablespoon
Worcestershire sauce

1/4 cup Dijon
mustard

1 1/2 cups olive oil

1/4 cup minced
fresh tarragon

3 tablespoons
drained capers

6 tablespoons each
minced scallions
and fresh parsley

✦

Process egg yolk,
cream, vinegar,
Worcestershire sauce
and mustard in
blender. Add oil
gradually, processing
constantly. Mix with
tarragon, capers,
scallions and parsley
in bowl. May chill,
covered, for up
to 1 day.

Before 1865, Wayne was a milk stop on the Paoli Local. In that year, James Henry Askin bought several hundred acres and established the community of "Louella," named for two of his daughters, Louise and Ella. In 1880, the town's name was changed to Wayne to commemorate the nation's most popular general, "Mad" Anthony Wayne.

BEEF TENDERLOIN

2 cups sour cream
6 tablespoons horseradish
2 teaspoons white vinegar
1 teaspoon sugar
1 teaspoon white pepper
9 pounds beef tenderloin
Freshly ground black pepper to taste

✦ Combine sour cream, horseradish, vinegar, sugar and white pepper in small bowl; mix well. Chill until serving time.
✦ Sprinkle tenderloin with black pepper; place in shallow baking pan. Roast at 425 degrees for 1 hour or to 140 degrees on meat thermometer.
✦ Cool and slice very thinly. Serve with small rolls and horseradish sauce.

Preparation time: 10 minutes   18 servings

GRILLED SPICED FLANK STEAK

1/2 teaspoon cinnamon
3/4 teaspoon ground coriander seeds
3/4 teaspoon cumin
3/4 teaspoon pepper
1 teaspoon salt
Olive oil
1 pound flank steak, trimmed

✦ Mix cinnamon, coriander seeds, cumin, pepper and salt in bowl. Rub olive oil into both sides of flank steak. Rub spice mixture into both sides. Seal in plastic bag. Marinate in refrigerator for 1 to 10 hours.
✦ Cook on hot oiled grill for 5 minutes on each side for medium-rare or until done to taste.

Preparation time: 20 minutes   4 servings

MARINATED FLANK STEAK

1/4 cup fresh orange juice
3 tablespoons reduced-sodium soy sauce
1 tablespoon fresh lemon juice
1 tablespoon molasses
1 tablespoon catsup
2 cloves of garlic, minced
1/8 to 1/4 teaspoon celery seeds
1/8 to 1/4 teaspoon dried dill or 1 tablespoon fresh
1 teaspoon Worcestershire sauce
1 (2-pound) flank steak, trimmed

✦ Mix orange juice, soy sauce, lemon juice, molasses,
catsup, garlic, celery seeds, dill and Worcestershire sauce
in bowl. Pour over flank steak in shallow dish, turning
steak to coat. Marinate, covered, in refrigerator for 2 to
48 hours, turning occasionally.
✦ Drain, reserving marinade. Cook steak over hot charcoal
until done to taste. Let stand for 10 minutes. Cut cross
grain into diagonal slices. Pour reserved marinade into
saucepan. Bring to a boil. Simmer for 5 minutes or until
reduced to a thick sauce. Serve with steak.

Preparation time: 15 minutes   6 servings

FILETS WITH ROSEMARY

2 (5-ounce) filet mignon steaks
1 tablespoon butter
2/3 cup canned beef broth
1/4 cup brandy
1 teaspoon chopped fresh rosemary
1/3 cup crumbled bleu cheese

✦ Panbroil steaks in butter in skillet for 4 minutes on each
side or until done to taste. Keep steaks warm in
200-degree oven.
✦ Add beef broth, brandy and rosemary to pan drippings.
Cook for 5 minutes or until sauce is reduced to 1/3 cup,
scraping pan frequently. Spoon sauce over steaks. Top
each steak with half the cheese.

Preparation time: 15 minutes   2 servings

TERIYAKI STEAKS

1 1/4 cups cider vinegar
1 1/4 cups tomato purée
1 cup pineapple juice
1 cup soy sauce
1 cup packed brown sugar
1/3 cup molasses
1/2 teaspoon fresh ginger
1/4 teaspoon garlic powder
6 to 8 sirloin or tenderloin steaks

✦ Combine vinegar, tomato purée, pineapple juice, soy
sauce, brown sugar, molasses, ginger and garlic powder in
saucepan, mixing well. Bring to a boil, stirring
constantly. Cool and pour over steaks in shallow dish.
Marinate, covered, in refrigerator for 24 hours. Drain,
reserving marinade.
✦ Cook steaks on hot grill to desired doneness. Heat
reserved marinade and serve with steaks.

Preparation time: 10 minutes   6 to 8 servings

FRENCH PEPPER STEAK

2 pounds beef tenderloin, cut into strips
3 tablespoons vegetable oil
2 tablespoons flour
1 (16-ounce) can whole tomatoes
1 pound fresh mushrooms, sliced
1 cup sliced onions
2 cups green bell pepper strips
1 teaspoon salt
Pepper to taste
1 cup red wine

✦ Sauté beef in hot oil in skillet until brown; remove to
bowl. Stir flour into skillet drippings. Cook until brown
and bubbly, stirring constantly.
✦ Add tomatoes, mushrooms, onions, green pepper strips,
salt, pepper, wine and beef. Cook, covered, for 30
minutes or until beef is tender, stirring occasionally.

Preparation time: 30 minutes   4 servings

In the 1880s, James Henry Askin sold "Louella" to Anthony Drexel and George Childs, two young businessmen from Philadelphia. Under their ownership, the town of Wayne, formerly Louella, was developed as one of the first planned communities in the country, providing residents with electricity, sewers and public water.

TURF-SURF TERIYAKI KABOBS

Teriyaki Marinade (at right)
2 pounds combined London broil, flank steak, tuna and
   swordfish, cut into cubes
8 to 10 fresh shiitake mushrooms
8 to 10 small onions or onion wedges
10 to 12 large chunks red and green bell pepper

✦ Pour Marinade over cubed beef and fish in shallow
   dish. Marinate, covered, in refrigerator for 6 to 12
   hours; drain.
✦ Thread mushrooms, onions, pepper, beef and fish
   alternately on skewers.
✦ Cook on hot grill for 10 to 12 minutes or until done to
   taste, turning once.

Preparation time: 15 minutes   4 servings

COMPANY BEEF STEW

2 pounds stew beef, cut into 1-inch cubes
5 carrots, cut into chunks
4 medium onions, cut into chunks
1 pound fresh mushrooms, sliced
4 stalks celery, cut into chunks
2 (8-ounce) cans sliced water chestnuts
1 (16-ounce) can green beans, drained
1 (22-ounce) can diced tomatoes, drained
1 cup burgundy
2 teaspoons salt
2 tablespoons brown sugar
5 tablespoons tapioca
1/4 cup Worcestershire sauce

✦ Combine beef, carrots, onions, mushrooms, celery,
   water chestnuts, green beans and tomatoes in large
   roasting pan. Mix wine, salt, brown sugar, tapioca
   and Worcestershire sauce in bowl. Pour over beef
   and vegetables.
✦ Bake, covered, at 325 degrees for 4 to 5 hours or until
   beef is tender. Do not stir.

Preparation time: 25 minutes   8 servings

TERIYAKI MARINADE

**1 cup prepared
teriyaki marinade**

**1 tablespoon minced
fresh ginger**

**2 teaspoons
minced garlic**

**1/4 cup pineapple or
orange juice**

2 tablespoons sake

**1/4 cup low-sodium
soy sauce**

Pinch of sugar

✦

Mix teriyaki marinade,

ginger, garlic,

pineapple juice, sake,

soy sauce and sugar

in bowl.

BEEF BURGUNDY

3 pounds beef rump roast, cut into 2-inch cubes
2 cups red burgundy
2 whole cloves
1 large bay leaf
8 peppercorns, crushed
1/2 teaspoon salt
2 cloves of garlic, minced
4 slices bacon, chopped
3 cups beef broth
1/2 teaspoon dried marjoram
1 teaspoon dried thyme
4 carrots, peeled, cut into chunks
2 onions, sliced
3/4 pound fresh mushrooms, sliced

✦ Place beef in shallow glass container. Add wine, cloves, bay leaf, peppercorns, salt and 1 clove of garlic. Marinate in refrigerator for 1 hour or longer, stirring occasionally.

✦ Cook bacon in large skillet until fat is rendered; remove bacon with slotted spoon and drain. Drain beef, reserving marinade. Pat beef dry with paper towel; place in bacon drippings in skillet. Add remaining clove of garlic. Sauté beef over high heat until brown on all sides. Discard garlic; place beef in Dutch oven.

✦ Heat reserved marinade to boiling point in saucepan. Add to beef. Add beef broth, marjoram and thyme. Bring mixture to a full boil. Boil for 10 minutes. Reduce heat. Simmer, uncovered, for 30 minutes, stirring occasionally. Add carrots, onions, mushrooms and bacon to beef.

✦ Bake, covered, at 350 degrees for 1 1/2 hours or until beef is tender.

Preparation time: 30 minutes   6 servings

BEEF BOURGUIGNON

2 pounds stew beef cubes
1 tablespoon flour
1 teaspoon salt
1 teaspoon pepper
2 cloves of garlic, chopped
1 large onion, chopped
1 (14-ounce) can beef broth
1/2 cup burgundy
1 (8-ounce) can tomato sauce
1 tablespoon sugar
8 whole peppercorns
3 whole cloves
1/2 bay leaf
1/4 cup chopped fresh parsley
1/4 cup dry sherry
6 carrots, peeled, sliced
1 or 2 stalks celery, sliced diagonally
6 ounces fresh mushrooms, sliced

✦ Place beef cubes in Dutch oven; sprinkle with flour, salt and pepper, stirring to coat. Add garlic, onion, beef broth, burgundy, tomato sauce and sugar. Heat to boiling point, stirring frequently. Remove from heat. Seal peppercorns, cloves, bay leaf and parsley in tea infuser or tie in cheesecloth. Add to Dutch oven.
✦ Bake at 325 degrees for 2$1/2$ to 2$3/4$ hours or until beef is almost tender. Add sherry.
✦ Cook carrots, celery and mushrooms in a small amount of water in saucepan until tender-crisp. In the last 15 to 20 minutes of cooking add vegetables to beef.

Preparation time: 30 minutes   6 servings

QUICK HOMEMADE CHILI

1 pound ground round beef
1/2 cup chopped onion
1/2 clove of garlic, minced
1/2 green bell pepper, minced
1 (15-ounce) can New Orleans-style or Spanish-style
   kidney beans
1 (15-ounce) can plum tomatoes, drained, chopped
1 (15-ounce) can tomato sauce
1 teaspoon salt
2 to 3 teaspoons chili powder

✦ Brown ground beef in skillet, stirring until crumbly;
  drain. Add onion, garlic and green pepper. Cook until
  onion is clear.
✦ Add remaining ingredients. Simmer, uncovered, for 45
  minutes, stirring occasionally. Garnish servings with
  shredded Cheddar cheese.

Preparation time: 10 minutes   6 servings

VEAL CHOPS WITH MUSTARD

2 (1-inch thick) veal loin chops
Dried sage and pepper to taste
1 1/2 tablespoons butter
1 teaspoon vegetable oil
2 1/2 tablespoons chopped shallots
1/3 cup unsalted beef broth
2 tablespoons minced fresh sage
2 teaspoons Dijon mustard
1/4 cup half-and-half

✦ Sprinkle veal chops with sage and pepper. Brown in butter
  and oil in heavy skillet over medium-high heat for 5
  minutes on each side. Reduce heat to medium. Cook for
  1 minute on each side for medium-rare or until done to
  taste. Keep warm in 200-degree oven.
✦ Sauté shallots in pan drippings until tender. Add
  remaining ingredients. Cook until thickened, stirring
  frequently. Serve with veal chops. Garnish with fresh
  sage leaves.

Preparation time: 10 minutes   2 servings

VEAL CHOPS WITH ORANGE SAUCE

4 (6-ounce) veal loin chops
Salt and pepper to taste
5 tablespoons butter
1 cup chopped, seeded peeled tomatoes
1/4 cup thinly sliced fresh basil
Orange Sauce (at right)
Fresh basil sprigs

✦ Season veal chops with salt and pepper. Cook chops in
1 tablespoon of the butter in heavy skillet over medium
heat for 4 minutes on each side or until cooked through.
Remove to warm platter. Keep warm in 200-degree oven.
✦ Reheat sauce over low heat. Whisk in remaining butter.
Stir in tomatoes, sliced basil and remaining orange peel.
Season with salt and pepper. Ladle Orange Sauce over
veal chops. Top with fresh basil.

Preparation time: 15 minutes   4 servings

VEAL MARSALA

2 pounds (1/4-inch thick) veal cutlets
2 1/2 cups sliced fresh mushrooms
1/2 cup sliced green onions
3 tablespoons butter
1/2 cup beef stock
2/3 cup dry marsala or dry sherry
Salt and pepper to taste
2 tablespoons chopped fresh parsley

✦ Flatten veal cutlets into 4-inch squares with meat mallet.
Sauté mushrooms and green onions in 1 tablespoon of
the butter in large skillet. Add 3 tablespoons of the beef
stock. Remove vegetables with slotted spoon to bowl.
Brown veal in 2 tablespoons butter and pan drippings
over medium heat for 1 minute on each side. Remove to
serving platter. Keep warm in 200-degree oven.
✦ Add marsala and remaining beef stock to pan drippings
in skillet. Bring to a boil. Simmer for 1 minute, scraping
pan frequently. Add vegetables. Season with salt and
pepper. Heat to serving temperature. Spoon sauce over
veal. Top with parsley.

Preparation time: 10 minutes   4 servings

ORANGE SAUCE

3/4 cup fresh
orange juice

1/2 cup dry
white wine

1/4 cup minced
shallots

2 tablespoons minced
orange peel

1/4 cup whipping
cream

✦

Combine orange juice,
wine, shallots and 1
tablespoon of the
orange peel in heavy
saucepan. Cook over
medium heat for 10
minutes or until
mixture is reduced to
3 tablespoons, stirring
frequently. Add cream.
Boil for 1 minute,
stirring constantly.
Remove from heat.
May be made 1 day
ahead; cover
and refrigerate.

Martin's Dam Club, a sawmill and gristmill in the 1880s, was established as a swimming club in 1924.

VEAL PAPRIKA

2 medium onions, chopped
3 tablespoons butter
1 tablespoon paprika
2 cloves of garlic, minced
2 1/2 pounds veal, cubed
1/4 cup cooking sherry
1/4 cup flour
1 (14-ounce) can beef broth
1 tablespoon mustard
1/4 cup chopped fresh parsley
2 cups sour cream
10 ounces fresh mushrooms, cut into quarters
8 ounces slivered almonds, toasted

✦ Sauté onions in 2 tablespoons of the butter in large saucepan. Add paprika and garlic. Cook for several minutes. Spoon mixture into large baking dish. Add veal, remaining 1 tablespoon butter and sherry to pan drippings. Cook until veal is brown on all sides, stirring frequently. Add veal to baking dish. Blend flour into pan drippings. Add beef broth, mustard and half the parsley; mix well. Add to baking dish; mix well.

✦ Bake, covered, at 350 degrees for 2 1/2 to 3 hours or until veal is tender, stirring 2 or 3 times while baking. Stir in sour cream, mushrooms and almonds.

✦ Bake, covered, for 30 minutes longer. Sprinkle with remaining parsley to serve.

Preparation time: 30 minutes   8 servings

MEDALLIONS OF VEAL

16 veal scallops
Flour
Salt and pepper to taste
2 cloves of garlic, minced
1/4 cup butter
1/4 cup vegetable oil
3 tablespoons Dijon mustard
2 tablespoons brandy or cognac
2 cups whipping cream
1 cup half-and-half
1 teaspoon chopped fresh rosemary

◆ Flatten veal scallops between sheets of waxed paper to 1/8-inch thickness with meat mallet. Dust with flour; season with salt and pepper.

◆ Cook veal several pieces at a time with garlic in 2 tablespoons butter and 2 tablespoons oil in large skillet until golden brown on each side. Remove veal to warm platter and add additional butter and oil as needed. Stir mustard and brandy into pan drippings, scraping skillet several times. Whisk in cream, half-and-half and rosemary. Cook until thickened, whisking constantly. Season with salt and pepper. Add a small amount of rosemary sauce to each serving of veal.

Preparation time: 15 minutes   8 servings

The Wayne Hotel, built in 1906, is now an historic landmark.

ROAST RACK OF LAMB

1 (1½-pound) rack of lamb, trimmed, at room
    temperature
Salt and pepper to taste
3 tablespoons coarse-grained mustard
½ cup fresh bread crumbs
¼ cup minced fresh parsley
1 teaspoon dried rosemary, crumbled
1 clove of garlic, minced

✦ Sprinkle lamb with salt and pepper. Brush lamb with 1
tablespoon of the mustard. Mix remaining mustard,
bread crumbs, parsley, rosemary and garlic in bowl. Press
evenly over top of lamb. Place lamb in roasting pan.

✦ Roast at 450 degrees for 10 minutes. Reduce oven
temperature to 400 degrees.

✦ Roast lamb for 45 minutes to 135 degrees on meat
thermometer for medium-rare or until done to taste.

✦ Let stand for 10 minutes. Carve between ribs.

Preparation time: 15 minutes   2 servings

BARBECUED BUTTERFLIED LAMB

1 or 2 cloves of garlic, minced
1 teaspoon salt
½ teaspoon each black pepper and thyme
1 teaspoon fines herbes
½ onion, coarsely chopped
½ cup each vegetable oil and fresh lemon juice
1 whole leg of lamb, boned, butterflied

✦ Process garlic, salt, pepper, thyme, fines herbes, onion,
oil and lemon juice in blender until onion is finely
chopped. Place lamb in glass dish; pierce deeply with
fork. Pour marinade over lamb.

✦ Marinate, covered, in refrigerator for 1 hour or longer,
turning occasionally. Drain, reserving marinade.

✦ Place lamb in broiler basket or insert 2 long skewers
diagonally through corners to help in turning.

✦ Broil over medium to hot coals for 45 to 60 minutes,
turning and basting with reserved marinade every 15
minutes. Serve immediately.

Preparation time: 10 minutes   4 servings

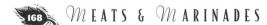

HERB ROASTED LAMB DIJON

2/3 cup Dijon mustard
2 tablespoons low-sodium soy sauce
2 large cloves of garlic, minced
1 1/2 teaspoons dried rubbed sage
1 1/2 teaspoons dried oregano
1 teaspoon fresh minced ginger
1 1/2 tablespoons olive oil
1 (2-pound) boneless leg of lamb, trimmed
9 medium potatoes, cut into halves
2 teaspoons olive oil
Salt and pepper to taste
3 tablespoons coarsely chopped fresh rosemary

✦ Process mustard, soy sauce, garlic, sage, oregano and ginger in blender until blended. Add 1 1/2 tablespoons olive oil in a fine stream, processing constantly at high speed until smooth. Rub half the mixture over surface of lamb. Roll from long side to enclose mixture, tieing with string to secure. Rub remaining mixture over surface. Chill, covered, for 8 to 10 hours.
✦ Place potatoes cut side up in shallow roasting pan; drizzle with 2 teaspoons olive oil. Season with salt and pepper; sprinkle with rosemary. Add lamb.
✦ Bake at 400 degrees for 15 minutes. Reduce oven temperature to 350 degrees. Turn potatoes; push to edges of roasting pan.
✦ Bake for 1 hour for medium-rare or until done to taste. Cut lamb into slices. Place on serving platter surrounded by potatoes. May serve heated pan drippings over lamb.

Preparation time: 30 minutes   6 servings

The Spread Eagle Tavern, built by John Siter in 1796, was one of the first taverns in the community. Development had "spread out" from the Old Eagle School nearby, hence the name. The inn had a reputation for good cheer and company, but fell into neglect with the advent of the railroad. Later it became a school for Lenni-Lenape Indian girls, then a boardinghouse. It is now the site of Spread Eagle Village.

BROILED LAMB CHOPS

6 (1/2-inch thick) lamb chops
2 large cloves of garlic, cut into halves
1 1/2 tablespoons olive oil
1 1/2 tablespoons dried rosemary, crumbled
Green Peppercorn Sauce (below)

✦ Rub lamb chops on both sides with garlic; brush with olive oil. Sprinkle both sides with rosemary. Chill, covered, for 4 to 10 hours.

✦ Broil or grill lamb for 4 minutes on each side for medium-rare or until done to taste. Serve Green Peppercorn Sauce with lamb.

Preparation time: 35 minutes   2 servings

GREEN PEPPERCORN SAUCE

1 small onion, minced
2 tablespoons butter
1 cup sliced fresh mushrooms
1 teaspoon minced fresh thyme
1 teaspoon minced fresh parsley
1/2 cup tawny port
1/3 cup low-salt chicken broth
2 tablespoons drained green peppercorns in brine
2 1/2 teaspoons Dijon mustard
1/2 cup whipping cream
Salt and pepper to taste

✦ Sauté onion in butter in skillet for 2 minutes. Add mushrooms, thyme and parsley. Sauté for 4 minutes. Add port. Boil for 3 minutes or until mixture is reduced by half, stirring frequently. Add chicken broth, peppercorns and mustard. Boil for 4 minutes or until slightly thickened, stirring constantly. Add cream to sauce. Boil for 5 minutes or until sauce is thickened, stirring occasionally. Season with salt and pepper.

Preparation time: 20 minutes   2 servings

Sarah Siter's House, built in 1798 from local stone, is the oldest existing house on Lancaster Pike in Radnor Township. Today it is part of the Braxton parcel.

MINTED LAMB IN RED WINE

4 onions, chopped
1/4 cup butter
4 slices bacon, chopped
31/2 pounds boned leg of lamb, cubed
1/2 cup flour
11/2 cups each red wine and beef stock
1/3 cup chopped fresh mint
1 tablespoon mint jelly
1/4 cup tomato paste
1/3 cup chopped fresh parsley
1 (28-ounce) can tomatoes, crushed

✦ Sauté onions in butter in large skillet until clear. Remove
to baking dish. Cook bacon in pan drippings until crisp;
drain. Cook lamb several pieces at a time in pan drippings
until brown on all sides. Add bacon and lamb to onions.
Stir flour into pan drippings. Stir in wine and beef stock.
Stir in mint, mint jelly, tomato paste, 1/4 cup of the
parsley and tomatoes with juice. Add to lamb; mix well.
✦ Bake, covered, at 375 degrees for 21/2 to 3 hours or until
lamb is tender, stirring occasionally. Garnish with parsley.

Preparation time: 30 minutes   6 servings

HONEY SESAME PORK ROAST

2/3 cup soy sauce
1 teaspoon ground ginger
3 cloves of garlic, minced
1 boneless pork loin roast
1/4 cup packed brown sugar
1/3 cup honey
11/2 tablespoons sesame oil

✦ Mix soy sauce, ginger and garlic in bowl. Pour over roast
in glass dish. Marinate, covered, in refrigerator for 3
hours or longer, turning twice; drain.
✦ Combine brown sugar, honey and sesame oil in saucepan.
Cook over low heat until sugar dissolves, stirring
constantly. Brush over roast in roasting pan.
✦ Roast at 350 degrees for 1 hour or to 160 degrees on
meat thermometer.

Preparation time: 15 minutes   4 servings

LOIN OF PORK WITH PORT SAUCE

1 (3-pound) boned loin of pork
2 tablespoons Dijon mustard
1/2 teaspoon dried thyme
1/2 teaspoon dried oregano
Salt and freshly ground pepper to taste
1 bay leaf
1/2 cup ruby port
1/2 cup chicken stock
3 cloves of garlic, cut into halves
Cranberry Port Sauce (below)

✦ Pat pork dry with paper towels; spread mustard over surface. Sprinkle with 1/2 teaspoon thyme and oregano. Season with salt and pepper to taste; top with bay leaf. Place pork in roasting pan. Add port, chicken stock and garlic.

✦ Roast at 350 degrees for 55 minutes for medium or until cooked through. Remove pork to platter, reserving pan drippings and garlic for sauce. Cut into thin slices. Serve with Cranberry Port Sauce.

Preparation time: 15 minutes   6 servings

CRANBERRY PORT SAUCE

1/2 cup ruby port
1 cup chicken stock
1/2 cup whipping cream
1/2 teaspoon dried thyme, crumbled
1/2 cup whole cranberry sauce
1 to 2 tablespoons red wine vinegar
1 1/2 teaspoons freshly grated orange peel
Pan drippings
Salt and pepper to taste

✦ Boil port and chicken stock in heavy saucepan until reduced by half. Add cream and thyme. Cook for 5 minutes, stirring occasionally. Stir in cranberry sauce, vinegar and orange peel. Degrease reserved pan drippings from pork; mash in reserved garlic. Add to sauce. Season with salt and pepper.

Preparation time: 15 minutes   3 cups

BROWN SUGAR PORK CHOPS

$1/4$ cup packed light brown sugar
$1/4$ cup apple juice
2 tablespoons vegetable oil
1 tablespoon soy sauce
$1/2$ teaspoon ground ginger
Salt and pepper to taste
1 teaspoon cornstarch
$1/4$ cup cold water
6 ($1/2$-inch thick) boneless loin pork chops

✦ Combine brown sugar, apple juice, oil, soy sauce, ginger, salt and pepper in saucepan. Cook over medium heat until brown sugar dissolves, stirring constantly. Mix cornstarch and water together. Add to sauce. Cook until mixture thickens, stirring constantly.
✦ Cook pork chops 6 inches from hot coals for 10 to 12 minutes, turning once. Brush with sauce. Grill for 5 minutes longer or until pork is glazed and cooked through, turning and brushing once with sauce.

Preparation time: 5 minutes   6 servings

PORK PICCATA

4 boneless pork chops
6 tablespoons flour
1 tablespoon lemon pepper
3 tablespoons butter
$1/4$ cup marsala or cream sherry
$1/4$ cup fresh lemon juice
$1/4$ cup capers

✦ Flatten pork chops to $1/8$-inch thickness with meat mallet. Dredge lightly in flour and lemon pepper. Cook in butter in skillet for 5 to 6 minutes or until golden brown and cooked through.
✦ Add marsala and lemon juice to skillet. Cook for 2 to 3 minutes or until sauce is thickened. Serve with capers.

Preparation time: 10 minutes   4 servings

TANGY PORK CHOPS

1/4 cup black currant preserves
1 1/2 tablespoons Dijon mustard
4 pork chops
Salt and pepper to taste
2 tablespoons vegetable oil
2 tablespoons white wine vinegar

✦ Mix preserves and mustard in bowl. Season pork chops with salt and pepper.
✦ Brown pork chops in oil in skillet; drain. Add preserves mixture. Simmer, covered, for 20 minutes. Remove pork chops to heated platter.
✦ Add vinegar to pan drippings. Cook until sauce is reduced by 1/3, stirring constantly. Spoon sauce over pork chops.

Preparation time: 5 minutes   4 servings

GRILLED PORK TENDERLOIN

1/2 cup soy sauce
1/2 cup dry cooking sherry
3 cloves of garlic, minced
1 1/2 tablespoons dry mustard
1 teaspoon ground ginger
1 teaspoon dried thyme
3 pounds pork tenderloin

✦ Mix soy sauce, sherry, garlic, mustard, ginger and thyme in bowl. Pour over pork in shallow glass dish. Marinate in refrigerator for 4 hours, turning occasionally.
✦ Cook on grill over low heat for 22 minutes on each side. Cut into thin slices.

Preparation time: 5 minutes   8 servings

APRICOT PORK TENDERLOIN

1¹/2 pounds boneless pork tenderloin
¹/4 cup soy sauce
¹/4 cup cider vinegar
2 tablespoons dark brown sugar
2 tablespoons honey
²/3 cup apricot preserves
1 to 1¹/2 teaspoons Dijon mustard

✦ Pat pork tenderloin dry with paper towels. Mix soy sauce, cider vinegar, brown sugar and honey in bowl. Pour over pork in shallow dish. Marinate, covered, in refrigerator for 8 to 10 hours, turning occasionally. Drain, reserving marinade. Place pork in baking dish; add ¹/4 cup reserved marinade.

✦ Bake at 350 degrees for 30 to 40 minutes, basting with reserved marinade every 10 minutes. Remove from oven; drain. Mix preserves and mustard. Spoon over pork.

✦ Bake for 10 minutes longer. Cut into thin slices. Spoon apricot glaze over pork.

Preparation time: 5 minutes   8 servings

ORANGE PORK TENDERLOIN

1 cup fresh orange juice
¹/3 cup soy sauce
¹/4 cup olive oil
2 tablespoons chopped fresh rosemary
3 cloves of garlic, minced
2 (12-ounce) pork tenderloins

✦ Mix orange juice, soy sauce, oil, rosemary and garlic in bowl. Pour over pork in shallow glass dish. Marinate, covered, in refrigerator for 1 to 10 hours. Drain, reserving marinade.

✦ Cook pork on hot grill for 15 to 20 minutes or until cooked through. May be baked at 400 degrees for 20 minutes. Cut pork into thin slices.

✦ Bring reserved marinade to a boil in small saucepan. Serve with pork.

Preparation time: 5 minutes   4 servings

MARINATED PORK

2 pork tenderloins, cut into medallions
2 tablespoons low-sodium soy sauce
1 tablespoon fresh lemon juice
1 tablespoon honey
1 clove of garlic, minced
1 tablespoon chopped fresh thyme
Pear and Apple Sauce (below)

✦ Place pork in shallow glass dish. Mix soy sauce, lemon juice, honey, garlic and thyme in bowl. Pour over pork. Marinate, covered, in refrigerator for several hours, turning occasionally. Drain, reserving 1/4 cup marinade for use in sauce.

✦ Cook pork in nonstick skillet until brown on both sides and tender. Serve Pear and Apple Sauce over pork.

Preparation time: 30 minutes   6 servings

PEAR AND APPLE SAUCE

2 medium pears
2 large apples
8 small spring onions, cut into halves
2 teaspoons sugar
1 to 2 teaspoons butter
1/4 cup reserved marinade
1 teaspoon cornstarch
1/2 cup chicken stock
1/4 cup water

✦ Cut each pear and each apple into 8 slices. Cook fruit with onions and sugar in butter in saucepan for 5 minutes or until light brown. Add reserved pork marinade. Blend in cornstarch. Add chicken stock and water. Simmer, covered, for 5 minutes or until fruit is tender, stirring occasionally. Serve over pork.

Preparation time: 10 minutes   6 servings

PORK TENDERLOIN WITH PORT

2 cups chicken stock
1 cup beef stock
1 pound boneless tenderloin
Salt and pepper to taste
1 tablespoon olive oil
1 1/2 pounds russet potatoes, peeled
1/2 cup butter
1/2 cup whipping cream
Pinch of ground nutmeg
1 large leek, sliced
3 shallots, finely chopped
1 cup port wine

✦ Combine chicken stock and beef stock in saucepan. Boil for 25 minutes or until reduced to 2/3 cup, stirring occasionally.

✦ Season pork with salt and pepper. Brown on both sides in hot olive oil in Dutch oven for 5 minutes.

✦ Bake pork at 425 degrees for 20 minutes or until cooked through. Remove to warm platter, reserving pan drippings in Dutch oven. Keep warm, tented with foil, in 200-degree oven.

✦ Cut potatoes into 1-inch pieces. Cook in salted water to cover in large saucepan until tender; drain. Mash potatoes in saucepan, adding butter, cream, salt, pepper and nutmeg. Keep warm in 200-degree oven.

✦ Cook leek and shallots in reserved drippings in Dutch oven for 8 minutes or until tender. Add reduced stock mixture and port. Boil for 4 minutes or until reduced by half.

✦ Cut pork into thin slices. Arrange mashed potatoes in center of serving plate surrounded by pork slices. Drizzle port sauce over pork.

Preparation time: 35 minutes   4 servings

In 1885, Strafford was named for Thomas Wentworth, Earl of Strafford, who was an English ancestor of John Landon Wentworth, a Pennsylvania Railroad executive. A punctual man, John built his house next to the train station so that he could hear the trains going by, on schedule.

STUFFED GREEN PEPPERS

4 green bell peppers
8 sweet Italian sausages
1 cup finely chopped onion
1 clove of garlic, minced
1 teaspoon curry powder
Salt and pepper to taste
1 1/2 cups cooked white or brown rice
1 egg, lightly beaten
1/4 cup chicken broth
2 tablespoons fresh bread crumbs
3 tablespoons freshly grated Parmesan cheese
2 tablespoons olive oil

✦ Cut green peppers into halves lengthwise; remove stems and seeds. Drop green peppers into boiling water in saucepan. Cook for 1 minute; drain.

✦ Remove sausage from sausage skin. Brown sausage in skillet, stirring until crumbly; drain. Add onion, garlic, curry powder, salt and pepper. Cook for 8 to 10 minutes, stirring frequently. Spoon into bowl. Add rice, egg and chicken broth; mix well. Stuff into green pepper halves. Place in baking pan. Mix bread crumbs and cheese in bowl. Sprinkle over green peppers; drizzle with olive oil.

✦ Bake at 400 degrees for 45 minutes or until peppers are heated through.

Preparation time: 15 minutes   4 servings

ALL-AMERICAN MARINADE

1 1/2 cups vegetable oil
3/4 cup soy sauce
1/4 cup Worcestershire sauce
2 tablespoons dry mustard
2 teaspoons salt
1 1/2 tablespoons chopped fresh parsley
1 tablespoon pepper
1/2 cup wine vinegar
1 teaspoon minced garlic
1/3 cup fresh lemon juice

✦ Process all ingredients in blender for 45 to 60 seconds or
  until well blended.
✦ Place beef or lamb in sealable plastic bag; add marinade
  and seal bag. Marinate in refrigerator for 24 to 36 hours.
✦ Great with tenderloin of beef, sirloin cuts, leg of lamb or
  rack of lamb.

Preparation time: 15 minutes   6 servings

BEEF MARINADE

3 tablespoons dry mustard
1/4 cup Worcestershire sauce
1 1/2 teaspoons salt
1/2 cup red wine vinegar
1 1/2 teaspoons dried parsley flakes
3 cloves of garlic, minced
1/2 cup fresh lemon juice
1/2 cup vegetable oil
3/4 cup soy sauce

✦ Combine all ingredients in bowl; mix well. Pour over
  London broil or other steak in shallow glass dish.
  Marinate, covered, in refrigerator for 1 to 2 hours.

Preparation time: 5 minutes   8 servings

SHERRY BEEF MARINADE

1/2 cup dry sherry
1/2 cup canola oil
1/2 cup low-sodium soy sauce
3 cloves of garlic, minced

✦ Combine all ingredients in bowl; mix well. Pour over beef in shallow glass dish. Marinate, covered, in refrigerator for 2 hours or longer; drain, reserving marinade. Baste beef frequently with reserved marinade while cooking.

Preparation time: 5 minutes   8 servings

ORIENTAL MARINADE

2 tablespoons vegetable oil
1/3 cup low-sodium soy sauce
2 tablespoons honey
1 tablespoon red wine vinegar
1 tablespoon freshly grated ginger
3 cloves of garlic, minced

✦ Combine all ingredients in bowl; mix well. Pour over London broil, swordfish steak or chicken in shallow glass dish. Marinate, covered, in refrigerator; drain, reserving marinade. Baste meat with marinade while cooking.

Preparation time: 10 minutes   6 servings

SOY HERB MARINADE

1/3 cup vegetable oil
1/3 cup soy sauce
1/2 teaspoon each chopped fresh oregano, basil and thyme
1 teaspoon chopped fresh rosemary

✦ Combine all ingredients in bowl; mix well. Pour over beef or chicken in shallow glass dish. Marinate, covered, in refrigerator for 2 to 6 hours; drain, reserving marinade.
✦ Use reserved marinade to baste meat while cooking or heat and serve as sauce for rice. May substitute dried herbs for fresh, using 1/2 the amount of fresh herbs.

Preparation time: 5 minutes   6 servings

BURGUNDY SALSA FOR PORK

2 cups chopped red onions
1 cup chopped seeded plum tomatoes
1/4 cup red wine vinegar
1 cup sugar
1 cup burgundy wine
2 tablespoons chili powder
Dash of Tabasco sauce
1 tablespoon Worcestershire sauce
1 teaspoon dry mustard
1 tablespoon salt
2 tablespoons (heaping) baking cocoa

✦ Combine all ingredients in bowl; mix well. Pour over 2 to
4 pounds pork tenderloin in shallow glass dish. Marinate,
covered, in refrigerator for 12 to 24 hours; drain,
reserving marinade. Heat marinade in saucepan; serve
over cooked pork.

Preparation time: 10 minutes   12 to 16 servings

ZIPPY MUSTARD SAUCE

2 eggs
1/2 cup sugar
5 tablespoons dry mustard
2 teaspoons salt
1 cup half-and-half
1/4 cup cider vinegar
White pepper to taste

✦ Combine eggs, sugar, mustard, salt and half-and-half
in double boiler. Cook over boiling water until thick,
stirring constantly. Add vinegar. Cool completely.
Add pepper.
✦ May store in refrigerator for 1 month. Serve with ham or
as a dip with cheese.

Preparation time: 5 minutes   10 to 12 servings

OLD ST. DAVID'S CHURCH

Built in 1715 in a quiet glen on the outskirts of
Penn's new colony, Old St. David's Church was designed for
the large number of settlers who weren't Quakers, especially the
Scots, Irish and some Welsh, and was geographically situated
in the valley to keep these two groups apart.

Reverend John Clubb, who arrived in 1714 to be
the church's first priest, is buried in the old cemetery and his
gravestone is the oldest in the Welsh tract. In 1788, Old St.
David's became the first American Protestant Episcopal parish,
with Slator Clay as its first rector.

The famous Revolutionary War hero, General
Anthony Wayne, is buried here, as well as the British
sympathizer Squire Moore, who is interred at the threshold
so that all who enter must walk on his grave.

In 1876, Henry Wadsworth Longfellow visited and
immortalized the lovely historic stone church with these words:

What an image of peace and rest,
Is this little church among the graves!
All is so quiet; the troubled breast,
The wounded spirit, the heart oppressed,
Here may find the repose it craves.

See how the ivy climbs and expands
Over this humble hermitage,
And seems to caress with its little hands
The rough, gray stones, as a child that stands
Caressing the wrinkled cheeks of age!

You cross the threshold;
and dim and small
Is the space that serves
for the Shepherd's Fold;
The narrow aisle, the bare, white wall
quaint and tall
Whisper and say: "Alas! We are old."

CHICKEN WITH GARLIC SAUCE

1 (6½- to 7-pound) roasting chicken
Olive oil
2 teaspoons dried rubbed sage
Salt and pepper to taste
2 heads of garlic
3 tablespoons dry white wine
3/4 cup plus 3 tablespoons chicken broth
2 tablespoons flour
1/4 teaspoon dried rubbed sage

✦ Rinse chicken; pat dry. Mix olive oil with 2 teaspoons sage. Brush chicken inside and out with mixture. Season chicken generously inside and out with salt and pepper. Tie chicken legs together; place in roasting pan. Separate garlic into individual cloves; do not peel. Arrange garlic around chicken. Drizzle additional olive oil over garlic.

✦ Roast at 425 degrees for 15 minutes. Remove garlic. Reduce oven temperature to 375 degrees. Roast for 1 hour and 10 minutes or until chicken juices run clear when thickest part of thigh is pierced. Remove to serving platter; tent with foil to keep warm.

✦ Squeeze garlic to release cloves. Place garlic in bowl; mash with fork. Pour pan juices into glass measuring cup; degrease. Add wine to roasting pan. Bring to a boil over medium-high heat, scraping up any browned bits. Add to pan juices in measuring cup. Add enough broth to measure 1 cup. Pour broth mixture into heavy saucepan.

✦ Blend 3 tablespoons broth with flour in small bowl. Add to saucepan. Stir in 1 teaspoon of the garlic purée and remaining 1/4 teaspoon sage. Bring to a boil. Cook for 5 minutes or until reduced to sauce consistency, stirring frequently. Serve with chicken.

Preparation time: 30 minutes   4 to 6 servings

TARRAGON-LIME CHICKEN

4 boneless skinless chicken breast cutlets
1/4 cup olive oil
3 tablespoons fresh lime juice
2 teaspoons dried tarragon
1/4 teaspoon dried oregano
Salt and freshly ground pepper to taste

✦ Rinse chicken; pat dry. Arrange in single layer in glass casserole. Whisk oil, lime juice, tarragon, oregano, salt and pepper in small bowl. Pour over chicken, turning to coat. Marinate at room temperature for 20 minutes or in refrigerator for longer period of time.
✦ Preheat broiler or barbecue. Cook for 6 minutes or until tender, turning once.

Preparation time: 10 minutes   4 servings

CHICKEN SAUTE

2 1/2 pounds chicken pieces
Salt and pepper to taste
3 tablespoons butter
1 1/2 tablespoons finely chopped shallots
3 tablespoons dry white wine
3/4 cup chicken broth
1 tablespoon butter
1 teaspoon (or more) flour

✦ Rinse chicken; pat dry. Season with salt and pepper. Melt 3 tablespoons butter in heavy skillet. Add chicken skin side down. Cook for 20 to 30 minutes or until tender and golden brown, turning once. Remove to serving platter and keep warm.
✦ Drain excess drippings from skillet. Add shallots to skillet. Cook quickly, stirring constantly. Add wine. Cook until reduced by 1/2. Add chicken broth. Simmer for 1 minute. Season with salt and pepper. Stir in remaining 1 tablespoon butter and flour. Cook until slightly thickened, stirring constantly. Serve with chicken.

Preparation time: 20 minutes   4 servings

St. David's Church, erected in 1715, played its part in the Revolutionary War a half-century later. The lead window sashes, which supported small, clear diamond-shaped windows in the church, were melted down and reshaped into bullets for the Continental Army.

CONFETTI CHICKEN

1 (3-pound) chicken
Salt and pepper to taste
2 tablespoons vegetable oil
1 onion, finely chopped
1 clove of garlic, minced
1/2 cup dry white wine
1 1/2 tablespoons vinegar
1 chicken bouillon cube, crumbled
1/2 cup water
1 (14-ounce) can peeled whole tomatoes
1 teaspoon basil
1 teaspoon sugar
3 anchovy fillets
1/4 cup milk
1 (2-ounce) jar black olives
1 tablespoon chopped fresh parsley

✦ Cut chicken into serving-size pieces. Rinse and pat dry. Season with salt and pepper. Brown in oil in skillet; remove to ovenproof baking dish. Drain skillet, leaving 1 tablespoon pan drippings in skillet. Add onion and garlic. Cook until onion is tender. Add wine and vinegar. Boil until reduced by 1/2. Add crumbled bouillon cube and water. Cook over high heat for 2 minutes, stirring constantly.

✦ Press undrained tomatoes through sieve. Add to wine mixture with basil and sugar. Cook for 1 minute. Pour over chicken. Bake, covered, at 375 degrees for 1 hour.

✦ Soak anchovies in milk in bowl for 5 minutes; drain on absorbent paper. Arrange chicken pieces on serving dish and keep warm. Bring pan juices to a boil in saucepan. Boil for 1 minute. Chop anchovies into small pieces and cut olives into halves. Add to saucepan. Stir in parsley. Cook for 1 minute. Pour over chicken pieces.

Preparation time: 45 minutes

4 servings

HONEY-GLAZED CHICKEN KABOBS

4 large boneless skinless chicken breasts
1 large yellow squash
1 large zucchini
2 medium red bell peppers
2 large onions
4 ounces medium fresh mushrooms
Honey-Mustard Glaze (at right)

✦ Heat coals; place grill 6 inches from coals. Rinse chicken; pat dry. Cut chicken and vegetables into bite-size pieces; cut mushrooms into halves. Thread onto four 12-inch skewers.

✦ Grill kabobs over coals for 8 to 10 minutes or until tender. Brush with Honey-Mustard Glaze. Grill for 5 minutes longer or until glazed and cooked through.

✦ May bake kabobs at 450 degrees for 15 to 20 minutes or until tender, turning frequently; then bake for 5 minutes longer, brushing frequently with glaze.

Preparation time: 20 minutes   4 to 6 servings

LEMON HERB CHICKEN TENDERS

1/4 cup flour
1/4 teaspoon each salt and pepper
Grated zest of 1 lemon
5 sprigs of parsley, minced
1 large clove of garlic, minced
4 boneless chicken breasts
3 tablespoons butter
1 tablespoon vegetable oil

✦ Mix flour, salt and pepper together; set aside. Mix lemon zest, parsley and garlic in small bowl; set aside. Rinse chicken; pat dry. Pound 1/4 inch thick between waxed paper. Cut into 1x4-inch strips.

✦ Dredge chicken in flour mixture, shaking off excess. Heat 1 tablespoon butter and oil in skillet over medium-high heat. Add chicken. Sauté for 4 minutes, turning once.

✦ Add parsley mixture and remaining 2 tablespoons butter. Cook for 1 minute, stirring constantly.

Preparation time: 20 minutes   2 to 4 servings

HONEY-MUSTARD GLAZE

3/4 cup honey

1/2 cup prepared spicy mustard

2 tablespoons soy sauce

1 tablespoon cider vinegar

2 tablespoons cornstarch

1/4 cup water

✦

Bring honey, mustard, soy sauce and vinegar to a boil in 2-quart saucepan. Blend cornstarch with water in 1-cup measure until smooth. Stir into honey mixture gradually. Bring to a boil. Boil for 1 to 2 minutes or until slightly thickened, stirring constantly.

CHICKEN NUGGETS

2 pounds boneless skinless chicken breasts
1 egg
1/2 cup milk
1 cup bread crumbs
1/2 teaspoon salt
1/2 teaspoon poultry seasoning
1/8 teaspoon onion powder or to taste
1/8 teaspoon garlic powder or to taste
1/4 cup margarine

✦ Rinse chicken; pat dry. Cut chicken into 2-inch pieces.
  Beat egg with milk in small bowl. Mix bread crumbs,
  salt, poultry seasoning, onion powder and garlic powder
  together. Dip chicken in milk mixture; coat with crumb
  mixture. Melt margarine on baking sheet with sides.
  Place chicken on baking sheet.
✦ Bake at 350 degrees for 20 minutes or until tender.

Preparation time: 15 minutes   6 servings

PARMESAN CHICKEN BREASTS

1/2 cup freshly grated Parmesan cheese
1/4 cup dry bread crumbs
1 teaspoon dried oregano leaves
1 teaspoon dried parsley flakes
1/4 teaspoon paprika
1/4 teaspoon salt
1/4 teaspoon pepper
6 boneless skinless chicken breast cutlets
2 tablespoons melted margarine

✦ Mix cheese, bread crumbs, oregano, parsley flakes, paprika,
  salt and pepper in bowl. Rinse chicken; pat dry. Dip
  chicken in margarine; coat with cheese mixture. Place
  in 10x15-inch baking pan sprayed with nonstick
  cooking spray.
✦ Bake at 400 degrees for 20 to 25 minutes or until
  chicken is cooked through.

Preparation time: 15 minutes   4 servings

CHICKEN PICCATA

1 pound chicken cutlets
3/4 cup flour
1/4 teaspoon each salt and pepper
3 tablespoons corn oil
1/4 cup each fresh lemon juice, white wine, butter, capers
   and chopped fresh parsley

✦ Rinse chicken; pat dry. Pound cutlets very thin. Dredge
   in mixture of flour, salt and pepper. Brown in hot oil in
   skillet. Remove to warmed plate and keep warm.
✦ Drain drippings from skillet. Add lemon juice, wine
   and any juices from warming plate. Cook for 1 to 2
   minutes or until thickened. Swirl in butter; add capers.
✦ Add chicken, turning to coat with sauce. Place on
   serving plate. Sprinkle with parsley. Garnish with thin
   slices of lemon peel.

Preparation time: 15 minutes   4 servings

CHICKEN ON TAP

2 pounds boneless skinless chicken breasts
1/2 cup flour
1 tablespoon salt
1/4 teaspoon pepper
3 tablespoons vegetable oil
1 cup thinly sliced onion
1 tablespoon tomato paste
1 teaspoon dried basil
1 cup beer
1/2 cup whipping cream
2 tablespoons minced parsley

✦ Rinse chicken; pat dry. Dredge in mixture of flour, salt
   and pepper. Brown in hot oil in large skillet over
   medium-high heat. Remove chicken; set aside.
✦ Add onion to skillet. Cook until translucent. Return
   chicken to skillet. Add mixture of tomato paste, basil and
   beer. Simmer, covered, over low heat for 20 minutes.
✦ Add cream and parsley. Cook until heated through.

Preparation time: 20 minutes   8 servings

St. David lived in an austere community of monks who engaged in hard labor, silence, continuous prayer and simple meals of bread, vegetables, water, wine and occasionally a little milk. For this reason St. David was surnamed the "Waterman."

CHICKEN MARENGO

1 (2 1/2-pound) chicken, cut up
1/2 cup flour
1 teaspoon each salt, freshly ground pepper and basil
1/4 cup each olive oil and melted butter
1 1/4 cups dry white wine
2 1/2 cups peeled Italian tomatoes
8 ounces fresh mushrooms, sliced
1 clove of garlic, minced
Chopped fresh parsley to taste

✦ Rinse chicken; pat dry. Dredge chicken in mixture of flour, salt, pepper and basil.
✦ Sauté in mixture of olive oil and butter in skillet. Remove chicken to large baking dish. Add remaining flour mixture to skillet, whisking until mixed. Add wine gradually, stirring until smooth and thickened. Add tomatoes, mushrooms and garlic; mix well. Pour over chicken.
✦ Bake, covered, at 350 degrees for 50 minutes or until chicken is cooked through. Sprinkle with parsley.

Preparation time: 40 minutes   4 to 6 servings

LEMON CHICKEN

3 boneless skinless chicken breasts
1/4 cup flour
1 teaspoon parsley flakes or 1 tablespoon fresh parsley
1/4 teaspoon white pepper
1/4 cup each butter and fresh lemon juice
1 teaspoon chicken bouillon granules
1/2 cup water

✦ Rinse chicken; pat dry. Shake with flour, parsley and pepper in sealable heavy plastic bag.
✦ Combine butter, lemon juice and bouillon granules in large skillet. Cook over medium-high heat until granules are dissolved, stirring constantly.
✦ Add chicken. Cook until browned; reduce heat. Simmer, covered, for 20 to 25 minutes or until tender, turning once. Remove to warm platter. Add water to drippings in skillet. Cook until heated through. Serve over chicken.

Preparation time: 15 minutes   4 servings

LEMON CHICKEN WITH LINGUINI

4 boneless skinless chicken breasts
1/4 cup flour
1 teaspoon salt
Freshly ground pepper to taste
2 tablespoons butter or margarine
1 tablespoon vegetable oil
1 clove of garlic, minced
1/4 cup dry white wine
1/3 cup chicken broth
1 tablespoon fresh lemon juice
1 tablespoon Dijon mustard
8 ounces linguini, cooked al dente
3 tablespoons lightly toasted pine nuts
Freshly grated Parmesan cheese to taste

✦ Rinse chicken; pat dry. Pound 1/4 inch thick between
  waxed paper. Coat with mixture of flour, salt and pepper.
✦ Heat butter and oil in skillet. Add chicken. Cook for 8
  minutes or until chicken is cooked through, turning
  once. Remove chicken and keep warm.
✦ Add garlic to skillet. Cook until translucent. Add wine,
  chicken broth, lemon juice and mustard. Cook until
  reduced to sauce consistency. Add chicken. Cook until
  heated through. Serve over linguini.
✦ Sprinkle with pine nuts and cheese. Garnish with
  lemon slices.

Preparation time: 25 minutes   6 servings

GRILLED CITRUS CHICKEN

Juice and grated zest of 1/2 lemon
Juice and grated zest of 1/2 lime
3 tablespoons olive oil
2 cloves of garlic, minced
1 tablespoon dry white wine
1 teaspoon salt
1/2 teaspoon freshly ground black pepper
1/8 teaspoon cayenne
6 boneless skinless chicken breast halves

✦ Combine lemon juice, lemon zest, lime juice, lime zest, olive oil, garlic, white wine, salt, black pepper and cayenne in large bowl; mix well. Rinse chicken; pat dry. Add to marinade. Marinate, covered, in refrigerator for 1 to 10 hours; drain.

✦ Grill over hot coals for 10 minutes or until chicken is cooked through, turning once.

Preparation time: 15 minutes   6 servings

DIJON CHICKEN AND SCALLIONS

1 tablespoon fresh lemon juice
1/4 teaspoon salt
1/4 teaspoon white pepper
3 tablespoons Dijon mustard
1/4 cup dry white wine
1/3 cup chopped scallions
2 tablespoons butter or margarine
4 or 5 skinless boneless chicken cutlets
3 tablespoons sour cream (optional)

✦ Mix lemon juice, salt, pepper, mustard and wine in bowl; set aside. Sauté scallions in butter in large skillet until tender.

✦ Rinse chicken; pat dry. Add to skillet. Cook over low or medium heat for 10 minutes, turning once.

✦ Add mustard mixture. Simmer, covered, for 20 to 30 minutes or until chicken is tender and cooked through. Add sour cream. Cook for 1 minute, stirring constantly.

Preparation time: 15 minutes   4 servings

In the mid-to late-19th century, the second wave of European immigrants arrived to take their place alongside the Welsh and English. In 1875, most of the farmers in the state were German (Amish), followed by the Scotch and Irish.

CHICKEN CRESCENT BUNDLES

3 chicken breasts, cooked
3 ounces cream cheese, softened
3 tablespoons melted butter
1/2 teaspoon salt
2 tablespoons milk
1 tablespoon chopped fresh chives
1/2 cup each cooked chopped fresh mushrooms and onion
1 (8-count) can crescent rolls
1/4 cup seasoned bread crumbs

✦ Cut chicken into bite-size pieces. Blend cream cheese with 2 tablespoons of the butter in bowl. Add chicken, salt, milk, chives, mushrooms and onion; mix well.
✦ Separate rolls into 4 rectangles, sealing perforations. Spoon chicken mixture onto center of each rectangle. Pull up corners of dough to center; seal. Brush with remaining butter; sprinkle with bread crumbs. Place on nonstick baking sheet.
✦ Bake at 350 degrees for 20 to 25 minutes or until brown.

Preparation time: 10 minutes   4 servings

SPICY ALMOND CHICKEN

4 to 6 boneless skinless chicken cutlets
3 tablespoons butter
1 (14-ounce) jar red currant jelly
1/2 cup each prepared mustard and slivered almonds
3 tablespoons brown sugar
2 tablespoons fresh lemon juice
1/2 teaspoon ground cinnamon

✦ Rinse chicken; pat dry. Brown in butter in large skillet over medium heat for 10 minutes. Place in greased 9x13-inch baking dish. Add remaining ingredients to skillet. Cook over medium heat until jelly dissolves, stirring occasionally. Pour over chicken.
✦ Bake, covered, at 350 degrees for 30 minutes. Bake, uncovered, for 10 minutes longer or until chicken is cooked through.

Preparation time: 30 minutes   4 to 6 servings

SPICY PEANUT CHICKEN

2 or 3 large boneless skinless chicken breasts
1 tablespoon each soy sauce and cornstarch
2 tablespoons each soy sauce and sherry
2 teaspoons sugar
1 teaspoon white vinegar
1/4 cup each chicken stock and peanut oil
1 teaspoon crushed red pepper
1/3 cup sliced scallions
1/2 teaspoon ground ginger
1/2 cup peanuts

✦ Rinse chicken; pat dry. Cut into 1/2-inch pieces. Mix
  1 tablespoon soy sauce with cornstarch in bowl; add
  chicken. Mix remaining 2 tablespoons soy sauce, sherry,
  sugar, vinegar and stock in small bowl; set aside.
✦ Heat peanut oil in wok or large skillet over high heat.
  Add red pepper. Cook until pepper turns black.
✦ Add chicken. Cook for 2 minutes or until chicken is
  cooked through; remove and set aside. Add scallions and
  ginger to wok; cook for 1 minute. Return chicken to
  wok. Cook for 2 minutes, stirring constantly. Add sherry
  mixture; reduce heat. Cook for 1 minute, stirring
  constantly. Stir in peanuts. Serve over hot cooked rice.

Preparation time: 45 minutes   4 servings

GRILLED SESAME CHICKEN

1 cup sunflower oil
1/4 cup sesame seed oil
1/2 cup soy sauce
1/4 cup vermouth
2 tablespoons Dijon mustard
6 boneless chicken breasts

✦ Mix first 5 ingredients in large bowl. Rinse chicken; pat
  dry. Marinate in mixture in bowl in refrigerator for 3 hours
  or longer, turning occasionally. Drain; reserve marinade.
✦ Grill chicken over low or medium flame for 7 to 8
  minutes per side; baste frequently during first 10 minutes
  of cooking time, allowing chicken's exterior to crisp
  without basting for remainder of cooking time.

Preparation time: 5 minutes   6 servings

Devon was named for an English tourist resort and means "deep valley." In 1883, a post office was established in Devon, officially putting it "on the map." The former mail stop had been in a stairwell of the railroad signal tower at the Spread Eagle Village site which was rather inaccessible.

CHICKEN AND SPINACH IN PHYLLO

3 boneless skinless chicken breasts
Vegetable oil
2 tablespoons olive oil
2 medium onions, chopped
10 ounces fresh spinach, chopped
8 ounces Muenster cheese, shredded
2 tablespoons dry white wine
1/4 teaspoon each salt and pepper
1 egg, slightly beaten
4 ounces phyllo (10 strudel leaves)
1/2 cup (or more) melted butter
2/3 cup dried bread crumbs
Paprika to taste

✦ Rinse chicken; pat dry. Pound very thin between
waxed paper. Sauté in vegetable oil in large skillet until
cooked through. Remove from skillet; drain. Cut into
1/2-inch pieces.

✦ Add olive oil and onions to skillet. Cook until tender,
stirring occasionally. Add spinach. Cook for 3 minutes or
until wilted, stirring frequently; remove from heat. Stir
in cheese, wine, salt and pepper. Pour beaten egg over
top; mix gently. Stir in chicken.

✦ Place 1 sheet of phyllo on waxed paper. Brush with melted
butter and sprinkle with 1 tablespoon bread crumbs.
Repeat process, stacking into 5 layers. Spoon half the
chicken mixture in a 2-inch wide strip along short side of
phyllo, leaving a 1/2-inch border on 3 sides. Roll like a
jelly roll from chicken mixture side, brushing with butter
so that phyllo continues to adhere. Butter seam and ends
and press to seal. Repeat process for second roll.

✦ Place rolls seam side down 2 inches apart on large
baking sheet. Brush with remaining butter. Cut halfway
through phyllo layers to make 1-inch wide pieces.
Sprinkle with paprika.

✦ Bake at 375 degrees for 15 to 20 minutes or until
golden brown. Cool on baking sheets on wire rack. Cut
through remaining uncut layers.

✦ May be prepared several hours ahead; place on baking
sheet, cover with waxed paper and clean damp towel and
chill until baking time.

Preparation time: 1 1/2 hours   8 servings

HOLIDAY CASSEROLE

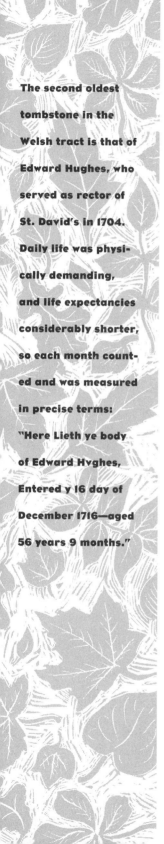

The second oldest tombstone in the Welsh tract is that of Edward Hughes, who served as rector of St. David's in 1704. Daily life was physically demanding, and life expectancies considerably shorter, so each month counted and was measured in precise terms: "Here Lieth ye body of Edward Hvghes, Entered y 16 day of December 1716—aged 56 years 9 months."

1/2 cup slivered almonds
1/4 cup butter
6 tablespoons flour
2 cups chicken broth
1 cup whipping cream
1 tablespoon minced onion
1 tablespoon minced fresh parsley
1 teaspoon salt
2 tablespoons sherry or dry white wine
1 jar pimentos
3 cups cooked rice
8 ounces frozen peas
2 1/2 cups chopped cooked chicken

✦ Sauté almonds in butter in skillet for 10 minutes; remove from heat. Stir in flour. Add chicken broth and whipping cream. Cook until thickened, stirring constantly. Add onion, parsley, salt, sherry, pimentos, rice, peas and chicken; mix well. Spoon into baking dish.

✦ Bake, covered, at 375 degrees for 20 minutes. Bake, uncovered, for 10 minutes longer or until bubbly.

Preparation time: 45 minutes   8 to 10 servings

CHICKEN PAPRIKA

1/2 cup butter
1 medium onion, chopped
1/2 cup chopped celery
1 teaspoon minced garlic
2 teaspoons paprika
1 teaspoon salt
1/2 teaspoon pepper
1 1/4 cups shredded cooked chicken
1/2 cup flour
1 (14-ounce) can chicken broth
1 cup half-and-half
2 cups cooked rice

✦ Melt butter in large stockpot over medium heat. Add onion, celery and garlic. Sauté until onion and celery are tender. Stir in paprika, salt, pepper and chicken.

✦ Sprinkle flour evenly over chicken mixture; mix well. Cook until heated through, stirring constantly. Add chicken broth gradually. Cook until mixture begins to thicken. Stir in half-and-half and rice. Cook for 5 to 10 minutes or until heated through. Spoon into 2-quart casserole.

✦ Bake, covered, for 25 to 30 minutes or until bubbly and heated through.

Preparation time: 30 minutes   6 servings

STUFFED CHICKEN BREASTS

1 (10-ounce) package frozen chopped spinach
6 boneless skinless chicken breasts
Salt and pepper to taste
1 (15-ounce) package ricotta cheese
1/2 cup coarsely chopped almonds
1/2 teaspoon minced garlic
1/2 teaspoon salt
1/8 teaspoon pepper, or to taste
1 egg
2 tablespoons milk
1 cup seasoned bread crumbs
1/2 cup creamy Italian dressing
1/4 cup sliced almonds

✦ Thaw spinach and squeeze dry. Rinse chicken; pat dry.
Pound 1/4 inch thick between waxed paper; season with
salt and pepper. Mix spinach, cheese, chopped almonds,
garlic, salt and pepper in medium bowl. Spread over
chicken; roll up and secure with wooden picks. Beat egg
with milk in pie plate. Dip chicken in egg mixture; coat
with crumbs. Place in greased 9x13-inch baking dish.

✦ Bake at 375 degrees for 30 to 45 minutes or until
chicken is cooked through. Remove wooden picks.
Drizzle with dressing and sprinkle with sliced almonds.

Preparation time: 15 minutes   8 servings

TURKEY CHILI

1¹/4 pounds turkey breast
Salt and freshly ground black pepper to taste
2 tablespoons vegetable oil, divided
1 medium onion, chopped
1 tablespoon minced garlic
¹/2 teaspoon salt
¹/2 teaspoon cumin
¹/4 teaspoon each cinnamon, dried basil, chili powder,
    red pepper flakes, freshly ground black pepper and
    dried sage
2 (15-ounce) cans black beans, drained
1 (14-ounce) can chicken broth
1 (4-ounce) can chopped green chiles, drained
1 cup frozen corn kernels
1 (7-ounce) jar roasted red peppers, chopped
¹/2 cup plain yogurt or nonfat sour cream
¹/2 teaspoon cumin
¹/4 teaspoon salt

✦ Rinse turkey; pat dry. Cut into 1-inch pieces; season
  with salt and black pepper to taste.
✦ Heat 1 tablespoon of the oil in large stockpot or Dutch
  oven over high heat. Add turkey. Cook until golden
  brown. Remove to plate and keep warm.
✦ Add remaining 1 tablespoon oil to stockpot. Stir in
  onion. Cook over medium heat for 2 minutes. Add
  garlic, ¹/2 teaspoon salt, ¹/2 teaspoon cumin, cinnamon,
  basil, chili powder, red pepper flakes, ¹/4 teaspoon black
  pepper and sage. Cook for 30 seconds.
✦ Purée half the beans with chicken broth in blender.
  Add to stockpot with remaining beans, chiles, corn and
  red peppers. Bring to a boil; reduce heat. Simmer for
  5 minutes.
✦ Return turkey to stockpot. Cook for 2 minutes or until
  heated through. Ladle into bowls.
✦ Mix yogurt, remaining ¹/2 teaspoon cumin and ¹/4
  teaspoon salt in bowl. Dollop each serving with yogurt
  mixture.

Preparation time: 1 hour   6 servings

TURKEY WITH PEANUT SAUCE

GINGERED VEGETABLES

1 pound fresh asparagus or fresh green beans

2 tablespoons vegetable oil

1 carrot, thinly sliced

1 teaspoon ground ginger

✦

Trim asparagus and cut into 2-inch pieces. Heat oil in skillet until very hot. Add carrot, asparagus and ginger. Stir-fry for 5 to 7 minutes or until cooked through.

8 ounces spaghetti
1 egg
1 tablespoon water
1/3 cup dry bread crumbs
1/4 cup sesame seeds
1 pound turkey cutlets
3 tablespoons salad oil
2 scallions, thinly sliced
2 chicken bouillon cubes
1/4 cup creamy peanut butter
1 tablespoon soy sauce
1/8 to 1/4 teaspoon crushed red pepper
2 cups water
Gingered Vegetables (at left)

✦ Cook spaghetti using package directions; drain. Beat egg with 1 tablespoon water in shallow dish. Mix bread crumbs with sesame seeds on waxed paper. Rinse turkey cutlets; pat dry. Dip into egg mixture and then into crumb mixture. Heat oil in skillet. Add turkey. Cook for 3 to 4 minutes or until browned. Remove turkey and cut into strips.

✦ Cook scallions in drippings in skillet for 2 minutes. Add bouillon cubes, peanut butter, soy sauce, red pepper and remaining 2 cups water; mix well. Bring to a boil over high heat. Cook for 5 minutes or until sauce is slightly thickened, stirring frequently.

✦ Toss pasta with Gingered Vegetables. Arrange on individual serving plates. Top with turkey. Spoon sauce over top.

Preparation time: 1 hour   4 servings

TURKEY TORTILLA CASSEROLE

10 to 12 (6-inch) corn tortillas
1/2 cup chopped onion
1/2 cup reduced-sodium chicken broth
1/4 cup chopped celery
3 cups chopped cooked turkey or chicken
1 (4-ounce) can chopped green chiles, drained
1 (10-ounce) can reduced-sodium cream of chicken soup
1 teaspoon pepper
1/2 cup shredded sharp Cheddar cheese
1/2 cup shredded Monterey Jack cheese
1 cup salsa
1/2 cup shredded sharp Cheddar cheese
1/2 cup shredded Monterey Jack cheese

✦ Tear tortillas into bite-size pieces; set aside. Bring onion,
chicken broth and celery to a boil in medium saucepan;
reduce heat. Simmer, covered, for 5 to 6 minutes or
until vegetables are tender-crisp; do not drain.

✦ Combine onion mixture, turkey, tortillas, chiles, soup and
pepper in large bowl; mix well. Stir in 1/2 cup Cheddar
cheese and 1/2 cup Monterey Jack cheese. Spoon into
lightly greased 9x13-inch baking dish. Top with salsa and
remaining cheeses.

✦ Bake at 350 degrees for 30 minutes or until heated
through and bubbly.

Preparation time: 45 minutes   8 to 10 servings

TURKEY CUTLETS INSALATA

1 teaspoon freshly grated orange peel
Sections of 1 orange
2 ounces fresh Parmesan cheese, shaved
1 large tomato, chopped
1 small bunch arugula, chopped
1/2 small red onion, thinly sliced
2 tablespoons olive oil
1 tablespoon fresh lemon juice
1/3 cup flour
11/2 cups fresh bread crumbs
2 teaspoons chopped fresh thyme or 3/4 teaspoon dried
1 egg
2 tablespoons water
4 turkey breast cutlets or 1/4-inch slices
1/2 teaspoon salt
1/4 teaspoon pepper
2 tablespoons olive oil

✦ Combine orange peel, orange sections, cheese, tomato,
  arugula and onion in bowl; mix well. Add 2 tablespoons
  oil and lemon juice; toss lightly to combine. Chill until
  serving time.
✦ Spread flour on waxed paper. Mix bread crumbs
  and thyme in shallow dish. Beat egg with water in
  shallow dish.
✦ Rinse turkey cutlets; pat dry. Sprinkle with salt and
  pepper. Dip in flour, then egg mixture, then crumb
  mixture. Heat remaining 2 tablespoons oil in large
  nonstick skillet over medium-high heat. Cook cutlets
  for 8 minutes or until browned and cooked through,
  turning once. Remove to serving plates. Top with salad.
✦ May substitute chicken, veal or pork cutlets for turkey.
  May substitute watercress or curly endive for arugula.

Preparation time: 45 minutes   3 servings

GINGER TARRAGON MARINADE

1/3 cup fresh lemon juice
1/4 cup low-sodium soy sauce
1 clove of garlic, minced
1/4 teaspoon powdered ginger
1/2 teaspoon dried tarragon or 2 teaspoons fresh

✦ Mix all ingredients in bowl. Use to marinate poultry.

Preparation time: 5 minutes   1/2 cup

ORIENTAL MARINADE

1 tablespoon dry sherry
1/4 cup light soy sauce
1 teaspoon minced garlic
1/2 teaspoon grated fresh ginger
2 teaspoons sugar
2 tablespoons peanut oil

✦ Mix all ingredients in bowl. Use to marinate poultry.

Preparation time: 5 minutes   1/2 cup

TAMARI MARINADE

1 cup vegetable oil
1/2 cup tamari sauce
1 teaspoon powdered ginger
1 tablespoon fresh lemon juice
8 cloves of garlic, sliced

✦ Mix all ingredients in bowl. Use to marinate poultry.

Preparation time: 5 minutes   1 1/2 cups

LIME-CHILE MARINADE

1/4 cup olive oil
1/3 cup fresh lime juice
1 clove of garlic, minced
2 teaspoons grated fresh ginger
1 tablespoon low-sodium soy sauce
1 small red chile, finely chopped
2 scallions, chopped

✦ Mix all ingredients in bowl. Use to marinate poultry.

Preparation time: 5 minutes   3/4 cup

PRISSY'S BLUE BALL INN

The Blue Ball Inn on Lancaster Road is a handsome stone house with a winding staircase and deep fireplaces, now privately owned. Built in 1795, it was home to Priscilla Robinson, also known as Prissy, until 1877. A hard-headed, gutsy woman, she survived the Civil War, supported the Underground Railroad of runaway slaves, and outlived all of her husbands, who were suspected to be three of the six skeletons found under the kitchen floor when it was remodeled in 1902.

The stories of Prissy and her inn are many, from the legendary barroom brawls that left many a dead body for disposal, to her run-ins with the Pennsylvania railroad, which cut through her backyard. Once, after a train had hit one of her cows, she dragged the carcass onto the tracks and spread slippery fat on the uphill stretch. All trains were halted until the reluctant railroad compensated her for the animal. In 1877, men working on the tracks unearthed a number of unidentified human remains, which hurt her business.

The Blue Ball Inn prospered in the early years of the Welsh settlement when Conestoga wagons, drovers, peddlers, farmers, and outlaws streamed past on Lancaster Pike, seeking accomodations. By 1902, the railroad had largely replaced wagons and coaches as a mode of travel, and many inns passed out of existence. The Blue Ball suffered the same fate, eventually becoming a private residence. The legend of Prissy Robinson remains, however, and she is thought to haunt the house to this day.

CHOCOLATE GLAZE ICING

1/4 cup whipping cream

1 cup semisweet chocolate chips

2 teaspoons light corn syrup

✦

Scald whipping cream in saucepan; remove from heat. Stir in chocolate chips and corn syrup. Let stand, covered with foil, for 15 minutes. Stir with wooden spoon until smooth.

ALMOND GLAZED COOKIES

$1/2$ cup butter, softened
$3/4$ cup sugar
1 egg
$1/2$ teaspoon almond extract
$1/4$ cup finely ground almonds
1 cup flour
1 cup sliced almonds
Chocolate Glaze Icing (at left)

✦ Cream butter and sugar in bowl until light and fluffy. Beat in egg and flavoring. Add ground almonds and flour, stirring just until mixed. Shape into $1 1/2$-inch balls. Roll in sliced almonds. Place 2 inches apart on nonstick cookie sheet.

✦ Bake at 350 degrees for 15 to 20 minutes or until edges are slightly browned. Cool on wire rack.

✦ Dip some cookies halfway into Chocolate Glaze Icing; drizzle Icing over remaining cookies. Chill until set.

Preparation time: 15 minutes   18 servings

FESTIVE EGGNOG COOKIES

$2 1/4$ cups flour
1 teaspoon baking powder
$1/2$ teaspoon each cinnamon and nutmeg
$3/4$ cup butter, softened
$1 1/4$ cups sugar
$1/2$ cup eggnog
2 egg yolks
1 teaspoon vanilla extract
$1 1/2$ teaspoons each sugar and nutmeg

✦ Mix flour, baking powder, cinnamon and $1/2$ teaspoon nutmeg together. Cream butter and $1 1/4$ cups sugar in mixing bowl until light and fluffy. Beat in eggnog, egg yolks and vanilla. Add flour mixture, stirring just until mixed.

✦ Drop by rounded teaspoonfuls onto nonstick cookie sheets. Sprinkle with mixture of remaining sugar and nutmeg. Bake at 300 degrees for 20 to 25 minutes or until light brown on bottom. Cool on wire rack.

Preparation time: 15 minutes   36 servings

ORANGE CINNAMON BISCOTTI

2 cups flour
1 1/2 teaspoons baking powder
1 teaspoon ground cinnamon
1/4 teaspoon salt
1 cup sugar
1/2 cup unsalted butter, softened
2 eggs
2 teaspoons freshly grated orange peel
1 teaspoon vanilla extract
8 ounces semisweet chocolate
2 tablespoons shortening
1/2 teaspoon orange extract

✦ Sift flour, baking powder, cinnamon and salt together.
Beat sugar and butter in large bowl. Add eggs 1 at a
time, beating well after each addition. Beat in orange peel
and vanilla. Add flour mixture, beating just until mixed.
Divide dough into 2 equal portions. Place each portion
on a buttered baking sheet. Shape each portion into
3/4x3-inch log. Bake at 325 degrees for 35 minutes or
until firm to the touch. Cool for 10 minutes.
✦ Cut logs diagonally into 1/2-inch slices. Arrange cut side
down on baking sheets. Bake for 12 minutes or until
golden brown on bottom. Turn biscotti over. Bake for
12 minutes longer or until golden brown on bottom.
Remove to wire racks to cool.
✦ Melt chocolate and shortening in double boiler over
simmering water. Stir in flavoring. Dip one end of
biscotti into chocolate mixture to coat. Let dry on
waxed paper.

Preparation time: 45 minutes   24 servings

Daylesford was named for an Austrian tourist resort, and was established in 1832 with the advent of the railroad.

Many Welsh families sold their farms and estates and moved west towards Lancaster, Pennsylvania, in the mid-1750s due to heavy taxes imposed on their valuable farm land.

CANDY CANE COOKIES

1 cup butter, softened
1 cup confectioners' sugar, sifted
$2^1/2$ cups flour
$1/8$ teaspoon salt
1 egg
$1/2$ teaspoon each vanilla and peppermint extract
$1/4$ teaspoon red food coloring

✦ Cream butter and confectioners' sugar in mixing bowl until light. Beat in next 5 ingredients. Divide into 2 equal portions. Beat food coloring into 1 portion. Chill dough, covered, for several hours.
✦ Shape 1 teaspoon red dough into 4-inch cylinder. Shape another cylinder of untinted dough. Twist together to form a candy cane. Repeat process with remaining dough. Place 2 inches apart on parchment-lined cookie sheet.
✦ Bake at 350 degrees for 8 to 10 minutes or until brown; do not overbake. Cool on wire rack.

Preparation time: 30 minutes   24 servings

CARAMEL NUT ACORNS

$2^1/2$ cups sifted flour
$1/2$ teaspoon baking powder
1 cup melted butter
$3/4$ cup packed brown sugar
1 teaspoon vanilla extract
1 cup (heaping) finely chopped pecans
8 ounces caramels
$1/4$ cup water

✦ Sift flour and baking powder together. Mix butter, brown sugar and vanilla in bowl. Stir in $1/3$ cup pecans. Add flour mixture gradually, mixing well after each addition.
✦ Shape dough by teaspoonfuls into balls. Flatten 1 side by pressing onto nonstick cookie sheet. Pinch tops to a point to resemble acorns. Bake at 350 degrees for 15 to 18 minutes or until brown. Cool completely.
✦ Melt caramels with water in double boiler over hot water. Dip $1/4$ inch of flat ends of cookies into caramel mixture. Dip into remaining pecans to coat.

Preparation time: 20 minutes   40 servings

I-CAN'T-STOP-EATING COOKIES

2¹/4 cups flour
1 teaspoon baking soda
¹/4 teaspoon salt
³/4 cup margarine, softened
¹/4 cup shortening
1¹/4 cups sugar
2 eggs
2¹/2 teaspoons vanilla extract
3 ounces semisweet chocolate, melted, cooled
3 ounces milk chocolate, melted, cooled
12 ounces semisweet chocolate, in ¹/2-inch chunks

✦ Mix flour, baking soda and salt together. Cream margarine, shortening and sugar in mixing bowl. Beat in eggs 1 at a time. Stir in vanilla and melted chocolate. Add flour mixture ¹/3 at a time, stirring just until mixed after each addition. Stir in chocolate chunks.
✦ Drop by spoonfuls 2 inches apart onto greased large cookie sheets. Bake at 350 degrees for 10 minutes or just until light brown. Cool on wire racks.

Preparation time: 15 minutes   60 servings

BLACK AND WHITE COOKIES

1 cup butter, softened
1¹/2 cups sugar
1 egg
1 teaspoon vanilla extract
2 cups flour
1 teaspoon each salt and baking soda
1 cup each semisweet chocolate chips, white chocolate chips and chopped walnuts

✦ Cream butter in mixing bowl until light. Beat in sugar gradually. Add egg and vanilla; beat well. Stir in remaining ingredients. Shape into 2-inch balls. Place 3 inches apart on nonstick cookie sheets.
✦ Bake at 350 degrees for 20 to 23 minutes or until edges are light brown. Cool on wire rack.

Preparation time: 15 minutes   20 servings

The legend of
Priscilla Robinson,
an owner of the
Blue Ball Inn, has
been peppered with
stories by many of
the Inn's subsequent
owners and inhabit-
ants and by unsolved
murders. She is said
to haunt the house,
rummaging through
drawers in search
of something fresh
to wear that is not
covered with the
blood of one of
her victims.

MACADAMIA NUT COOKIES

2 cups flour
1 teaspoon baking soda
1/2 teaspoon salt
1/2 cup softened butter
1/2 cup shortening
3/4 cup packed brown sugar
1/2 cup sugar
1 egg
1 1/2 teaspoons vanilla extract
6 ounces white chocolate, cut into chunks
7 ounces coarsely chopped macadamia nuts

✦ Mix flour, baking soda and salt together. Cream butter and shortening at medium speed in mixing bowl until smooth. Add brown sugar and sugar, beating well. Beat in egg and vanilla. Add flour mixture gradually, beating well after each addition. Stir in white chocolate and nuts.

✦ Drop by rounded teaspoonfuls 2 inches apart onto nonstick cookie sheets. Bake at 350 degrees for 8 to 10 minutes or until light brown. Cool slightly on cookie sheets. Remove to wire racks to cool completely.

Preparation time: 45 minutes   24 servings

GOLDEN LEMON THINS

1/2 cup butter, softened
3/4 cup packed brown sugar
1 egg
3/4 cup sifted flour
1/2 cup finely chopped almonds
1/4 cup quick-cooking oats
1 tablespoon grated lemon peel
1/2 teaspoon lemon extract

✦ Cream butter in mixing bowl. Beat in brown sugar gradually. Blend in egg. Stir in remaining ingredients.

✦ Drop by scant teaspoonfuls 3 inches apart onto greased cookie sheets. Bake at 350 degrees for 7 to 10 minutes or until edges are golden brown. Remove from cookie sheets immediately.

Preparation time: 20 minutes   36 servings

RASPBERRY THUMBPRINTS

2 cups butter, softened
1 cup packed brown sugar
1 tablespoon vanilla extract
3 egg yolks
4 cups flour
2 cups (or more) finely chopped pecans
1 cup (or more) raspberry jam, jelly or preserves

◆ Mix butter, brown sugar, vanilla and egg yolks in bowl. Add flour gradually, mixing well after each addition. Shape into 1-inch balls. Roll in pecans. Place on nonstick cookie sheets. Make indentation in each cookie with thumb. Fill indentation with jam.
◆ Bake at 350 degrees for 10 to 14 minutes or until brown.

Preparation time: 20 minutes   96 servings

ENGLISH TOFFEE

2 cups butter
2 tablespoons water
2 cups sugar
1/2 teaspoon salt
2 cups finely chopped walnuts
2 cups chocolate chips

◆ Melt butter with water in 4-quart saucepan over medium heat. Stir in sugar and salt. Bring to a boil, stirring constantly. Boil gently until mixture begins to lighten in color. Stir in 1 cup of the walnuts. Cook to 298 degrees on candy thermometer, stirring constantly.
◆ Pour mixture into buttered 10x15-inch jelly roll pan, spreading to edges. Cool slightly. Sprinkle chocolate chips over toffee. Let stand for 2 minutes. Spread chocolate chips evenly over top. Sprinkle with remaining 1 cup walnuts.
◆ Let stand for 3 to 4 hours. Cut crosswise into 1-inch strips. Remove from pan and cut into 1-inch squares. There will be some breakage; save the crumbs for an ice cream topping. Store in airtight container for several weeks in refrigerator or several months in freezer.

Preparation time: 15 minutes   36 servings

Before she died in 1888 at one hundred years of age, Priscilla Robinson requested that her coffin be made of chestnut wood, so that when she went to hell she would "go through cracklin'."

WHITE CHOCOLATE TRUFFLES

2 tablespoons whipping cream
3 ounces white chocolate, finely chopped
1 teaspoon unsalted butter, softened
2 teaspoons brandy
3/4 cup coarsely chopped pecans, lightly toasted

✦ Bring whipping cream to a boil in small saucepan; remove from heat. Add chocolate, stirring until completely melted. Add butter; mix until smooth. Stir in brandy and 1/4 cup of the pecans.
✦ Chill, covered, in bowl for 4 hours or until firm. Shape by teaspoonfuls into balls; roll in remaining 1/2 cup pecans. Chill for 1 hour or until firm.
✦ May store for 1 week in airtight container in refrigerator.

Preparation time: 30 minutes   16 servings

MOCHA BLONDE BROWNIES

2 cups flour
2 teaspoons baking powder
1/2 teaspoon salt
11/4 cups each packed dark and light brown sugar
3/4 cup butter
3 tablespoons instant coffee powder
1 tablespoon hot water
2 eggs
2 tablespoons vanilla extract
1 cup chopped pecans (optional)
2 cups semisweet chocolate chips

✦ Sift flour, baking powder and salt together. Melt brown sugars and butter in medium saucepan over medium-low heat. Dissolve coffee powder in hot water. Stir into butter mixture. Cool to room temperature. Beat in eggs and vanilla with hand-held mixer; do not overmix. Add flour mixture gradually, mixing well with a wooden spoon after each addition. Stir in pecans and chocolate chips. Spread evenly in buttered jelly roll pan.
✦ Bake at 350 degrees for 20 to 25 minutes or until light brown; do not overbake. Cut cooled brownies into 2-inch squares.

Preparation time: 45 minutes   24 servings

There were at least four types of inns in the 19th century, based on the social standing of those who frequented them. "Stage stands," which catered to stagecoach travelers, were at the top of the social ladder. "Wagon stands," patronized by wagoners who slept on bags of hay or oats on the taproom floor, were several notches down. Still lower were "drove stands" for the men who herded the livestock to market. The lowest type of inn was the "taphouse," receiving those who were not welcome elsewhere.

RASPBERRY BROWNIES

1¹/4 cups flour
1 teaspoon baking powder
¹/2 teaspoon salt
5 ounces unsweetened chocolate
1 cup unsalted butter
2 cups sugar
4 eggs
2 teaspoons vanilla extract
1 cup chopped pecans, toasted
³/4 cup raspberry preserves

✦ Mix flour, baking powder and salt together. Melt chocolate and butter in large saucepan, stirring until smooth; remove from heat. Whisk in sugar, eggs and vanilla. Add flour mixture; whisk to blend. Stir in pecans. Pour 2 cups of the batter into 9x13-inch baking dish sprayed with nonstick baking spray. Freeze for 15 minutes or until firm. Spread preserves over frozen batter. Spoon remaining batter over preserves. Let stand until frozen layer thaws.

✦ Bake at 350 degrees for 35 minutes or until wooden pick comes out clean.

Preparation time: 30 minutes   12 to 14 servings

DOUBLE-CHOCOLATE BROWNIES

4 eggs
2 cups sugar
1 cup butter
4 ounces unsweetened chocolate
1 cup sifted flour
1 cup chocolate chips

✦ Beat eggs with sugar in bowl until mixture is thickened and sugar is dissolved. Melt butter and unsweetened chocolate in saucepan. Cool slightly. Stir into egg mixture; beat until blended. Stir in flour. Add chocolate chips. Spread evenly in greased and floured 8x12-inch baking pan.

✦ Bake at 350 degrees for 35 to 45 minutes or until wooden pick comes out clean.

Preparation time: 30 minutes   20 servings

Known as "Peggy Dane's," the Spring House opposite the water tank in Berwyn was a wagon stand or tavern of good reputation. Here many drivers of Conestoga wagons quenched their thirst and rested before heading west to Ohio and beyond.

KAHLUA CHIP BROWNIES

2 cups flour
2 teaspoons baking powder
1/2 teaspoon salt
3 tablespoons instant coffee powder
1 tablespoon water
2 cups packed brown sugar
3/4 cup butter
2 eggs
2 tablespoons Kahlúa or other coffee liqueur
6 ounces white chocolate, chopped into 1/2-inch chunks
3/4 cup coarsely chopped pecans or walnuts

✦ Sift flour, baking powder and salt together. Heat coffee powder and water in heavy medium saucepan over medium-low heat until coffee powder dissolves, stirring constantly. Add brown sugar and butter. Cook until butter is melted, stirring constantly. Pour into large bowl. Cool to room temperature, stirring occasionally. Add eggs and coffee liqueur; whisk to combine. Add flour mixture; mix well. Stir in white chocolate and pecans. Spread in greased 9x13-inch baking pan.
✦ Bake at 350 degrees for 30 to 35 minutes or until wooden pick comes out clean.

Preparation time: 30 minutes   12 servings

CHOCOLATE PEANUT BUTTER BARS

1 cup butter or margarine
1 cup peanut butter
1 (1-pound) package confectioners' sugar
1 1/2 cups graham cracker crumbs
2 cups semisweet chocolate chips, melted

✦ Melt butter in medium saucepan; remove from heat. Stir in peanut butter, confectioners' sugar and graham cracker crumbs, mixing well. Press into 9x13-inch dish. Spread with melted chocolate. Chill for 30 minutes or longer. Cut into bars.

Preparation time: 30 minutes   24 servings

COCONUT-BUTTERSCOTCH BARS

3/4 cup sifted flour
1/2 teaspoon baking powder
1/2 teaspoon salt
1/4 cup margarine, softened
1 cup packed brown sugar
1 egg
1 teaspoon vanilla extract
1 1/2 cups shredded coconut
1 tablespoon melted butter
1 tablespoon sugar

✦ Sift flour, baking powder and salt together. Beat
margarine, brown sugar, egg and vanilla in mixing bowl
until light. Add flour mixture and 1 cup of the coconut;
mix well. Spoon into 8x8-inch baking pan lined with
greased waxed paper. Sprinkle with mixture of remaining
1/2 cup coconut, butter and sugar.
✦ Bake at 350 degrees for 35 minutes. Cut into 2-inch
bars while warm. Cool in pan.

Preparation time: 20 minutes   16 servings

ENGLISH TOFFEE BAR COOKIES

2 cups flour
1 teaspoon cinnamon
1 cup butter, softened
1 cup sugar
1 egg yolk
1 egg white, slightly beaten
1 cup chopped pecans or walnuts

✦ Sift flour with cinnamon. Cream butter and sugar in
mixing bowl until light. Add egg yolk; mix well. Mix in
flour mixture gradually. Spread in greased 10x15-inch
baking pan. Spread egg white over dough. Sprinkle with
pecans, pressing lightly into dough.
✦ Bake at 275 degrees for 1 hour. Cut into 1 1/2-inch bars.
Cool in pan.

Preparation time: 20 minutes   72 servings

**Berwyn means
"white boundary" in
Welsh; it is the name
of a mountain range
in Wales.**

CRANBERRY WALNUT BARS

3/4 cup chopped walnuts
1 (12-ounce) package fresh cranberries
1 cup water
1 1/4 cups sugar
2 tablespoons unsalted butter
1 tablespoon amaretto
1 3/4 cups flour
1/2 cup sugar
1/4 cup finely ground walnuts
3/4 cup unsalted butter
1 egg, beaten
2 tablespoons milk
Sugar to taste

+ Spread walnuts on baking sheet. Bake at 300 degrees for 5 minutes or until dry.
+ Bring cranberries, water and 1 1/4 cups sugar to a boil in medium saucepan; reduce heat. Simmer for 15 minutes or until berries pop and thicken; remove from heat. Stir in 2 tablespoons butter and amaretto. Let stand, covered, until berries cool and thicken. Stir in walnuts.
+ Mix flour, 1/2 cup sugar and walnuts in bowl. Cut in 3/4 cup butter until crumbly. Add mixture of egg and milk, mixing until soft dough forms. Divide dough into 2 portions. Wrap in plastic wrap and chill.
+ Roll dough into two 10x14-inch rectangles. Press 1 portion over bottom and up sides of buttered 9x13-inch baking pan. Spread with cranberry mixture. Top with remaining dough; press down gently. Sprinkle lightly with additional sugar.
+ Bake at 375 degrees for 25 to 30 minutes or until center is light and edges are golden brown. Cut into 36 bars. Let stand to cool.

Preparation time: 40 minutes   36 servings.

The first American locomotives, in operation around 1832, were wood-burning and had very tall smokestacks. Behind the engine was a small flat car, carrying wood fuel and barrels of water, followed by three to six passenger cars. These were entered from the side, and when the train was in motion it was not possible to pass from one coach to another.

PUMPKIN CRUNCH BARS

1 cup flour
1/2 cup rolled oats
1/2 cup packed brown sugar
1/2 cup butter
1 (16-ounce) can pumpkin
1 (12-ounce) can evaporated milk
2 eggs
3/4 cup sugar
1 teaspoon cinnamon
1/2 teaspoon ground ginger
1/2 teaspoon salt
1/4 teaspoon ground cloves
1/2 cup chopped pecans
1/2 cup packed brown sugar
2 tablespoons butter
1/4 cup rolled oats

✦ Beat flour, 1/2 cup oats, 1/2 cup brown sugar and 1/2 cup butter at low speed in mixing bowl until crumbly. Press into 9x13-inch baking pan. Bake at 350 degrees for 15 minutes or until light brown.

✦ Mix pumpkin, evaporated milk, eggs, sugar, cinnamon, ginger, salt and cloves in bowl. Pour into prepared crust. Bake for 20 minutes.

✦ Mix pecans, 1/2 cup brown sugar, 2 tablespoons butter and 1/4 cup oats in bowl. Sprinkle over pumpkin filling. Bake for 15 to 20 minutes or until filling is set. Cool in pan on wire rack. Cut into bars.

Preparation time: 25 minutes   12 servings

SNICKER BAR SQUARES

1 1/2 cups flour
1 1/2 cups old-fashioned rolled oats
1 1/2 cups packed brown sugar
1/2 teaspoon baking soda
1/4 teaspoon salt
3/4 cup chilled butter, cut into pieces
2 cups semisweet miniature chocolate chips
1 cup chopped peanuts
1/2 cup whipping cream
1 (14-ounce) package caramels

✦ Combine flour, oats, brown sugar, baking soda and salt
in food processor container. Cut in butter by pulsing
several times until crumbs begin to stick together.
Reserve 2 cups crumb mixture. Press remaining mixture
into 9x13-inch baking pan. Sprinkle with chocolate
chips and peanuts.

✦ Bring whipping cream to a simmer in heavy medium
saucepan over medium heat. Add caramels. Cook until
caramels are melted, stirring constantly until smooth.
Pour over crust. Sprinkle with reserved crumb mixture.

✦ Bake at 350 degrees for 15 minutes or until edges
are golden brown. Loosen from sides of pan. Cool
completely; cut into squares. Chill for 3 hours or until
cold throughout. Serve cold.

Preparation time: 25 minutes   36 servings

The first trains in the early 1800s did not run after dark because the locomotive had no headlight. Sparks emitted from the wood-burning engine often set fire to forests and fields, passengers' clothing and occasionally a coach car. The train usually attained a running speed of ten to fifteen miles an hour, making the time of arrival and departure a matter of conjecture. Time-tables were not taken seriously until after 1850.

ZUCCHINI DESSERT BARS

1¼ cups packed brown sugar
½ cup margarine or butter, softened
2 eggs
1 teaspoon vanilla extract
2 cups flour
2 teaspoons baking soda
¾ teaspoon ground cinnamon
½ teaspoon ground nutmeg
¼ teaspoon ground cloves
1½ cups shredded zucchini
1 cup raisins
3 ounces cream cheese, softened
6 tablespoons margarine or butter, softened
1 teaspoon vanilla extract
2 cups confectioners' sugar

✦ Mix brown sugar, ½ cup margarine, eggs and vanilla in
large bowl. Add flour, baking soda, cinnamon, nutmeg
and cloves; mix well. Stir in zucchini and raisins. Spread
in 9x13-inch baking pan.
✦ Bake at 350 degrees for 25 to 35 minutes or until layer
tests done. Cool completely.
✦ Mix cream cheese, 6 tablespoons margarine and vanilla
in bowl. Add confectioners' sugar gradually, beating until
of spreading consistency.
✦ Spread frosting over cooled baked layer. Cut into bars.

Preparation time: 35 minutes   24 servings

WAYNESBOROUGH

Waynesborough, built in 1745, is the birthplace of one of the most famous war heroes in American history, General Anthony Wayne, who was also born in the same year. The house was enlarged in 1765 by Wayne's father, and again in 1810 by his son. For 242 years, the house embraced seven generations of Waynes. The sixteen-acre property is now owned by Easttown Township and is maintained as a park. The house is open to the public for tours and is administered by the Philadelphia Society for the Preservation of Landmarks.

General Anthony Wayne distinguished himself in many battles with the British during the Revolutionary War. He fought at Brandywine, Germantown, Valley Forge, and Monmouth. He became a national hero after his victory in 1779 at Stony Point on the Hudson River, and helped lead the battles that defeated the British in Georgia and the Carolinas.

George Washington appointed him commander-in-chief of the Legions of America in 1792. Wayne was the only such commander who was not a President. He continued to serve his country by defeating the British and Indians in the Northwest Territory, opening up new frontiers for settlement. The notoriety that followed his victory over the Indian nations at Fallen Timbers led to many honors, including the naming of Fort Wayne, Indiana, the General Wayne Inn in Merion, and the town of Wayne in 1880.

DARK CHOCOLATE SAUCE

1¹/₂ cups
whipping cream

²/₃ cup packed dark
brown sugar

¹/₄ cup unsalted
butter, softened

4 ounces bittersweet
chocolate, chopped

3 ounces
unsweetened
chocolate, chopped

3 to 4 tablespoons
amaretto

✦

Bring cream and

brown sugar to a boil

in heavy saucepan,

whisking until brown

sugar dissolves. Stir

in butter and choco-

late until melted. Stir

in amaretto. Cool

slightly. May keep in

refrigerator for 1

week; reheat to serve.

ALMOND ICE CREAM CAKE

1¹/₂ cups chocolate wafer crumbs (30 wafers)
¹/₄ cup melted unsalted butter
2 pints coffee ice cream, softened
1¹/₂ cups whipping cream, chilled
1 teaspoon vanilla extract
1¹/₂ cups crushed amaretti cookies
¹/₂ cup sliced blanched almonds, toasted
Dark Chocolate Sauce (at left)

✦ Mix chocolate wafer crumbs and butter in bowl. Press mixture onto bottom and 1 inch up side of greased 8-inch springform pan. Freeze for 30 minutes or until firm.
✦ Spread with ice cream. Freeze until firm.
✦ Beat cream in mixing bowl until soft peaks form. Add vanilla; beat until stiff. Fold in amaretti cookie crumbs. Spread over ice cream, smoothing top. Sprinkle with almonds. Freeze, covered with plastic wrap and foil, for 4 hours to overnight. Wrap warm wet kitchen towel around springform pan. Remove side. Place cake on serving plate. Serve with Dark Chocolate Sauce.

Preparation time: 1¹/₄ hours   10 servings

COUNTRYSIDE APPLE CAKE

4 cups chopped peeled tart apples
3 eggs, beaten
1 cup vegetable oil
2 cups flour
1 cup each sugar and packed brown sugar
1 teaspoon each salt and cinnamon
1¹/₂ teaspoons baking powder
Cinnamon and sugar mixture

✦ Combine apples, eggs and oil in bowl. Add mixture of flour, sugar, brown sugar, salt, cinnamon and baking powder. Oil tube or bundt pan; coat with mixture of cinnamon and sugar. Spoon batter into pan.
✦ Bake at 350 degrees for 1 hour or until cake tests done. Cool in pan for several minutes; invert onto serving plate.

Preparation time: 20 minutes   16 servings

BUTTER RUM CAKE

1/2 cup melted butter
1 cup packed brown sugar
1/2 to 3/4 cup chopped pecans
1 (2-layer) package yellow butter cake mix
1 (4-ounce) package French vanilla instant pudding mix
4 eggs
1/3 cup water
1/3 cup light rum
1/3 cup canola oil
1/3 cup light rum

✦ Spread melted butter in bottom of bundt pan. Sprinkle with brown sugar; sprinkle with pecans.
✦ Mix cake mix, pudding mix and eggs in mixing bowl. Add water, 1/3 cup rum and oil; mix well. Spoon into bundt pan.
✦ Bake at 325 degrees for 45 minutes or until cake tests done. Cool in pan for several minutes; invert onto serving plate. Drizzle with remaining 1/3 cup rum.

Preparation time: 10 minutes   16 servings

BLUEBERRY CARROT CAKE

2 cups flour
2 teaspoons baking powder
1 teaspoon baking soda
2 teaspoons cinnamon
1 teaspoon salt
1 cup sugar
1/2 cup packed brown sugar
4 large eggs
4 medium carrots, grated
2 cups fresh blueberries
1 cup chopped walnuts

✦ Mix flour, baking powder, baking soda, cinnamon, salt, sugar and brown sugar in mixing bowl. Add eggs; beat well. Stir in carrots, blueberries and walnuts. Spoon into greased and floured bundt pan.
✦ Bake at 350 degrees for 1 hour or until cake tests done. Cool in pan for 20 minutes. Invert onto serving plate.

Preparation time: 30 minutes   16 servings

"Mad" Anthony Wayne earned his nickname for two outstanding characteristics. First, he was known for his bravery and for starting a fight at the slightest provocation. Second, he was quite hand-some and dashing in a "mad cap" way, in the lingo of the day.

BLUEBERRY LEMON POUND CAKE

1^1/2 cups butter, softened
1/2 cup sugar
3/4 cup packed light brown sugar
1/3 cup freshly grated lemon zest
6 eggs, beaten
1/3 cup milk
1^1/2 tablespoons vanilla extract
2^2/3 cups flour
1 teaspoon baking powder
1^1/4 teaspoons salt
3 cups fresh blueberries
1^1/2 tablespoons flour
1/3 cup fresh lemon juice
1/2 cup sugar

✦ Cream butter, 1/2 cup sugar, brown sugar and lemon zest
  in mixing bowl until light and fluffy. Beat eggs with milk
  and vanilla in bowl. Sift 2^2/3 cups flour, baking powder
  and salt together. Add to creamed mixture alternately
  with egg mixture, beginning and ending with flour
  mixture and mixing just until combined.
✦ Toss blueberries with 1^1/2 tablespoons flour. Fold half
  the blueberries into batter. Layer the batter and
  remaining blueberries 1/3 at a time in greased and floured
  bundt pan.
✦ Bake at 350 degrees for 1 hour or until cake tests done.
✦ Heat lemon juice and 1/2 cup sugar in saucepan until
  sugar dissolves, stirring constantly.
✦ Poke holes in hot cake with wooden spoon handle. Brush
  with half the hot syrup. Let stand for 10 minutes.
✦ Invert onto wire rack. Poke holes in cake. Brush with
  remaining syrup.

Preparation time: 30 minutes   Yield: 10 to 12 servings

SECOND-TO-NONE CARROT CAKE

1 pound carrots, peeled, cut into $^1/2$-inch pieces
Salt to taste
1 cup canola oil
1 (8-ounce) can juice-pack crushed pineapple, drained
4 large eggs
1 tablespoon vanilla extract
3 cups flour
$2^1/2$ cups sugar
1 tablespoon cinnamon
1 tablespoon baking soda
1 teaspoon salt
$1^1/2$ cups coarsely chopped walnuts
Lemony Cream Cheese Frosting (at right)

✦ Cook carrots with salted water to cover in large saucepan for 12 minutes or until tender; drain. Process in blender until puréed. Cool slightly.
✦ Whisk oil, pineapple, eggs and vanilla in bowl. Add carrot purée; mix well. Mix flour, sugar, cinnamon, baking soda and 1 teaspoon salt together. Stir into batter. Stir in walnuts. Spoon batter into 3 buttered 9-inch cake pans lined with waxed paper.
✦ Bake at 350 degrees for 35 minutes or until cake tests done. Cool in pans for several minutes; remove to wire racks to cool completely. Spread Lemony Cream Cheese Frosting between layers and over top and side of cake. Garnish with walnuts.
✦ May be made 1 day ahead and refrigerated. Let stand for 3 hours at room temperature before serving.

Preparation time: 30 minutes   12 servings

LEMONY CREAM CHEESE FROSTING

16 ounces cream cheese, softened

1$^1/4$ cups unsalted butter, softened

1 tablespoon fresh lemon juice

2 teaspoons vanilla extract

5$^2/3$ cups confectioners' sugar, sifted

✦

Beat cream cheese, butter, lemon juice and vanilla in mixing bowl until light and fluffy. Add confectioners' sugar gradually, beating until creamy. Chill until of spreading consistency.

CHOCOLATE CHIP FUDGE CAKE

3/4 cup unsalted butter
6 ounces unsweetened chocolate, chopped
6 eggs
3 cups sugar
1/2 teaspoon salt
1 tablespoon vanilla extract
1 1/2 cups flour
1 1/2 cups chocolate chips
Mocha Frosting (at left)

✦ Melt butter and chocolate in double boiler over hot water. Cool to lukewarm.
✦ Beat eggs, sugar, salt and vanilla in mixing bowl. Add melted chocolate mixture; mix well. Stir in flour and chocolate chips. Pour into 2 greased 9-inch cake pans lined with waxed paper.
✦ Bake at 350 degrees for 30 to 35 minutes or until cake tests done. Cool in pans for several minutes; remove to wire racks to cool completely. Spread Mocha Frosting between layers and over top and side of cake.

Preparation time: 15 minutes   10 servings

CHOCOLATE CHIP CRUMB CAKE

1/2 cup butter, softened
2 cups each flour and sugar
1 teaspoon each salt and baking soda
1 teaspoon vanilla extract
1 cup sour cream
2 eggs
1 cup chocolate chips
1 1/2 tablespoons butter, softened

✦ Cut butter into mixture of flour and sugar in bowl until crumbly. Reserve 3/4 cup for topping. Combine salt, baking soda, vanilla, sour cream and eggs with remaining mixture; mix well. Spoon into greased and floured 9x13-inch cake pan. Sprinkle with chocolate chips. Mix reserved topping with remaining butter; sprinkle over top.
✦ Bake at 350 degrees for 40 minutes or until cake tests done. Serve warm or cold.

Preparation time: 15 minutes   16 servings

MOCHA FROSTING

1 1/4 cups sugar

1 tablespoon instant coffee powder

1 cup whipping cream

5 ounces unsweetened chocolate, finely chopped

1/2 cup unsalted butter

1 1/2 teaspoons vanilla extract

✦

Combine sugar, instant coffee powder and cream in saucepan. Bring to a boil, stirring constantly. Remove from heat. Stir in chocolate and butter until melted. Stir in vanilla. Chill until of spreading consistency.

CHOCOLATE ZUCCHINI CAKE

1/2 cup butter, softened
1/2 cup vegetable oil
1 3/4 cups sugar
2 eggs
1 teaspoon vanilla extract
1/2 cup sour milk
2 1/2 cups flour
1/4 cup baking cocoa
1/2 teaspoon baking powder
1 teaspoon baking soda
1/2 teaspoon ground cinnamon
1/2 teaspoon ground cloves
2 cups finely chopped unpeeled zucchini (2 to 3 medium)
1/2 cup semisweet chocolate chips

✦ Cream butter, oil and sugar in mixing bowl. Add eggs, vanilla and milk; mix well. Mix flour, baking cocoa, baking powder, baking soda, cinnamon and cloves together. Add to batter; mix well. Stir in zucchini. Spoon into greased 9x13-inch cake pan. Sprinkle with chocolate chips.
✦ Bake at 325 degrees for 40 to 45 minutes or until cake tests done.
✦ Serve with whipped cream.
✦ Combine 1/2 cup milk with 1/2 tablespoon cider vinegar to make sour milk. May omit cloves.

Preparation time: 20 minutes   15 servings

During the Revolutionary War, General Anthony Wayne employed midnight attacks, ambushes and attacking isolated enemy scouting parties as his favored and successful methods of fighting in the Pennsylvania countryside that he knew so well.

CHOCOLATE CHAMBORD CAKE

1/2 cup butter, softened

1 1/4 cups sugar

2 eggs yolks

1 1/4 cups cake flour

2 teaspoons baking powder

1/4 teaspoon salt

1/3 cup baking cocoa

2/3 cup milk

1 teaspoon vanilla extract

2 egg whites, stiffly beaten

5 tablespoons seedless raspberry jam

5 tablespoons Chambord or other raspberry flavor liqueur

2 cups whipping cream

1/4 cup sifted confectioners' sugar

2 1/2 cups fresh raspberries

✦ Cream butter and sugar in mixing bowl until light and fluffy. Add egg yolks; beat well. Mix flour, baking powder, salt and baking cocoa together. Add to creamed mixture alternately with milk, beating at low speed after each addition until blended. Add vanilla. Fold in stiffly beaten egg whites. Spoon batter into 2 greased 9-inch cake pans lined with waxed paper.

✦ Bake at 350 degrees for 18 minutes or until cake tests done. Cool in pans for several minutes; remove to wire racks to cool completely. Heat raspberry jam in saucepan over low heat until melted, stirring constantly. Remove from heat. Stir in liqueur.

✦ Beat whipping cream until soft peaks form. Add confectioners' sugar, beating until stiff.

✦ Place 1 cake layer on serving plate. Brush with raspberry jam mixture; arrange half the fresh raspberries over top. Spread half the whipped cream mixture over raspberries. Add second layer; brush with remaining jam mixture. Top with remaining whipped cream. Arrange remaining raspberries on top.

Preparation time: 45 minutes   12 servings

WHITE CHOCOLATE CAKE

8 ounces white chocolate
1 teaspoon vanilla extract
2 1/2 cups cake flour
1 teaspoon baking powder
1/2 teaspoon salt
1 cup butter, softened
2 cups sugar
4 egg yolks
1/2 cup white crème de cacao
1 cup whipping cream
4 egg whites
Pinch of cream of tartar
Salt to taste
1 cup chopped pecans
1 cup flaked coconut

✦ Melt white chocolate in double boiler over hot water, stirring constantly. Remove from heat. Add vanilla; mix well. Set aside.
✦ Sift flour, baking powder and 1/2 teaspoon salt together.
✦ Cream butter and sugar in mixing bowl until light and fluffy. Beat in egg yolks 1 at a time. Add melted chocolate; beat until blended. Add flour mixture alternately with crème de cacao, beginning and ending with dry ingredients and mixing well after each addition.
✦ Beat cream in mixing bowl until soft peaks form; fold into batter.
✦ Beat egg whites in mixing bowl until foamy. Add cream of tartar and salt to taste, beating until stiff. Fold into batter. Fold in pecans and coconut. Spoon batter into nonstick tube pan.
✦ Bake at 325 degrees for 1 hour and 10 minutes or until cake tests done. Cool in pan for several minutes; remove to wire rack to cool completely.

Preparation time: 30 minutes   16 servings

The Paoli Massacre occurred September 20, 1777. The British learned the secret colonial password, "Here we are, and there they go," and surprised eighty of Washington's sick and wounded men encamped in Paoli. The Americans surrendered, but were charged and bayoneted nonetheless; not one survived.

SOUR CREAM COFFEE CAKE

3 cups sifted flour
1 1/2 teaspoons baking powder
1 1/2 teaspoons baking soda
1/4 teaspoon salt
1 1/2 cups butter, softened
1 1/2 cups sugar
1 1/2 teaspoons vanilla extract
3 eggs
1 1/2 cups sour cream
1/4 cup coarsely chopped walnuts
1 1/2 teaspoons cinnamon
1/4 cup packed dark brown sugar
2 tablespoons vanilla extract
2 tablespoons water
Confectioners' sugar

✦ Sift flour, baking powder, baking soda and salt together.
Cream butter and sugar in mixing bowl until light and
fluffy. Beat in 1 1/2 teaspoons vanilla. Add eggs 1 at a
time, beating well after each addition. Add sour cream
and flour mixture; mix well. Mix walnuts, cinnamon
and brown sugar in bowl. Layer batter and cinnamon
mixture 1/3 at a time in greased 10-inch tube pan. Mix 2
tablespoons vanilla and water together. Drizzle over
batter.

✦ Bake at 325 degrees for 1 hour to 1 hour and 10
minutes or until coffee cake tests done. Cool in pan for
several minutes; remove to wire rack to cool completely.
Place coffee cake on serving plate; dust with confectioners' sugar.

Preparation time: 20 minutes   16 servings

ITALIAN CREAM CAKE

1/2 cup each softened margarine and shortening
2 cups sugar
5 egg yolks
1 cup buttermilk
1 teaspoon baking soda
2 cups flour
1 cup chopped pecans
2 cups shredded coconut
2 teaspoons vanilla extract
5 egg whites, stiffly beaten
Cream Cheese Frosting (at right)

✦ Cream margarine, shortening and sugar in mixing bowl until light. Beat in egg yolks 1 at a time. Add mixture of buttermilk and baking soda alternately with flour; mix well. Stir in pecans, coconut and vanilla. Fold in egg whites. Spoon into greased and floured tube pan.
✦ Bake at 350 degrees for 1 hour or until cake tests done. Cool in pan for several minutes; remove to wire rack to cool completely. Spread with Cream Cheese Frosting.

Preparation time: 45 minutes   16 servings

CHOCOLATE POUND CAKE

1 cup butter, softened
1/2 cup shortening
2 1/2 cups sugar
1 1/2 teaspoons vanilla extract
5 eggs
3 cups sifted flour
1/2 cup baking cocoa
1 teaspoon salt
1/2 teaspoon baking powder
1 cup milk

✦ Cream butter, shortening and sugar in mixing bowl until light. Beat in vanilla. Add eggs 1 at a time. Add dry ingredients alternately with milk; mix well. Spoon into greased and floured tube pan.
✦ Bake at 325 degrees for 1 1/4 hours. Cool in pan for several minutes; remove to wire rack to cool completely.

Preparation time: 15 minutes   16 servings

CREAM CHEESE FROSTING

1/2 cup butter, softened

8 ounces cream cheese, softened

1 (1-pound) package confectioners' sugar

1 teaspoon vanilla extract

✦

Cream butter and cream cheese in mixing bowl until light and fluffy. Add confectioners' sugar and vanilla, beating until of spreading consistency.

PEACH SPONGE CAKE

8 egg yolks, beaten
3/4 cup water
1 1/2 cups sugar
1/4 cup soybean oil
1 teaspoon vanilla extract
1 teaspoon freshly grated lemon peel
2 cups flour
2 teaspoons baking powder
8 egg whites
1/2 teaspoon cream of tartar
2 pounds fresh peaches
Lemon juice
1/2 cup sugar
1/2 cup peach schnapps
2 quarts whipping cream, whipped

+ Beat egg yolks with water, 1 1/2 cups sugar, oil, vanilla and lemon peel in mixing bowl. Add flour mixed with baking powder gradually. Beat at high speed for 3 minutes.
+ Beat egg whites with cream of tartar in mixing bowl until stiff peaks form. Fold into egg yolk mixture gently. Pour into lightly greased tube pan.
+ Bake at 325 degrees for 1 hour or until cake tests done. Cool in pan. Remove from pan. Peel peaches; cut into thin slivers. Dip in mixture of lemon juice and water to prevent browning; place in bowl. Add 1/2 cup sugar and schnapps; mix gently. Let stand for 15 minutes. Drain and reserve juices.
+ Reserve a few peach slices for topping. Cut cake horizontally into 3 layers; moisten each layer with reserved peach juices. Place one layer of cake on cake plate. Spread with some of the whipped cream and half the remaining peaches. Add additional cake layer, peach juice, some of the whipped cream and remaining peaches. Moisten remaining cake layer with peach juices; place on top. Frost top and side with remaining whipped cream. Chill in refrigerator. Decorate with reserved fresh peach slices just before serving.

Preparation time: 1 1/4 hours   12 servings

FRENCH APPLE TARTS

2 large Golden Delicious apples, peeled, cored
2 tablespoons fresh lemon juice
1¹/2 teaspoons vanilla extract
1 egg
1 tablespoon milk
¹/3 cup sugar
¹/2 teaspoon cinnamon
¹/2 (17-ounce) package frozen puff pastry, thawed
¹/3 cup apricot preserves
¹/2 teaspoon vanilla extract
Sliced almonds
Whipped cream

✦ Cut apples into thin slices. Mix apples, lemon juice and 1¹/2 teaspoons vanilla in bowl. Let stand for several minutes; drain. Beat egg and milk in small bowl. Mix sugar and cinnamon together.

✦ Roll out pastry on floured surface to 10-inch square. Cut into four 5-inch squares. Brush each square with egg mixture; place in nonstick baking pan. Overlap apple slices on pastry, leaving ¹/4-inch border around edge. Sprinkle with cinnamon mixture.

✦ Bake at 350 degrees for 30 minutes or until crust is brown. Remove to wire rack.

✦ Mix preserves and remaining ¹/2 teaspoon vanilla in small saucepan. Heat until preserves are melted, stirring constantly. Brush glaze over apples; sprinkle with almonds. Top with whipped cream. Serve warm or at room temperature.

Preparation time: 30 minutes   4 servings

CARAMEL APPLE PIE

28 light caramels
1/2 cup evaporated milk
6 cups sliced peeled tart apples
1 cup sugar
1/3 cup flour
2 teaspoons chopped fresh lemon peel
2 to 4 teaspoons fresh lemon juice
8 ounces cream cheese, softened
1 egg
1/3 cup sugar
1/3 cup chopped walnuts
Fluted Pastry (below)

✦ Melt caramels in evaporated milk in double boiler over boiling water, stirring frequently.
✦ Combine apples, 1 cup sugar, flour, lemon peel and lemon juice in bowl; mix well. Cook mixture in saucepan until thickened if apples are juicy. Spoon apples over Fluted Pastry. Drizzle caramel sauce in strips over apples.
✦ Beat cream cheese, egg and 1/3 cup sugar in bowl until smooth. Spoon over apples between strips of caramel sauce. Sprinkle with walnuts.
✦ Bake at 375 degrees for 30 to 35 minutes or until apples are tender and pastry is light brown.

Preparation time: 45 minutes   15 servings

FLUTED PASTRY

3 cups sifted flour
1/4 cup sugar
1 1/2 teaspoons salt
1/2 cup butter
1/4 cup vegetable oil
1 egg
1/4 cup cold water

✦ Sift flour, sugar and salt into bowl. Cut in butter until crumbly. Mix oil, egg and cold water in bowl. Add to dry ingredients, stirring until combined. Shape into a square. Roll out to fit 10x15-inch baking pan. Place on pan. Shape rim around edge; flute top of rim.

Preparation time: 15 minutes   15 servings

Berwyn dates back to 1690 and was originally known as "Travelgwyn" which is Welsh for "white trouble." It referred to the white hills overlooking the Dee River in Wales.

APPLE WALNUT CRUMB PIE

3 pounds tart apples, peeled, cored
1/4 cup unsalted butter
Juice of 1/2 lemon
2/3 cup sugar
1/2 teaspoon salt
Cloves and nutmeg to taste
1 teaspoon cinnamon
2 tablespoons cornstarch
2 teaspoons vanilla extract
2 tablespoons rum
11/2 cups chopped walnuts
1/3 cup packed brown sugar
1/4 cup flour
1 teaspoon cinnamon
1/4 cup unsalted butter
Vanilla Cookie Crust (at right)

✦ Cut apples into slices. Combine apples and 1/4 cup butter in large saucepan over medium heat, stirring to coat apples as butter melts. Add lemon juice, sugar, salt, cloves, nutmeg and 1 teaspoon cinnamon. Simmer until apples are tender, stirring frequently. Mix cornstarch, vanilla and rum together. Add to apples. Cook for 1 minute, stirring constantly. Cool slightly.

✦ Mix chopped walnuts, brown sugar, flour and 1 teaspoon cinnamon in bowl. Cut in 1/4 cup butter until crumbly. Spoon apple mixture into chilled Vanilla Cookie Crust, heaping higher in center. Sprinkle walnut mixture over top. Bake at 375 degrees for 40 minutes or until brown. Cool on wire rack for 2 to 3 hours before slicing. Serve with whipped cream or ice cream.

Preparation time: 30 minutes   10 servings

VANILLA COOKIE CRUST

7 ounces
finely ground
vanilla wafers

1 cup finely
ground walnuts

2 tablespoons
confectioners' sugar

1 teaspoon
cinnamon

1/4 cup melted butter

✦

Combine all ingredients in bowl; mix well. Press over bottom and side of 9-inch pie plate. Line with foil. Bake at 400 degrees for 10 minutes. Remove foil. Bake for 5 to 10 minutes longer or until light brown. Cool to room temperature. Freeze for 30 minutes.

CHOCOLATE STRAWBERRY PIE

1 cup graham cracker crumbs
3 tablespoons sugar
1/3 cup melted butter
1/2 cup chocolate chips
8 ounces cream cheese, softened
1/4 cup packed brown sugar
1/2 teaspoon vanilla extract
1 cup whipping cream, whipped
1 pint fresh strawberries
2 tablespoons chocolate chips
1 teaspoon shortening

✦ Mix graham cracker crumbs, sugar and melted butter in bowl. Press onto bottom and up side of greased 9-inch pie plate.
✦ Bake at 350 degrees for 10 minutes. Cool completely on wire rack.
✦ Microwave 1/2 cup chocolate chips in glass dish for 30 to 45 seconds or until melted. Cool slightly.
✦ Beat cream cheese in bowl until light and fluffy; add brown sugar and vanilla. Fold in whipped cream and melted chocolate. Spoon into cooled crust. Chill for 8 hours or longer.
✦ Reserve 1 whole strawberry. Cut remaining strawberries into thick slices. Arrange slices over pie with whole strawberry in center. Combine remaining chocolate chips and shortening in saucepan. Melt over low heat, stirring constantly. Drizzle over strawberries.

Preparation time: 40 minutes   8 servings

ICE CREAM PIE

3 tablespoons butter
1 cup chocolate chips
2 cups crisp rice cereal
1 quart chocolate chip mint ice cream, softened

✦ Melt butter and chocolate chips in saucepan. Stir in rice cereal. Remove from heat. Mash with fork to consistency of graham cracker crumbs. Press onto bottom and up side of 9-inch pie plate. Freeze until firm. Spoon ice cream into shell. Freeze until serving time.

Preparation time: 10 minutes   6 servings

PRALINE PEACH OF A PIE

1/2 cup packed light brown sugar
1 1/2 teaspoons flour
3 tablespoons unsalted butter, chopped
1/2 cup pecans
2 tablespoons quick-cooking tapioca
1/2 cup sugar
1/4 teaspoon cinnamon
1/8 teaspoon nutmeg
4 1/3 cups sliced, peeled fresh peaches (about 9)
1/4 teaspoon vanilla extract
Pastry Shell (at right)

◆ Mix brown sugar and flour in bowl. Cut in butter until crumbly. Stir in pecans. Chill, covered, in refrigerator.
◆ Combine tapioca, sugar, cinnamon, nutmeg, peaches and vanilla in bowl. Let stand for 10 minutes. Spoon peach filling into Pastry Shell. Sprinkle pecan topping over top.
◆ Bake at 425 degrees in the lower third of oven for 30 minutes or until golden brown. Cool on wire rack.

Preparation time: 35 minutes   8 servings

SOUR CREAM PECAN PIE

3 eggs
1/2 cup sour cream
1/2 cup dark corn syrup
1 teaspoon vanilla extract
1 cup sugar
1/8 teaspoon salt
2 tablespoons melted butter
1 3/4 cups pecan halves
1 unbaked (9-inch) pie shell

◆ Beat eggs in bowl. Stir in sour cream, corn syrup, vanilla, sugar, salt and butter until well mixed. Stir in pecans. Spoon into pie shell.
◆ Bake at 400 degrees for 30 to 45 minutes or until filling is puffy and crust is brown. Cool on wire rack.

Preparation time: 15 minutes   8 servings

PASTRY SHELL

1 1/4 cups
unbleached flour

1 teaspoon sugar

1/4 teaspoon salt

6 tablespoons
unsalted butter,
chopped

2 tablespoons
shortening

3 tablespoons
ice water

◆

Combine flour, sugar
and salt in bowl. Cut
in butter and
shortening until
crumbly. Stir in ice
water until combined,
adding additional
water if needed.
Shape into ball.
Chill, covered, for
1 hour. Roll dough
into 12-inch circle
on floured surface.
Fit into 9-inch
deep-dish pie plate,
fluting edges.

TARTLET SHELLS

1/4 cup flour

1/2 teaspoon each salt and sugar

1/2 cup cold unsalted butter, chopped

1/8 to 1/4 cup ice water

✦

Process flour, salt and sugar in food processor. Add butter, processing until crumbly. Add ice water 1 tablespoon at a time. Shape into 4 balls. Chill, covered, for 15 minutes. Roll 1/8 inch thick between waxed paper. Fit into 4-inch tartlet pans sprayed with nonstick baking spray. Bake at 375 degrees for 12 to 15 minutes or until golden brown. Cool on wire rack.

RED RASPBERRY TARTLETS

1/2 cup red currant jelly
Tartlet Shells (at left)
1/2 cup whipping cream
1 tablespoon framboise
1 pint fresh red raspberries

✦ Melt jelly in small saucepan; strain. Brush inside bottom and sides of baked Tartlet Shells with some of the jelly. Whip cream and framboise in mixing bowl until soft peaks form. Spoon into Tartlet Shells. Arrange raspberries on top; brush with remaining jelly. Chill until serving time.

Preparation time: 25 minutes   4 servings

FRESH FRUIT TART

1 (8-ounce) package refrigerator sugar cookie dough
8 ounces cream cheese, softened
1/3 cup sugar
1/2 teaspoon vanilla extract
Assorted fresh fruit such as strawberries, bananas,
    blueberries, kiwifruit or raspberries, cut into slices
2 tablespoons hot water
1/2 cup apricot preserves

✦ Line 14-inch tart pan with sliced cookie dough, overlapping slightly.
✦ Bake at 375 degrees for 10 minutes or until brown. Cool slightly.
✦ Beat cream cheese, sugar and vanilla in bowl. Spread over baked layer. Arrange fruit in circles over top. Mix hot water and preserves in bowl. Brush top of fruit with glaze. Chill before slicing. May substitute 1/2 recipe of your favorite cookie dough for refrigerator dough.

Preparation time: 25 minutes   8 servings

STRAWBERRY GLAZE PIE

3 1/2 cups fresh strawberries
3/4 cup sugar
2 tablespoons cornstarch
1/4 teaspoon salt
1 cup water
2 tablespoons strawberry gelatin
1 baked (9-inch) pie shell
Whipped cream

✦ Wash strawberries; remove tops and drain. Combine sugar, cornstarch, salt and water in saucepan. Cook over low heat for 10 to 15 minutes or until thickened and clear, stirring constantly. Remove from heat. Stir in gelatin until dissolved. Line bottom of pie shell with glaze. Alternate layers of strawberries and glaze in pie shell until all are used. Chill until serving time. Top with whipped cream.

Preparation time: 15 minutes   8 servings

ALMOND MOCHA TORTONI

2 cups whipping cream
1/4 cup sugar
2 tablespoons instant coffee powder
2 egg yolks, slightly beaten
2 teaspoons vanilla extract
2 egg whites, stiffly beaten
2/3 cup semisweet chocolate chips
1/2 cup minced toasted almonds
Grated unsweetened chocolate to taste

✦ Whip cream in bowl. Stir in sugar and coffee powder. Add egg yolks and vanilla; mix well. Fold into egg whites in large bowl.
✦ Melt chocolate chips in double boiler over hot water; cool slightly. Fold melted chocolate and almonds into egg white mixture. Spoon into foil-lined muffin cups. Freeze until firm. Wrap each tortoni well; place in plastic box and store in freezer until needed. Let stand for several minutes to soften. Top with grated chocolate.

Preparation time: 40 minutes   12 to 14 servings

Paoli was settled in 1719 by William Evans. It remained nameless until his son Joshua opened a tavern on the Darby-Yellow Springs Road, and named it for the popular Corsican patriot, General Pasquale de Paoli, who championed liberty and self-determination for his native island in the mid-1700s.

APPLE CRISP

6 cups sliced, peeled tart apples
2 tablespoons brown sugar
1 cup flour
3/4 cup sugar
1 teaspoon baking powder
3/4 teaspoon salt
1 egg
1/3 cup melted butter or margarine
1 teaspoon (heaping) cinnamon sugar

✦ Place apples in baking dish. Sprinkle with brown sugar. Mix flour, sugar, baking powder, salt and egg in bowl. Spoon over apples. Drizzle with melted butter. Sprinkle with cinnamon sugar.
✦ Bake at 375 degrees for 30 minutes or until lightly browned.
✦ Serve warm with vanilla ice cream or hard sauce.

Preparation time: 25 minutes   6 to 8 servings

GRANNY SMITH APPLE CRISP

6 Granny Smith apples, peeled, thinly sliced
3/4 cup sugar
1/4 teaspoon nutmeg
1/2 teaspoon cinnamon
1/2 cup melted butter
1/2 cup flour
1/4 cup sugar
1/2 cup rolled oats, or to taste

✦ Place apples in large pie plate until overflowing. Mix 3/4 cup sugar, nutmeg and cinnamon together. Combine with apples and toss lightly. Mix butter, flour, 1/4 cup sugar and oats in bowl. Pour over apple mixture.
✦ Bake at 350 degrees for 1 hour.
✦ Serve warm or cold. May serve with ice cream.

Preparation time: 20 minutes   8 servings

BLUEBERRY CHEESE SQUARES

2/3 cup graham cracker crumbs
1 tablespoon sugar
2 tablespoons melted butter
8 ounces cream cheese, softened
1 egg
1/2 cup sugar
1/2 teaspoon vanilla extract
1 (16-ounce) package fresh or frozen blueberries
1/4 cup sugar
1 tablespoon cornstarch
1 teaspoon fresh lemon juice

✦ Mix graham cracker crumbs, 1 tablespoon sugar and
butter in bowl. Press into 8x8-inch baking pan.
✦ Mix cream cheese, egg, 1/2 cup sugar and vanilla in bowl.
Pour over crust. Bake at 350 degrees for 30 minutes.
Cool completely.
✦ Heat remaining ingredients in saucepan until mixture
boils and thickens, stirring frequently. Pour over cream
cheese mixture. Chill for 6 hours. Cut into squares.

Preparation time: 1 hour   9 to 12 servings

WHITE CHOCOLATE CREME BRULEE

5 egg yolks
3/4 cup sugar
2 cups whipping cream
3 ounces white chocolate, chopped
1/4 teaspoon vanilla extract

✦ Whisk egg yolks with 1/4 cup of the sugar in bowl. Bring
whipping cream and 1/4 cup of the sugar to a simmer in
saucepan; reduce heat to low. Add white chocolate
gradually, whisking until smooth. Whisk into egg yolk
mixture gradually. Stir in vanilla. Ladle into four
10-ounce custard cups. Place in baking pan. Fill baking
pan with boiling water halfway up sides of custard cups.
✦ Bake at 300 degrees for 1 hour or until set. Cool
completely. Chill, covered, overnight.
✦ Sprinkle 1 tablespoon sugar over each custard. Broil
until sugar caramelizes.

Preparation time: 1 hour   4 servings

BLACK TIE CHEESECAKE

Not all large homes
on the Main Line
were the domains of
wealthy men. The
gracious Hollystone
home on Valley and
White Horse Roads
in Paoli belonged to
a tenant farmer. A
simple but elegant
design, Hollystone
launched the career
of a young architect,
Richard Brognard
Okie, around 1897.

1¹/4 cups graham cracker crumbs
¹/3 cup melted butter
¹/4 cup packed light brown sugar
1 teaspoon cinnamon
32 ounces cream cheese, softened
1¹/2 cups sugar
2 tablespoons flour
4 extra-large eggs
2 egg yolks
1¹/3 cups whipping cream
1 teaspoon vanilla extract
1¹/2 cups coarsely chopped Oreo cookies
2 cups sour cream
1 teaspoon vanilla extract
8 ounces semisweet chocolate, chopped
1 teaspoon vanilla extract

✦ Mix graham cracker crumbs, butter, brown sugar and cinnamon in bowl. Press onto bottom and up side of 10-inch springform pan. Chill for 30 minutes or until firm.
✦ Beat cream cheese at low speed in mixing bowl until smooth. Beat in 1¹/4 cups of the sugar and flour. Beat in eggs and egg yolks. Stir in ¹/3 cup of the cream and 1 teaspoon vanilla. Layer half the batter, chopped cookies and remaining batter in prepared pan; smooth top with spatula. Bake at 425 degrees for 15 minutes. Reduce temperature to 225 degrees. Bake for 55 to 60 minutes or until cheesecake tests done, covering loosely with foil if top browns too quickly. Increase temperature to 350 degrees. Mix sour cream, remaining ¹/4 cup sugar and 1 teaspoon vanilla in bowl. Spread over cheesecake. Bake for 7 minutes. Chill, covered with plastic wrap, overnight.
✦ Scald remaining 1 cup cream in heavy saucepan over high heat. Add chocolate and 1 teaspoon vanilla. Cook for 1 minute, stirring constantly. Remove from heat and stir until chocolate is melted. Chill for 10 minutes.
✦ Place cheesecake on platter; remove springform. Pour chocolate mixture over cheesecake, allowing glaze to drip down side. Garnish with Oreo halves placed cut side down around outer edge of cheesecake; place maraschino cherry in center. Chill until serving time.

Preparation time: 45 minutes   20 servings

LADYFINGER CHEESECAKE

3 packages ladyfingers
3/4 cup sugar
20 ounces cream cheese, softened
1 teaspoon vanilla extract
2 cups whipping cream, whipped
1/2 pint fresh strawberries, cut into halves

✦ Line bottom and side of springform pan with ladyfingers. Cream sugar and cream cheese in mixing bowl until light and fluffy. Beat in vanilla. Fold in whipped cream.
✦ Layer half the creamed mixture, remaining ladyfingers and remaining creamed mixture in prepared pan. Top with strawberries. Chill, covered with plastic wrap, for 9 to 10 hours.

Preparation time: 45 minutes   12 servings

FRESH LEMON CHEESECAKE

32 ounces cream cheese, softened
1 cup sugar
1 tablespoon fresh orange juice
4 eggs
1 cup sour cream
3 tablespoons fresh lemon juice
2 tablespoons freshly grated lemon peel

✦ Beat cream cheese in mixing bowl until light. Beat in sugar and orange juice. Add eggs 1 at a time, beating well after each addition. Fold in sour cream, lemon juice and lemon peel. Pour into greased 9-inch springform pan.
✦ Bake at 300 degrees for 1 1/4 hours or until outside edge is set but center still moves slightly when pan is shaken. Turn off oven. Let stand in closed oven for 1 hour. Chill, covered with plastic wrap, overnight.

Preparation time: 20 minutes   8 to 10 servings

CHOCOLATE FUDGE SAUCE

2 cups semisweet chocolate chips

2 tablespoons melted unsalted butter

1/2 teaspoon vanilla extract

1/2 cup whipping cream

✦

Melt chocolate chips in double boiler over hot water. Whisk in butter and vanilla as chocolate is melting. Whisk cream in gradually. Cook for 5 minutes or until blended and smooth, stirring constantly; remove from heat. Let stand to cool; sauce will thicken as it cools.

TRIPLE CHOCOLATE TERRINE

7 ounces bittersweet chocolate
6 ounces milk chocolate
4 ounces white chocolate
3 cups whipping cream
2/3 vanilla bean
Chocolate Fudge Sauce (at left)
Fresh raspberries

✦ Break each of the chocolates into 1-inch pieces, keeping each kind separate. Heat the whipping cream almost to a simmer in saucepan. Spoon 1 1/4 cups into 1 bowl, 1 cup into another and 3/4 cup into a third bowl.

✦ Whisk bittersweet chocolate with 1 1/4 cups cream until smooth. Whisk milk chocolate with 1 cup cream until smooth. Whisk white chocolate with 3/4 cup cream until smooth. Stir seeds from vanilla bean into white chocolate mixture. Chill mixtures, loosely covered, for 3 hours or until mixtures are thick but can still be poured.

✦ Line loaf pan with foil, leaving some foil above edge of pan. Beat white chocolate mixture in mixing bowl until soft peaks form; do not overbeat. Spoon into loaf pan; smooth top. Freeze for 5 minutes. Beat milk chocolate mixture in mixing bowl until soft peaks form; do not overbeat. Spread over white chocolate layer. Freeze for 5 minutes. Beat bittersweet chocolate mixture in mixing bowl until soft peaks form; do not overbeat. Spread over milk chocolate layer. Chill, covered with plastic wrap, for 3 hours or until firm.

✦ Lift foil to unmold terrine; remove foil. Cut terrine into 1/2-inch slices. Spoon a small amount of Chocolate Fudge Sauce onto each plate. Top with slice of terrine. Let stand for 5 minutes. Garnish with fresh raspberries.

Preparation time: 1 hour   8 to 10 servings

FRESH FRUIT COMPOTE

1/2 cup each sugar and water
1/2 vanilla bean, split lengthwise
2 oranges
16 (1/2-inch) fresh pineapple cubes
8 fresh strawberries, cut into halves
2 kiwifruit, cut into 1/3-inch slices
1 large banana, cut into 1/2-inch rounds
2 tablespoons golden raisins (optional)

✦ Mix sugar and water in heavy saucepan. Scrape in seeds from vanilla bean; add bean. Bring to a boil over medium-high heat. Cook until sugar is dissolved, stirring constantly. Cool completely. Discard vanilla bean and pour syrup into bowl.
✦ Trim peel and zest from oranges; cut oranges into sections. Fold orange sections, pineapple, strawberries, kiwifruit, banana and raisins into syrup. Let stand for 30 minutes. Garnish with pineapple leaves or mint leaves.

Preparation time: 15 minutes   4 to 6 servings

LEMON SOUFFLE

2 envelopes unflavored gelatin
1/2 cup cold water
8 egg yolks
1 cup each sugar and fresh lemon juice
1/2 teaspoon salt
8 egg whites, softly beaten
1 cup sugar
2 cups whipping cream, whipped

✦ Sprinkle gelatin over cold water in saucepan. Let stand for 5 to 10 minutes to soften. Heat until gelatin is dissolved, stirring constantly. Cool to room temperature.
✦ Beat egg yolks, 1 cup sugar, lemon juice and salt in mixing bowl over warm water until mixture is lemon colored and light and fluffy. Stir in gelatin mixture. Beat 1 cup sugar into egg whites gradually until stiff peaks form. Fold into gelatin mixture. Fold in whipped cream gently.
✦ Pour into individual molds, a larger soufflé dish or a collared mold. Chill until set. Serve with raspberry sauce.

Preparation time: 1 hour   8 servings

RASPBERRY COULIS

1 (10-ounce)
package frozen
raspberries, thawed

1/3 cup sugar

2 tablespoons
Grand Marnier

✦

Place raspberries

in food processor

container. Process

until smooth. Press

through sieve or food

mill to remove seeds.

Stir in sugar and

Grand Marnier. Chill

until serving time.

SASSY LEMON SOUFFLE

1 envelope unflavored gelatin
1/4 cup cold water
6 egg yolks
1 1/4 cups sugar
3/4 cup fresh lemon juice
Grated peel of 2 lemons
4 egg whites, stiffly beaten
1 1/2 cups whipping cream, whipped
Raspberry Coulis (at left)

✦ Tie a waxed paper collar around 1-quart soufflé dish with
collar extending 2 inches above rim. Brush inside of
collar with vegetable oil or spray with unflavored nonstick
cooking spray.

✦ Soften gelatin in cold water in small bowl. Beat egg
yolks with sugar in non-aluminum saucepan over low
heat. Cook until thickened and hot; do not boil. Add
gelatin mixture, stirring until dissolved. Stir in lemon
juice and lemon peel. Cool to room temperature,
stirring occasionally.

✦ Fold egg whites into lemon mixture. Fold in whipped
cream. Pour into prepared soufflé dish; mixture will rise
above rim. Freeze overnight. Remove from freezer 30
minutes before serving time; remove collar. Garnish with
whipped cream rosettes and candied violets.

✦ Spoon a small amount of Raspberry Coulis onto
individual plates. Place spoonful of soufflé in center
of coulis.

Preparation time: 1 hour   8 to 10 servings

AUNT ORELIA'S MEXICAN FLAN

1 cup sugar
8 eggs
2/3 cup sugar
1/4 teaspoon salt
2 (12-ounce) cans evaporated milk
2 teaspoons vanilla extract
1/4 cup golden rum

✦ Caramelize 1 cup sugar in loaf pan over low heat, stirring constantly; remove from heat. Beat eggs in bowl until well blended. Stir in 2/3 cup sugar and salt. Beat in evaporated milk. Stir in vanilla and rum. Pour over caramelized sugar in pan. Place pan in shallow baking dish filled with hot water.
✦ Bake at 350 degrees for 1 hour or until knife inserted near center comes out clean. Cool to room temperature. Chill overnight.
✦ Loosen edge of flan gently with knife. Invert onto serving plate. Scrape caramelized sugar over top of flan. May sprinkle confectioners' sugar on individual plates before serving. Garnish with fresh strawberries.

Preparation time: 45 minutes   8 servings

THREE-MELON COINTREAU

1 watermelon
2 cantaloupes
2 honeydew melons
1 cup Cointreau
1 cup chopped fresh mint leaves

✦ Cut watermelon into halves lengthwise; scoop out pulp, reserving 1 shell. Cut all melons with scoop. Combine with Cointreau in bowl; mix well. Chill until serving time. Pour into reserved watermelon shell. Sprinkle with chopped mint.

Preparation time: 20 minutes   10 servings

BLACK-WHITE MACAROON TART

2 egg whites
1/3 cup sugar
2 cups sweetened flaked coconut
2 tablespoons flour
2 egg yolks
2/3 cup whipping cream
6 ounces bittersweet chocolate, chopped
2 tablespoons light rum
6 ounces white chocolate, chopped
2 tablespoons light rum
6 ounces white chocolate, chopped
1/2 cup sour cream
1 (10-ounce) package frozen raspberries, thawed, strained

✦ Butter bottom and side of 10-inch round tart pan with removable bottom. Line pan with parchment paper; butter paper.

✦ Whisk egg whites with 1/3 cup sugar in bowl until foamy. Mix coconut and flour in bowl. Blend into egg white mixture. Spread evenly in prepared pan. Bake at 325 degrees for 20 to 25 minutes or until firm and golden brown. Loosen and remove macaroon shell; peel away paper. Place shell on serving plate.

✦ Whisk egg yolks and whipping cream together in saucepan. Simmer to 160 degrees on candy thermometer or until thickened, stirring constantly; remove from heat. Add bittersweet chocolate, stirring until melted. Stir in rum. Let stand to cool, stirring frequently.

✦ Melt white chocolate in saucepan. Add sour cream, stirring until smooth. Let stand to cool, stirring frequently.

✦ Alternate layers of dark chocolate mixture and white chocolate mixture in shell until both mixtures are completely used. Shake shell gently to settle filling as layers are added. Draw knife through layers to swirl together. Chill, covered, for 8 hours or until set.

✦ Press raspberries through sieve; scrape away excess pulp. Swirl sauce on individual plates. Cut tart into slices. Place 1 slice on each raspberry swirl. Garnish each serving with a fresh raspberry and a mint leaf.

Preparation time: 45 minutes   8 to 12 servings

SUMMER SPONGE CAKE TRIFLE

1 cup flour
1 teaspoon baking powder
2 eggs
1 cup sugar
1/4 teaspoon salt
1 teaspoon vanilla extract
1 tablespoon melted butter
1/2 cup boiling milk
2 cups whipping cream
2 tablespoons sugar
1 cup currant jelly, whipped thin
4 cups thinly sliced, peeled fresh peaches
4 cups thinly sliced fresh strawberries

✦ Sift flour and baking powder together. Beat eggs slightly in mixing bowl. Beat in 1 cup sugar gradually. Stir in salt and vanilla. Add mixture of butter and milk. Add flour mixture; beat well. Spoon into greased and floured 8-inch round cake pan. Bake at 350 degrees for 25 to 35 minutes or until cake tests done. Cut cooled cake into four 1/2-inch thick layers. Beat whipping cream with 2 tablespoons sugar.

✦ Place 1 cake layer in glass bowl. Spread with 1/4 of the jelly. Add layer of peaches, strawberries and whipped cream. Continue layering until all ingredients are used, ending with fruit. Garnish with additional whipped cream. May peel peaches after first placing in boiling water for 30 to 45 seconds.

Preparation time: 1 hour   10 to 12 servings

There is a catchy phrase used to remember the names of the train stations on the Main Line: "Old Maids Never Wed And Have Babies, Period." Overbrook, Merion, Narberth, Wynnewood, Ardmore, Haverford, Bryn Mawr and Paoli.

BERRY GRAND MARNIER SAUCE

2 cups fresh raspberries
1/2 cup confectioners' sugar
1 tablespoon fresh lemon juice
1/8 to 1/4 cup Grand Marnier

✦ Purée raspberries in food processor or blender. Add confectioners' sugar, lemon juice and Grand Marnier. Process until of desired sauce consistency. Strain through strainer or food mill to remove seeds.

Preparation time: 10 minutes   1 cup

CHOCOLATE STRAWBERRIES

6 ounces semisweet chocolate
3 1/2 tablespoons unsalted butter
6 1/2 teaspoons brandy
24 large fresh strawberries

✦ Combine chocolate, butter and brandy in double boiler over hot water over moderate heat. Cook until chocolate and butter are melted, stirring frequently until blended and smooth; remove from heat. Hold strawberries by the leaves; dip half way in chocolate mixture. Place on platter lined with waxed paper. Chill for 10 minutes or longer. Serve on dessert tray.

Preparation time: 20 minutes   24 servings

GRAND MARNIER CREAM

2/3 cup whipping cream
1 teaspoon each vanilla extract and brandy
1 1/2 teaspoons Grand Marnier
1/4 cup sugar
2 tablespoons sour cream

✦ Chill beaters and mixing bowl in freezer. Beat whipping cream, vanilla, brandy and Grand Marnier in mixing bowl at medium speed for 1 minute. Add sugar and sour cream. Beat for 3 minutes or until soft peaks form; do not overbeat. Serve with strawberries.

Preparation time: 15 minutes   1 1/2 cups

RASPBERRY CHAMBORD DIP

4 ounces cream cheese, softened
$1/2$ cup sour cream
1 tablespoon sugar
$1/4$ cup whipping cream
1 tablespoon seedless raspberry jelly
1 teaspoon Chambord
$1/2$ teaspoon vanilla extract

✦ Blend cream cheese and sour cream in bowl. Add sugar,
  cream, jelly, Chambord and vanilla; mix until smooth.
✦ Serve with bite-size fresh fruit.

Preparation time: 10 minutes $1^1/4$ cups

COFFEE BAR

Cinnamon sticks
Ground cinnamon
Whipped cream
Raw sugar
Sugar cubes
Sugar sticks
Confectioners' sugar
Artificial sweetener packets
Peppermint sticks
Cocoa powder
Lemon curls
Orange curls
Bottle of Kahlúa
Bottle of Grand Marnier
Skim and whole milk
Freshly brewed hot coffee

✦ Present first 12 ingredients in water goblets arranged
  decoratively and compactly on varying levels.
✦ Serve hot coffee in cups of desired size and allow guests
  to customize the servings from the coffee bar.

Preparation time: 20 minutes   Variable servings

THE SATURDAY CLUB

The Saturday Club grew out of the need for women
in the community to enrich their own lives outside the home.
The first meeting was held on Saturday, February 16, 1886, in
Wayne Hall adjacent to Wayne Presbyterian Church. On
Saturdays, men came to town to conduct business, and the
women, who often rode along, came in search of their own
fellowship. "Dare to be Wise" was the motto they adopted, and
their meeting programs usually took the form of papers
presented to each other on such topics as literature, science, art,
music, and, of course, the household. In 1894, the meetings
were changed to Tuesdays when Saturday became a school and
business holiday. In 1898, members pooled their resources to
buy a lot and build a clubhouse on West Wayne Avenue.
It was modeled after William Shakespeare's home in England,
and is now on the National Historic Register.

The Saturday Club grew further in the mid 1900s
to serve women in all circumstances. An Evening Section
was added for those women who were joining the
workforce, and the Junior Saturday Club was formed for
women remaining at home.

Today, the Junior Saturday Club of Wayne has a
vital membership of 125 women who donate their time and
energy to local groups and community service projects,
and their resources to numerous nonprofit and educational
organizations in need. To raise funds for its philanthropies, the
club published its first successful cookbook, *Philadelphia Main
Line Classics,* in 1982. Proceeds from this book have enabled the
club to distribute over $130,000 in directed grants to local
charities. This second volume, *Main Line Classics II, Cooking Up
A Little History*, will help the Junior Saturday Club carry
on its valuable work in the community.

FESTIVE BEEF TENDERLOIN
DINNER FOR TEN

Crab Meat Balls

Red Pepper Soup

Three-Greens Salad with Sautéed Walnuts
and Dijon Vinaigrette

Roast Tenderloin of Beef

French Bean Sauté

Garlic Roasted Potatoes

Irish Cream Cheesecake

CRAB MEAT BALLS

1 pound fresh crab meat, finely chopped
4 slices white bread, crusts removed, crumbled
White Sauce (at right)
1/2 red or green chile, seeded, finely chopped
1 green onion, finely chopped
1 tablespoon chopped fresh parsley
Salt and pepper to taste
2 eggs, beaten
Dry bread crumbs
Vegetable oil for deep-frying

✦ Mix crab meat with fresh bread crumbs in large bowl.
✦ Stir in White Sauce, chile, green onion, parsley, salt and pepper. Cool completely.
✦ Shape with floured hands into 1-inch balls. Dip into beaten eggs; coat with dry bread crumbs. Deep-fry 6 crab meat balls at a time in 350-degree oil for 3 minutes or until golden brown and crisp; drain on paper towels. Sprinkle lightly with salt. Serve with cocktail sauce.

Preparation time: 30 minutes   10 servings

RED PEPPER SOUP

4 small onions, sliced
4 large red bell peppers, thinly sliced
6 tablespoons butter
1/2 potato, peeled, grated
3 cups chicken broth
1/2 cup whipping cream
2 tablespoons fresh lemon juice
Salt and pepper to taste
2 tablespoons snipped fresh dill
10 sprigs of fresh dill

✦ Sauté onions and red peppers in butter in saucepan for 30 minutes. Add potato and broth. Cook for 15 minutes.
✦ Purée in batches in blender. Combine purée, cream, lemon juice, salt and pepper and snipped dill in saucepan.
✦ Heat to serving temperature. Top servings with dill sprigs.

Preparation time: 30 minutes   8 to 10 servings

WHITE SAUCE

1 tablespoon
melted butter

1 tablespoon flour

1/2 cup milk

✦

Blend butter and flour
in small saucepan. Stir
in milk. Bring to a boil
over medium heat.
Cook until thickened,
stirring constantly.

SAUTEED WALNUTS

1/4 cup butter

3 cups walnut halves

✦

Heat butter in skillet over low heat until bubbly. Add walnuts. Sauté until golden brown; drain on paper towels.

THREE-GREENS SALAD

2 heads Boston lettuce
2 heads red leaf lettuce
2 heads green leaf lettuce
Dijon Vinaigrette (below)
Sautéed Walnuts (at left)
12 ounces Stilton cheese, crumbled
24 cherry tomatoes, halved

✦ Separate lettuce leaves, rinse and pat completely dry; tear and place in salad bowl.
✦ Add desired amount of Vinaigrette; toss lightly. Arrange on individual chilled salad plates.
✦ Divide Sautéed Walnuts, cheese and tomatoes into equal portions on prepared salad plates.
✦ Serve immediately.

Preparation time: 15 minutes   10 servings

DIJON VINAIGRETTE

1 tablespoon Dijon mustard
1 tablespoon minced shallots
1 1/2 teaspoons salt
Freshly ground pepper to taste
3/4 cup balsamic vinegar
2 1/4 cups olive oil

✦ Whisk mustard, shallots, salt, pepper and balsamic vinegar in medium bowl.
✦ Add olive oil in a fine stream, whisking constantly until emulsified.
✦ Whisk before adding to salad if vinaigrette separates while standing.

Preparation time: 15 minutes   10 servings

ROAST TENDERLOIN OF BEEF

$1/2$ ounce dried morel mushrooms
1 cup hot water
4 ounces shallots, minced
2 tablespoons unsalted butter
$1/3$ cup red wine vinegar
1 cup canned beef broth
1 cup dry red wine
Salt and pepper to taste
1 (6-pound) loin end, trimmed tenderloin
3 tablespoons vegetable oil
$1/2$ cup water
2 tablespoons unsalted butter

✦ Rinse morels well; soak in 1 cup hot water for 30 minutes. Drain, reserving liquid. Pour liquid through fine sieve lined with dampened paper towels. Mince morels; set aside.

✦ Sauté shallots in 2 tablespoons butter in small saucepan over medium-low heat until tender. Add vinegar. Cook until mixture is almost dry.

✦ Add reserved mushroom liquid. Add morels, broth and wine. Boil until mixture is reduced to about $1 1/2$ cups. Season with salt and pepper.

✦ May prepare sauce to this point up to 2 days in advance. Cool, cover and refrigerate.

✦ Rub tenderloin with oil; season with salt and pepper. Place in roaster.

✦ Roast at 500 degrees for 10 minutes. Reduce to 325 degrees for 45 minutes or to 130 degrees on meat thermometer for medium-rare.

✦ Place tenderloin on cutting board. Let stand, loosely covered with foil, for 20 minutes. (Tenderloin should come from oven just as guests sit down for first course.)

✦ Reheat morel sauce. Add $1/2$ cup water to drippings in roasting pan. Cook over low to medium heat for 5 minutes or until thickened, stirring to deglaze pan.

✦ Whisk pan juices and juices from standing tenderloin into morel sauce. Heat to serving temperature; whisk in 2 tablespoons butter.

✦ Place sliced tenderloin on plates. Add generous amount of sauce. Serve remaining sauce in gravy boat.

Preparation time: 1 hour   10 servings

1891: Mrs. George R. Stocker, club president in 1888, foreshadowed the modern women's movement in this speech: "The club movement for women is a factor for modern progress. It has stimulated an intellectual and social life without, in the least, detracting from the duties of wife-hood and motherhood. It is impossible for me to comprehend the narrow groove in which the majority of women have been forced to live, move and have their being in the past. Club life has revealed women to each other; it has established fellowship on purely human foundation."

FRENCH BEAN SAUTÉ

1 pound fresh French beans (haricots verts)
1 red bell pepper
1 yellow bell pepper
1/2 clove of garlic
1/4 cup butter
1 tablespoon vegetable oil (optional)

✦ Cut blunt ends from beans. Cut bell peppers julienne.
✦ Rub cut side of garlic over surface of large sauté pan. Add butter and oil.
✦ Sauté vegetables in butter mixture over medium-high heat for 3 to 4 minutes or until vegetables are tender-crisp. Be careful not to burn butter.

Preparation time: 20 minutes   10 servings

GARLIC ROASTED POTATOES

3 pounds baking potatoes
1/3 cup olive oil
1 tablespoon minced fresh garlic
1 to 2 tablespoons dried oregano
Salt and freshly ground pepper to taste

✦ Scrub potatoes. Cut each into approximately eight 2-inch pieces. Place in baking dish.
✦ Add olive oil, garlic, oregano, salt and pepper; toss to coat.
✦ Bake at 400 degrees for 30 to 40 minutes or until tender and brown, tossing every 15 minutes. Drain excess oil during baking time.

Preparation time: 20 minutes   10 servings

IRISH CREAM CHEESECAKE

6 whole graham crackers
1/4 cup melted butter
24 ounces cream cheese, softened
7 tablespoons sugar
1 tablespoon flour
2 eggs
6 tablespoons sour cream
1/3 cup Baileys Irish Cream
2 teaspoons vanilla extract
1/2 cup whipping cream
9 ounces semisweet chocolate, chopped
Chocolate curls

✦ Process graham crackers in food processor until finely ground. Add butter; process until mixed. Press over bottom of 9-inch springform pan. Bake at 350 degrees for 8 minutes or until golden brown. Cool on wire rack.

✦ Beat cream cheese and sugar in mixing bowl until smooth. Beat in flour and eggs 1 at a time. Blend in sour cream, Irish Cream and vanilla. Pour over crust. Bake at 350 degrees for 10 minutes. Reduce oven temperature to 250 degrees. Bake for 40 minutes longer. Turn off oven. Let cheesecake stand in closed oven for 1 hour.

✦ Loosen cheesecake from side of pan; do not remove pan. Chill overnight.

✦ Bring cream to a simmer in heavy saucepan. Add semisweet chocolate. Heat over low heat until melted and smooth, stirring constantly. Cool to lukewarm.

✦ Place cheesecake on rack placed on baking sheet. Remove side of pan. Pour chocolate glaze over top; spread over top and side with spatula. Chill for 30 minutes or until set. Remove to serving plate. Top with chocolate curls.

Preparation time: 45 minutes   12 servings

1892: The colors dark green, for freshness, and white, for purity, were chosen as the Saturday Club colors. The motto "Dare to Be Wise" was adopted, and the mountain laurel was selected as the club emblem. Annual membership dues were two dollars.

DELECTABLE FLANK STEAK
DINNER FOR TEN

Salmon Dill Cream Cheese

Tomato and Red Pepper Dip

Mixed Green Salad

Stuffed Flank Steak

Wild Rice and Orzo

Baby Squash and Baby Carrots

Heath Bar Torte

SALMON DILL CREAM CHEESE

16 ounces cream cheese, softened
4 ounces smoked salmon
1 1/2 tablespoons minced shallots or red onion
1 1/2 teaspoons snipped fresh dill
1 teaspoon tomato paste

✦ Combine cream cheese, salmon, shallots, dill and tomato
  paste in food processor container; process until smooth.
✦ Serve with assorted favorite crackers.

Preparation time: 10 minutes   3 cups

TOMATO AND RED PEPPER DIP

2 (7-ounce) jars roasted red peppers
8 sun-dried tomato halves
1 clove of garlic, minced
Pinch of salt
1 1/2 tablespoons fresh lemon juice
1 tablespoon chopped fresh parsley
4 ounces cream cheese, chopped, softened
1/2 cup sour cream
Salt and pepper to taste
Lightly toasted pita triangles

✦ Drain red peppers; pat dry. Soak tomatoes in hot water
  to cover in a bowl for 5 minutes; drain and pat dry. Mash
  garlic with pinch of salt into a paste.
✦ Process peppers, tomatoes and garlic with lemon juice
  and parsley in food processor until smooth. Add cream
  cheese, sour cream, salt to taste and pepper; process
  until smooth.
✦ Place in serving bowl. Garnish with additional parsley.
  Serve with pita triangles.

Preparation time: 20 minutes   2 1/4 cups

1893: The Saturday Club, with a membership of sixty-five, including eleven men, expanded its scope from an intellectual and social group to a philanthropic organization dedicated to providing goods and services to needy households and hospitals in the area.

1907: The Junior Saturday Club was formed for girls seventeen to twenty-three years of age. The first president of this section was elected in 1921.

MIXED GREEN SALAD

Arugula, radicchio, red cabbage and green leaf lettuce
8 to 10 cloves of garlic, thinly sliced
3/4 cup olive oil
1/4 cup balsamic vinegar
4 teaspoons brown sugar
8 ounces pine nuts
Parmesan cheese curls

✦ Prepare salad greens in desired amounts in large bowl.
✦ Sauté garlic in olive oil in skillet over low heat until lightly browned. Add vinegar and brown sugar. Add to salad; toss to mix.
✦ Toast pine nuts on baking sheet at 300 degrees for 2 to 4 minutes. Add to salad. Top with Parmesan cheese.

Preparation time: 20 minutes   10 servings

STUFFED FLANK STEAK

1 pound fresh spinach, trimmed
1 cup bread crumbs
1 cup freshly grated Parmesan cheese
1/2 cup olive oil
3 cloves of garlic
6 pounds flank steaks, butterflied
Salt and pepper to taste
6 ounces thinly sliced prosciutto
5 red bell peppers, roasted, peeled, halved, seeded
1 fresh hot cherry pepper, seeded, minced

✦ Rinse spinach; drain but do not dry. Cook, covered, in saucepan over medium heat for 5 minutes or until wilted; drain in colander, pressing dry. Purée with next 4 ingredients in food processor.
✦ Open steaks; sprinkle with salt and pepper. Add layers of prosciutto, roasted peppers, spinach mixture and cherry pepper. Roll as for jelly roll from long side; tie with string at 2-inch intervals. Brush with additional olive oil; sprinkle with salt and pepper. Place in baking dish.
✦ Bake at 350 degrees for 40 minutes for medium-rare. Cool slightly before slicing.

Preparation time: 25 minutes   10 servings

WILD RICE AND ORZO

2 cups wild rice
1 cup orzo
2 medium onions, chopped
2 cloves of garlic, crushed
2 tablespoons butter
1/4 cup honey
2 teaspoons light soy sauce
2 teaspoons fresh lemon juice
1 tablespoon chopped fresh parsley

✦ Cook wild rice in a generous amount of boiling water in large pot for 25 minutes; drain. Cook pasta in a generous amount of boiling water in another pot for 10 minutes or until tender; drain.

✦ Sauté onions and garlic in butter in large skillet until tender. Add rice, orzo, honey, soy sauce, lemon juice and parsley; mix well. Heat to serving temperature, stirring constantly. May prepare a day ahead and reheat.

Preparation time: 15 minutes   10 servings

1915: The club founded the first kindergarten in Wayne, and also organized the community Christmas tree.

BABY SQUASH AND BABY CARROTS

1 bag baby carrots, scraped
1/2 (1-pint) carton baby zucchini squash
1/2 (1-pint) carton baby yellow squash
1/4 cup finely chopped fresh parsley
1/4 cup finely chopped fresh dill
2²/3 tablespoons butter

✦ Cook carrots in a generous amount of boiling water in large saucepan for 1 minute. Add squash. Cook for 2 minutes; drain.

✦ Sauté parsley and dill in butter in skillet until heated through. Add carrots and squash. Sauté until tender-crisp. Serve immediately.

Preparation time: 10 minutes   10 servings

HEATH BAR TORTE

6 egg whites
2 teaspoons vanilla extract
1/2 teaspoon cream of tartar
Dash of salt
2 cups sugar
2 cups whipping cream, whipped
8 Heath bars, finely chopped
1/2 cup toasted slivered almonds

✦ Beat egg whites with vanilla, cream of tartar and salt in mixing bowl until soft peaks form. Add sugar gradually, beating until stiff peaks form. Draw 2 plate-size circles on baking parchment on baking sheet. Spread meringue over circles.

✦ Bake at 275 degrees for 1 hour. Turn off oven. Let meringues stand in closed oven for 2 hours. Remove from parchment.

✦ Fold whipped cream and chopped candy together gently in large bowl. Layer meringues and whipped cream mixture 1/2 at a time on serving plate. Top with almonds.

Preparation time: 20 minutes   10 servings

ENTIRELY ITALIAN DINNER
FOR SIX

Bruschetta

Insalata di Fantasia

Osso Buco

Garlic Bread

Pasta with Tomato Sauce

Tiramisu

BRUSCHETTA

12 to 14 fresh ripe plum tomatoes
1 tablespoon minced garlic
2 tablespoons minced shallots
1 cup fresh basil leaves, coarsely chopped
1 teaspoon fresh lemon juice
Salt and freshly ground pepper to taste
1/3 cup extra virgin olive oil
3 cloves of garlic, slivered
1/4 cup extra-virgin olive oil
1 loaf Italian bread, sliced 1/2 inch thick

✦ Cut tomatoes into 1/4-inch pieces; place in bowl. Add minced garlic, shallots, basil, lemon juice, salt, pepper and 1/3 cup olive oil; toss to mix.
✦ Sauté garlic cloves in 1/4 cup olive oil in small skillet for 2 to 3 minutes or until golden brown; discard garlic and reserve oil.
✦ Toast bread; cut each slice into halves. Brush with garlic oil; top with tomato mixture. Serve immediately.

Preparation time: 20 minutes   6 servings

INSALATA DI FANTASIA

1 large head radicchio, julienned
2 large Belgian endive, sliced into rounds
1 bunch arugula, trimmed
1/4 cup extra-virgin olive oil
2 tablespoons fresh lemon juice
Salt and freshly ground pepper to taste
1 avocado, peeled, pitted, chopped
1 (7-ounce) can hearts of palm, drained, sliced
    into rounds

✦ Combine radicchio, endive and arugula in large salad bowl. Add olive oil and lemon juice; toss to mix. Add salt and pepper.
✦ Top with avocado and hearts of palm. Serve immediately.

Preparation time: 25 minutes   6 servings

OSSO BUCO

1 medium onion, thinly sliced into rings
1 cup each finely chopped celery and carrots
1 bay leaf
1/4 cup butter
1 teaspoon freshly grated lemon peel
6 (6-ounce) meaty crosscut veal shanks
1/4 cup flour
1/4 teaspoon each freshly ground pepper, dried basil,
    marjoram and thyme
3 tablespoons olive oil
1 (1-pound) can Italian plum tomatoes
1 cup each dry white wine and rich homemade beef broth

◆ Sauté onion, celery, carrots and bay leaf in butter in
  skillet for 5 minutes or until onion is tender. Stir in
  lemon peel; remove from heat.
◆ Coat veal with mixture of flour and seasonings. Cook in
  olive oil in large Dutch oven over medium-high heat
  until brown on both sides. Drain and chop tomatoes,
  reserving juice. Add wine to veal; bring to a boil. Add
  broth, sautéed vegetables, tomatoes and reserved juice.
  Bring to a boil.
◆ Bake, covered, at 375 degrees for 1 hour or until tender.
  Discard bay leaf. Remove veal shanks to serving platter.
  Cook pan juices until reduced by 1/3. Pour over veal.

Preparation time: 20 minutes   6 servings

GARLIC BREAD

1 loaf Italian bread
1 tablespoon olive oil
1 clove of garlic, crushed
1 teaspoon dried parsley
1 tablespoon freshly grated Parmesan cheese

◆ Cut bread lengthwise into 2 pieces; place cut side up on
  baking sheet. Mix olive oil, garlic and parsley in small
  bowl. Spread on bread; sprinkle with cheese.
◆ Broil until golden brown. Slice and serve immediately.

Preparation time: 10 minutes   6 servings

1930s: Membership swelled to the hundreds. The club worked closely with local schools and the Mothers' Association (now the PTA). A series of first-aid classes was held at the clubhouse.

PASTA WITH TOMATO SAUCE

2 medium red bell peppers, quartered
2 medium onions, sliced
2 cloves of garlic, crushed
2 tablespoons olive oil
6 green scallions, chopped
1/2 teaspoon chopped fresh roasted chile
1/2 cup drained sun-dried tomatoes, thinly sliced
1/2 cup dry white wine
1 1/4 cups cream
1/3 cup sour cream
1/3 cup shredded fresh basil
3/4 cup freshly grated Parmesan cheese
12 ounces penne pasta, cooked

✦ Grill or broil peppers until skins are blistered and blackened; cool. Peel and cut into thin strips.
✦ Sauté onions and garlic in olive oil in skillet until tender. Add peppers, scallions, chile and tomatoes. Cook until scallions are tender. Stir in next 5 ingredients. Heat to serving temperature, stirring constantly. Stir into penne.
✦ Garnish with additional Parmesan cheese and fresh basil.

Preparation time: 20 minutes   6 servings

TIRAMISU

3 egg yolks, beaten
2 tablespoons confectioners' sugar
2 teaspoons sweet marsala wine
2 tablespoons orange-flavor liqueur
8 ounces mascarpone cheese
6 tablespoons cold strong coffee or espresso
12 ladyfingers, broken into thirds
2 ounces milk chocolate, grated

✦ Beat egg yolks with confectioners' sugar in mixing bowl until thick and lemon colored. Beat in wine and 1 table-spoon liqueur gradually. Add cheese; beat until smooth. Blend coffee with 1 tablespoon liqueur in separate bowl.
✦ Layer ladyfinger pieces, coffee mixture, cheese mixture and chocolate 1/2 at a time in 6 wine glasses. Chill, covered, for 2 hours or longer.

Preparation time: 20 minutes   6 servings

FALL HARVEST DINNER
FOR EIGHT

Black Olive Dip

Seafood Phyllo Cups

Butternut Squash Soup

Snow Pea and Endive Salad

Pork Tenderloin with Mustard Sauce

Curried Apple Rice

Green Bean Sauté

Pumpkin Cheesecake

BLACK OLIVE DIP

1/2 cup mayonnaise
1/2 cup sour cream
2 tablespoons fresh lime juice
3/4 teaspoon Tabasco sauce
1 (4-ounce) can chopped black olives, drained
3/4 cup finely chopped green onions
1/2 cup freshly chopped cilantro
1 clove of garlic, finely chopped
Salt and pepper to taste

✦ Blend mayonnaise, sour cream, lime juice and Tabasco sauce in bowl. Add olives, green onions, cilantro, garlic, salt and pepper; mix well.
✦ Chill, covered, for 1 to 8 hours. Serve with corn chips.

Preparation time: 15 minutes   8 servings

SEAFOOD PHYLLO CUPS

8 ounces phyllo dough, thawed
1/2 cup melted butter
3/4 cup mayonnaise
1/3 cup freshly grated Parmesan cheese
1/3 cup shredded Swiss cheese
1 (6-ounce) jar marinated artichokes, drained, chopped
8 ounces fresh crab meat, flaked
Tabasco sauce to taste
5 scallions, thinly sliced

✦ Layer 5 sheets phyllo dough on work surface, brushing each layer with melted butter. Cut into 3-inch squares with sharp knife. Fit each square butter side down into miniature muffin cup. Repeat to make about 24 cups.
✦ Bake in preheated 350-degree oven for 10 minutes or until lightly browned; do not overbake.
✦ Combine mayonnaise, cheeses, artichokes, crab meat, Tabasco sauce and half the scallions in bowl; mix well.
✦ Increase oven temperature to 400 degrees. Fill each phyllo cup with 1 teaspoon crab meat mixture. Bake for 7 minutes longer.
✦ Top with remaining scallions. Serve immediately.

Preparation time: 40 minutes   8 servings

1951: During the Cold War, a Civil Defense Committee was formed to provide emergency housing for homeless people in the event of a "disaster." An oyster supper sponsored by the club raised one hundred dollars toward the restoration of Independence Hall in Philadephia. In 1951, the club tradition of an Antiques Show fund raiser was started to support improvements to the clubhouse.

BUTTERNUT SQUASH SOUP

3 medium potatoes, peeled, chopped
4 to 5 pounds butternut squash, peeled, chopped
3 medium onions, chopped
9 cups chicken stock
2 1/2 tablespoons honey
1 teaspoon (or more) curry powder
Salt and pepper to taste
3/4 cup sour cream
Sour cream for garnish
3 or 4 fresh chives, chopped

✦ Simmer potatoes, squash and onions in chicken stock in large saucepan for 20 minutes or until tender. Cool.
✦ Purée vegetable mixture with honey, curry powder, salt and pepper. Chill in refrigerator.
✦ Blend mixture with 3/4 cup sour cream in large saucepan. Heat to serving temperature; do not boil.
✦ Ladle into soup cups. Garnish with sour cream and chives.

Preparation time: 40 minutes   8 servings

SNOW PEA AND ENDIVE SALAD

1 1/4 pounds snow peas, trimmed
1 1/2 teaspoons salt
6 heads Belgian endive
3 tablespoons red wine vinegar
2 tablespoons Dijon mustard
9 tablespoons olive oil
3 tablespoons chopped shallots
Freshly ground pepper to taste

✦ Blanch snow peas in boiling water with 1 teaspoon salt in large saucepan for 30 seconds; drain. Rinse with cold water and drain well. Place in salad bowl.
✦ Peel outer leaves from endive; arrange spoke fashion on serving platter. Chop remaining endive; add to snow peas.
✦ Whisk vinegar, mustard and 1/2 teaspoon salt in small bowl. Whisk in olive oil gradually. Add shallots and pepper. Add to snow pea mixture; toss to coat. Mound in center of endive-lined platter.

Preparation time: 35 minutes   8 servings

1954–1960: Membership swelled to 319. A Senior Citizens Club was formed to provide recreation for older people. The club sponsored a "United Nations Weekend" in which more than forty U.N. members and their families were invited to Wayne for a weekend. The Public Affairs Committee assisted in a survey of park and recreation needs in Radnor township. Boxes of clothes, food and money were provided to the Royer Greaves School for the Blind, as well as to the Peter Pan School for Retarded Children.

MUSTARD SAUCE

1/2 cup sour cream

1/2 cup mayonnaise

1 tablespoon finely chopped scallions

1 1/2 teaspoons red wine vinegar

1 tablespoon dry mustard

1 tablespoon grainy Dijon mustard

Salt and pepper to taste

✦

Blend sour cream and mayonnaise in bowl. Add scallions, vinegar, dry mustard, Dijon mustard, salt and pepper; mix well.

PORK TENDERLOIN

4 1/2 pounds pork tenderloin
1/2 cup soy sauce
1/2 cup dry sherry
2 cloves of garlic, minced
1 tablespoon dry mustard
1 teaspoon ground ginger
1 teaspoon dried thyme
Mustard Sauce (at left)

✦ Marinate tenderloin in mixture of soy sauce, sherry, garlic, dry mustard, ginger and thyme in sealed food storage bag in refrigerator overnight.
✦ Drain tenderloin; place in roasting pan. Bake at 325 degrees for 1 1/4 hours or until tenderloin is cooked through.
✦ Let stand for several minutes for easier slicing. Slice, place on serving platter and serve with Mustard Sauce on the side.

Preparation time: 25 minutes   8 servings

CURRIED APPLE RICE

1/4 cup melted butter
3 to 4 teaspoons curry powder
2 Golden Delicious apples, cored, coarsely chopped
1 large onion, chopped
1 cup sliced celery
2 cups uncooked long grain rice
1/2 cup raisins
4 cups apple cider or apple juice
1 teaspoon salt

✦ Blend butter and curry powder in large skillet. Add apples. Sauté for 2 minutes; remove apples with slotted spoon to bowl.
✦ Add onion and celery to skillet. Sauté for 1 minute. Add remaining ingredients. Bring to a boil; reduce heat.
✦ Simmer, tightly covered, for 20 to 25 minutes or until rice is tender and liquid is absorbed. Stir in apples gently.

Preparation time: 30 minutes   8 servings

GREEN BEAN SAUTÉ

2 pounds fresh green beans, trimmed
1/4 cup olive oil
2 tablespoons unsalted butter
Salt and freshly ground pepper to taste

✦ Blanch green beans in boiling water in large saucepan
for 4 minutes or just until tender-crisp and bright
green; drain.
✦ Heat olive oil and butter in large skillet over medium-high
heat. Add green beans. Sauté for 4 to 5 minutes.
✦ Season with salt and pepper. Serve immediately.

Preparation time: 15 minutes   8 servings

PUMPKIN CHEESECAKE

1 1/2 cups graham cracker crumbs
3 tablespoons sugar
1 teaspoon ground ginger
6 tablespoons melted unsalted butter
24 ounces cream cheese, softened
1 cup sugar
1 3/4 cups pumpkin purée, at room temperature
1 teaspoon freshly grated orange zest
2 teaspoons ground cinnamon
1/2 teaspoon each ground cloves and nutmeg
6 eggs, at room temperature, lightly beaten

✦ Cover bottom and outside of 9-inch springform pan with
foil. Butter inside of pan. Mix crumbs, 3 tablespoons
sugar and 1 teaspoon ginger in bowl. Add butter
gradually, tossing until well mixed. Press over bottom
and 1 3/4 to 2 inches up side of pan. Chill for 30 minutes.
✦ Beat cream cheese at medium speed in mixing bowl for 2
to 3 minutes or until light. Beat in 1 cup sugar. Add
pumpkin, zest and spices; beat until smooth.
✦ Add eggs gradually, beating well after each addition. Pour
into prepared pan; smooth top.
✦ Bake at 325 degrees for 60 to 70 minutes or until lightly
puffed. Remove from oven. Let stand until cool. Remove
foil. Refrigerate overnight. Loosen from side of pan.
Place on serving plate. Remove side of pan.

Preparation time: 1 hour   8 to 12 servings

1960: The Evening
Section was formed
to maintain an
organized center for
community service
and social events for
members who had
outgrown the Junior
section, or who were
employed during
the day.

SPRING FLING FOR EIGHT

Scallop-Bacon Brochettes

Roquefort Grapes

Cream of Watercress Soup

Strawberry Spinach Salad

Stuffed Leg of Lamb

Wild Rice-Mushroom Casserole

Asparagus with Red Pepper

Jamocha Ice Cream Bombe with
Coffee Hot Fudge Sauce

SCALLOP-BACON BROCHETTES

16 slices bacon
1 pound sea scallops
1 cup mayonnaise
1 tablespoon horseradish
4 teaspoons fresh dill
2 teaspoons fresh lemon juice

✦ Cut bacon crosswise into halves. Arrange in single layer in shallow baking pan. Bake at 350 degrees until bacon has rendered drippings but will be pliable even when cool. Drain on paper towels; cool to lukewarm.
✦ Cut scallops as desired to yield 32 pieces. Wrap each piece in bacon; secure with wooden pick or small skewer. Arrange on foil-lined baking sheet. Bake at 400 degrees for 8 minutes; drain on paper towels.
✦ Mix mayonnaise, horseradish, dill and lemon juice in small bowl. Serve as dipping sauce with scallops.

Preparation time: 25 minutes   8 servings

ROQUEFORT GRAPES

1 (10-ounce) package almonds, coarsely chopped
8 ounces cream cheese, softened
4 ounces Roquefort cheese, crumbled
2 tablespoons whipping cream
1 1/2 pounds seedless red grapes

✦ Spread almonds in single layer on baking sheet. Bake at 275 degrees until toasted to light golden color, stirring occasionally.
✦ Combine cheeses and cream in mixing bowl; beat until smooth. Rinse grapes; pat dry. Stir grapes in cheese mixture to coat; roll in almonds. Place on tray lined with waxed paper. Chill until serving time.
✦ Arrange grapes on serving plate to resemble grape cluster.

Preparation time: 45 minutes   8 servings

1970–1975: The club supported many projects—the County Cancer Project, Radnor Ambulance, Fire and Police Pension Funds, the Neighborhood League's Nutrition Program for Radnor Middle School students, and a program for Haverford State Hospital patients. Several hundred dollars in scholarships were awarded to deserving students. In 1975, the 90th year of the club was celebrated with a guest appearance by Maggie Kuhn, founder of the Gray Panthers.

CREAM OF WATERCRESS SOUP

6 tablespoons butter
2 large bunches watercress, rinsed, patted dry
2 red potatoes, peeled, thinly sliced
Salt and pepper to taste
6 tablespoons flour
6 cups chicken stock
1 cup whipping cream

✦ Melt butter in large saucepan over medium-low heat. Reserve several watercress leaves for topping. Add remaining watercress, potatoes, salt and pepper to saucepan. Cover with buttered waxed paper and lid. Cook for 15 minutes, stirring occasionally.
✦ Add flour. Cook for 3 minutes, stirring constantly. Stir in stock. Simmer for 15 minutes, stirring occasionally.
✦ Purée soup in food processor; return to saucepan. Blend in cream and salt and pepper. Heat to serving temperature over medium-low heat, stirring constantly.
✦ Ladle into soup bowls. Top with reserved watercress.

Preparation time: 20 minutes   8 servings

STRAWBERRY SPINACH SALAD

1/3 cup vegetable oil
1/4 cup cider vinegar
1/3 cup sugar
1 small onion, finely chopped
1/4 teaspoon Worcestershire sauce
1/4 teaspoon each paprika and salt
2 tablespoons sesame seeds
1 tablespoon poppy seeds
1 (12-ounce) package fresh spinach, torn
2 cups fresh strawberries, sliced

✦ Combine oil, vinegar, sugar, onion, Worcestershire sauce, paprika and salt in blender container. Process until smooth. Stir in sesame and poppy seeds.
✦ Rinse spinach; pat dry. Combine with strawberries in large salad bowl. Add dressing; toss lightly.

Preparation time: 20 minutes   8 servings

STUFFED LEG OF LAMB

1 (6-pound) leg of lamb, boned, flattened
1 large clove of garlic, finely chopped
Salt and pepper to taste
2 tablespoons olive oil
1 (13-ounce) can artichoke hearts, drained, chopped
1 medium onion, finely chopped
1/4 cup chopped fresh parsley
1/2 teaspoon dried oregano
1/2 teaspoon dried rosemary
1/2 teaspoon dried thyme
2 tablespoons olive oil
1/3 cup freshly grated Parmesan cheese
1/2 cup fresh bread crumbs
1 egg, lightly beaten
1 to 2 tablespoons olive oil

✦ Bring lamb to room temperature. Sprinkle with garlic, salt, pepper and 2 tablespoons olive oil; set aside.
✦ Sauté artichokes, onion, parsley, oregano, rosemary and thyme in 2 tablespoons olive oil in skillet for 3 to 4 minutes or until onion is tender but not brown; remove from heat. Add cheese, bread crumbs and egg; mix well. Adjust seasonings.
✦ Spread artichoke mixture over lamb; roll up carefully to enclose filling. Tie securely at 2-inch intervals. Place seam side down in shallow roasting pan. Rub with 1 to 2 tablespoons olive oil.
✦ Roast at 375 degrees for 1 1/2 hours or to 140 degrees on meat thermometer. Let stand at room temperature for 10 minutes. Slice 3/4 to 1 inch thick and place on serving platter.
✦ Strain and skim pan juices. Spoon over lamb slices. Garnish with sprigs of fresh herbs.

Preparation time: 30 minutes   8 servings

1976–1978: The first club newsletter, the "Satur-Lite," was started. Two years of research by club members resulted in the application for placement of the clubhouse on the Pennsylvania Register of Historical Sites. In 1978, the building was placed on the National Register of Historic Sites.

WILD RICE-MUSHROOM CASSEROLE

1 cup wild rice
1/2 cup slivered almonds
1 pound fresh mushrooms, sliced
2 tablespoons chopped scallions
Salt and pepper to taste
1/4 cup butter
3 cups chicken broth

✦ Sauté wild rice, almonds, mushrooms, scallions, salt and pepper in butter in large skillet over medium heat for 20 minutes or until almonds are lightly browned.
✦ Pour into oiled 2-quart baking dish. Stir in chicken broth.
✦ Bake, tightly covered, at 350 degrees for 1 1/2 hours or until wild rice is tender.

Preparation time: 15 minutes   8 servings

ASPARAGUS WITH RED PEPPER

32 fresh asparagus spears, peeled, trimmed
1 red bell pepper

✦ Steam asparagus in steamer for 3 to 4 minutes or until tender; drain.
✦ Cut red pepper into thin strips. Wrap 4 spears at a time with strip of red pepper, tieing each into bundle. Place on serving plate.

Preparation time: 30 minutes   8 servings

JAMOCHA ICE CREAM BOMBE

1/4 cup strong hot coffee
1 tablespoon coffee liqueur
1 teaspoon sugar
18 to 20 ladyfingers, split horizontally
8 ounces cream cheese, softened
1/4 cup sugar
1 teaspoon vanilla extract
1/2 cup vanilla ice cream
1/2 cup semisweet chocolate chips
1 pint coffee ice cream
Coffee Hot Fudge Sauce (at right)

✦ Line 5-cup round-bottom bowl or mold with plastic wrap, leaving generous overhang around edge.
✦ Blend coffee, liqueur and 1 teaspoon sugar in small bowl. Brush rounded sides of lady fingers with coffee mixture.
✦ Line bottom and side of prepared bowl with ladyfingers, arranging rounded sides against bowl; fill any gaps with ladyfinger trimmings. Drizzle any remaining coffee mixture over ladyfingers. Chill, covered, in refrigerator until needed.
✦ Beat cream cheese with 1/4 cup sugar and vanilla until smooth; set aside. Stir vanilla ice cream in chilled bowl until creamy. Fold ice cream and chocolate chips into cream cheese mixture. Freeze, covered with heavy-duty foil, for 2 to 4 hours or until firm, stirring occasionally.
✦ Spread mixture evenly over ladyfingers as to form bowl. Freeze, covered with heavy foil, for 2 to 4 hours or until firm.
✦ Stir coffee ice cream in chilled bowl until creamy. Spoon into ladyfinger-lined bowl; smooth top. Arrange remaining ladyfingers over top, covering completely. Fold plastic wrap over ladyfingers; cover tightly with foil. Freeze until firm.
✦ Remove foil and open plastic wrap; invert onto serving plate. Remove plastic wrap carefully. Let stand at room temperature for 10 to 15 minutes to soften.
✦ Cut into wedges; place on dessert plates. Drizzle with Coffee Hot Fudge Sauce.

Preparation time: 1 1/2 hours   8 servings

COFFEE HOT FUDGE SAUCE

1/4 cup butter

3/4 cup semisweet chocolate chips

2/3 cup sugar

2 teaspoons instant coffee crystals

1 (5-ounce) can evaporated milk

✦

Heat butter and chocolate chips in small heavy saucepan over very low heat until melted, stirring constantly. Add sugar and coffee crystals. Stir in evaporated milk gradually. Bring to a boil, stirring constantly. Simmer for 8 minutes, stirring frequently.

SUMMER CELEBRATION DINNER
FOR TWENTY-FIVE

Texas Caviar

Homemade Boursin

Salmon-Stuffed Mushrooms

Shrimp Vinaigrette

Grilled London Broil with Dijon Sauce

Mixed-Up New Potato Salad

Pesto Tomatoes and Mozzarella

Sweet-Sour Broccoli Salad

Spinach Feta Pasta Salad

Fresh Fruit Basket

Outrageous Chocolate Cake

Toffee Nut Blondies

Lemon Hazelnut Squares

TEXAS CAVIAR

2 (16-ounce) cans black-eyed peas, drained, rinsed
Kernels of 4 ears of blanched corn
1 tomato, chopped
4 green onions, chopped
1 cup chopped fresh parsley
1 tablespoon minced fresh cilantro
2 cloves of garlic, minced
1 (8-ounce) bottle Italian salad dressing

✦ Drain rinsed black-eyed peas. Combine with corn, tomato, green onions, parsley, cilantro and garlic in large bowl. Add salad dressing; mix well.
✦ Marinate for 3 to 4 hours. Place in serving bowl. Serve with corn chips.

Preparation time: 15 minutes   24 servings

HOMEMADE BOURSIN

16 ounces cream cheese, softened
1 tablespoon whipping cream or milk
1/2 teaspoon minced fresh garlic
1/4 cup minced fresh parsley
1/4 cup minced fresh dill
1/3 cup minced scallions
1/2 teaspoon salt
1/2 teaspoon pepper
1/4 teaspoon Tabasco sauce (optional)

✦ Combine cream cheese and cream in food processor container or mixer fitted with paddle attachment; process until smooth. Add remaining ingredients; process until smooth.
✦ Store in covered container in refrigerator.
✦ Bring to room temperature before serving. Serve with assorted crackers of choice.

Preparation time: 15 minutes   12 servings

1982: The Junior Saturday Club introduced a cookbook, **Philadelphia Main Line Classics**, to raise money for its many causes. Now in its sixth printing, this book has enabled the club to donate more than $130,000 to charities, including the Children's Heart Hospital, Juvenile Rheumatoid Arthritis, Multiple Sclerosis Foundation, Daemon House, Bryn Mawr Hospital's Neonatal Intensive Care Unit, and many other groups.

SALMON-STUFFED MUSHROOMS

6 ounces smoked salmon, minced
12 ounces cream cheese, softened
4 to 6 tablespoons minced fresh dill or 1 to 2 tablespoons
    dried
2 tablespoons (about) fresh lemon juice
2 to 4 shallots, minced
1 pound fresh white mushrooms, stems removed

✦ Combine salmon, cream cheese, dill, lemon juice and
  shallots in bowl or food processor fitted with steel blade;
  mix until smooth. Adjust seasonings.
✦ Fill mushroom caps with salmon mixture; place on
  serving plate. Chill until serving time.

Preparation time: 40 minutes   10 servings

SHRIMP VINAIGRETTE

1 pound large shrimp, cooked, peeled, deveined
1/2 cup olive oil
3 tablespoons white wine vinegar
3 tablespoons Dijon mustard
1 tablespoon chopped shallots
1 teaspoon finely minced ginger
2 cloves of garlic, finely minced
1 tablespoon chopped fresh dill
Pinch of sugar
Salt and pepper to taste
20 snow peas, trimmed

✦ Place shrimp in large bowl. Combine olive oil, vinegar,
  mustard, shallots, ginger, garlic, dill, sugar, salt and
  pepper in jar; shake vigorously to mix. Pour over shrimp;
  mix gently to coat. Chill for 2 to 4 hours, stirring
  occasionally.
✦ Blanch pea pods in boiling water in small saucepan for
  30 seconds; plunge into ice water. Drain well and split
  lengthwise into halves.
✦ Remove shrimp from marinade; wrap pea pod half
  around each shrimp and secure with wooden pick. Place
  on serving plate. Chill until serving time.

Preparation time: 45 minutes   10 servings

1996: With this second volume, Main Line Classics II, the club will continue to support local groups such as the Surrey Club for seniors, the Women's Resource Center, Main Line Senior Services, Meals on Wheels, and Thorncroft Therapeutic Riding for physically handicapped persons. Outreach beyond the community includes support of a soup kitchen in Philadelphia, a homeless shelter, and the Christmas Angel Tree project.

GRILLED LONDON BROIL

12 pounds London broil or flank steaks
6 cups soy sauce
3 cups vegetable oil
6 cloves of garlic
1 1/2 cups dry sherry
9 tablespoons brown sugar
1 tablespoon freshly ground pepper
1 tablespoon minced fresh ginger
Salt to taste
Dijon Sauce (below)

✦ Place steaks in large container. Mix soy sauce, oil, garlic, sherry, brown sugar, pepper, ginger and salt in bowl. Pour over steaks.
✦ Marinate in refrigerator for 8 hours, turning occasionally.
✦ Drain, reserving marinade. Grill as desired, brushing occasionally with reserved marinade. Slice diagonally. Arrange slices on platter. Serve with Dijon Sauce.

Preparation time: 10 minutes   25 servings

DIJON SAUCE

2 1/4 cups mayonnaise
2 1/4 cups sour cream
3/4 cup Dijon mustard
6 tablespoons chopped fresh parsley

✦ Blend mayonnaise, sour cream and mustard in bowl. Stir in parsley. Chill until serving time.

Preparation time: 10 minutes   5 1/4 cups

There's a house
that has stood
by the side
of the road,
Since the
village had
one country
store.
In this house
many women
have labored
and served,
And have
sought,
through the years,
to be sharing
the load,
Of a panic
or illness
or war.

MIXED-UP NEW POTATO SALAD

Now the club

has grown

larger than

founders

could know,

And we meet

with our

neighbors again,

For there's work

we'll be doing

for those of all

creeds,

For the young

and the old,

with their hopes

and their needs,

While we're

praying for peace

among men.

Susan
Dorothea
Keeney,
for 75th Club
Anniversary,
1961.

2 pounds new red potatoes
12 ounces fresh green beans, trimmed
3 tablespoons minced scallions
$1/4$ to $1/2$ cup minced red bell pepper
3 tablespoons red wine vinegar
$1/2$ teaspoon salt
1 clove of garlic, minced
1 teaspoon Dijon mustard
$1/2$ teaspoon grainy mustard
$1/2$ cup olive oil
Freshly ground pepper to taste
$1/4$ cup each finely minced fresh parsley, summer savory
    and chives
8 ounces bacon, crisp-fried, crumbled
$1/4$ cup finely minced fresh basil

✦ Scrub potatoes; slice $1/8$ inch thick. Cook in boiling water to cover over medium heat for 8 to 10 minutes or just until tender; drain.

✦ Cook green beans in boiling water to cover for 3 to 4 minutes or until tender-crisp; rinse with cold water and drain well.

✦ Combine potatoes, green beans, scallions and red pepper in large bowl; set aside.

✦ Blend vinegar, salt, garlic and mustards in small bowl. Add olive oil 1 tablespoon at a time, whisking constantly. Add pepper, parsley, savory and chives and pour over potato mixture; mix gently.

✦ Marinate for 2 to 3 hours. Top with bacon and basil.

Preparation time: 45 minutes   12 servings

PESTO TOMATOES AND MOZZARELLA

12 ounces fresh mozzarella cheese
3 large tomatoes, sliced 1/4 inch thick
2 large cloves of garlic, minced
1/2 teaspoon salt
2/3 cup firmly packed fresh basil leaves
2/3 cup firmly packed fresh mint leaves
2/3 cup firmly packed fresh parsley
1/3 cup pine nuts
1/3 cup freshly grated Parmesan cheese
1/2 cup olive oil
1 tablespoon (about) balsamic vinegar
Freshly ground black pepper to taste
Fresh basil, mint and parsley sprigs

✦ Slice mozzarella cheese 1/4 inch thick. Alternate tomato
  and mozzarella cheese slices on large platter, overlapping
  slices slightly.
✦ Mash garlic with salt to a smooth paste. Combine with
  basil, mint and parsley leaves, pine nuts, Parmesan
  cheese, olive oil and vinegar in food processor or blender
  container; process until puréed.
✦ Spoon pesto in ring around center of tomato and
  mozzarella cheese slices. Sprinkle with pepper; top with
  herb sprigs.

Preparation time: 20 minutes   12 servings

SWEET-SOUR BROCCOLI SALAD

1 bunch broccoli, chopped
1 small red onion, chopped
1/3 to 1/2 cup raisins
1/2 cup walnuts
1/2 cup mayonnaise
1 tablespoon sugar
1 teaspoon white vinegar
8 ounces bacon, crisp-fried, crumbled

✦ Mix broccoli, onion, raisins and walnuts in salad bowl.
✦ Blend mayonnaise, sugar and vinegar in small bowl. Add
  to broccoli mixture; mix lightly to coat. Refrigerate for
  several hours. Add bacon; toss to mix.

Preparation time: 20 minutes   6 servings

HERBED DRESSING

1 tablespoon red wine vinegar

1/2 cup vegetable oil

2 tablespoons sugar

1/2 teaspoon salt

1/4 teaspoon each thyme, rosemary, marjoram and freshly ground pepper

1 clove of garlic, minced

✦

Combine wine vinegar, oil, sugar, salt, thyme, rosemary, marjoram, pepper and garlic in small bowl; mix well.

SPINACH FETA PASTA SALAD

1 pound fresh spinach, rinsed
8 ounces small bow-tie pasta, cooked, drained, cooled
Herbed Dressing (at left)
2 medium tomatoes, chopped
8 ounces feta cheese, crumbled
1 cup sliced black olives
2 tablespoons chopped fresh parsley

✦ Pat spinach dry. Line large salad bowl with largest spinach leaves. Chop remaining spinach coarsely. Combine with pasta in large bowl.

✦ Add 1/2 cup Herbed Dressing; toss lightly. Add tomatoes, cheese and olives; toss to mix. Spoon into spinach-lined salad bowl. Sprinkle with parsley.

Preparation time: 20 minutes   6 servings

FRESH FRUIT BASKET

1 honeydew melon
1 cantaloupe
1 watermelon
4 kiwifruit, peeled, sliced
1 quart fresh blueberries

✦ Cube melon pulp or scoop into balls.

✦ Combine honeydew, cantaloupe, watermelon, kiwifruit and blueberries in large bowl; mix gently. Chill for 3 to 4 hours.

✦ Serve chilled.

Preparation time: 20 minutes   12 servings

OUTRAGEOUS CHOCOLATE CAKE

8 ounces semisweet chocolate
1 cup butter, softened
1 1/2 cups sugar
5 eggs, beaten
Ganache (at right)
1 cup fresh raspberries

✦ Melt chocolate in double boiler over hot water. Cool slightly. Blend in butter 1 tablespoon at a time. Add sugar; beat for 1 minute. Add eggs; beat well.

✦ Pour into buttered 8-inch round cake pan lined with buttered waxed paper. Place in larger baking pan. Add boiling water halfway up side of cake pan.

✦ Bake at 350 degrees for 1 1/4 hours. Cool. Chill for 2 hours. Invert onto cake plate. Spread with Ganache. Chill until serving time. Top with raspberries to serve.

Preparation time: 40 minutes   14 to 16 servings

TOFFEE NUT BLONDIES

1/4 cup butter or margarine
1/2 cup each sugar and packed light brown sugar
1 egg, lightly beaten
1 teaspoon vanilla extract
1 tablespoon coffee liqueur
2 teaspoons instant coffee powder
3/4 cup flour
1 teaspoon baking powder
1/8 teaspoon salt
1 cup chopped walnuts
1 cup chocolate-covered toffee bits

✦ Melt butter in medium saucepan; remove from heat. Blend in sugar and brown sugar; cool slightly. Add egg, vanilla, liqueur and coffee powder; mix well.

✦ Add mixture of flour, baking powder and salt; stir just until mixed. Stir in walnuts and toffee bits.

✦ Spread in 8x8-inch baking pan lined with greased foil. Bake at 350 degrees for 35 to 40 minutes or until blondies pull from side of pan. Cool on wire rack. Cut into 2-inch squares.

Preparation time: 20 minutes   16 servings

GANACHE

2 cups semisweet chocolate chips

1 cup whipping cream

✦

Melt chocolate chips with cream in heavy saucepan, stirring frequently. Bring to a boil; boil briefly. Chill in refrigerator.

LEMON HAZELNUT SQUARES

1 cup flour
1/3 cup sugar
1/4 teaspoon salt
6 tablespoons chilled butter, cut up
1/4 cup toasted chopped hazelnuts
3/4 cup sugar
2 eggs
3 tablespoons fresh lemon juice
1 tablespoon freshly minced lemon zest
1/2 teaspoon baking powder
Pinch of salt
Confectioners' sugar

✦ Process flour, 1/3 cup sugar, 1/4 teaspoon salt, butter and hazelnuts in food processor until crumbly. Press over bottom of 8x8-inch baking pan lined with buttered foil. Bake at 350 degrees for 15 to 18 minutes or until golden brown around edges.

✦ Process 3/4 cup sugar, eggs, lemon juice and zest, baking powder and pinch of salt in food processor until smooth. Pour over hot crust. Bake for 20 minutes or just until light brown at edges and springy to the touch.

✦ Cool on wire rack. Lift foil carefully from pan; peel off foil. Cut into 2-inch squares.

✦ Sift confectioners' sugar over squares; arrange on serving plate.

Preparation time: 15 minutes   16 servings

CO-CHAIRMEN
Barbara C. Zonino
Patricia V. Leidy

RECIPE TESTING
Amy Y. Hartsock, Chairman
Victoria Cosgriff, Co-Chairman
Sally M. Scorzetti, Co-Chairman
Carol C. Shepard, Co-Chairman

RECIPE COLLECTION
Nancy H. Hirschfeld, Co-Chairman
Marty J. Bedeian, Co-Chairman
Jill A. Bonn, Co-Chairman

DESIGN COORDINATION & EDITING
Elisabeth M. Yeager, Chairman

RESEARCH & WRITING
Jill A. Bonn

MARKETING
Karen P. Dalby, Chairman

PUBLICITY
Patrice H. German, Chairman

TREASURER
Paige Miller

DESIGN & ILLUSTRATION
Susan Stewart Vaughn

✦

The Cookbook Committee wishes to acknowledge
and thank the Junior Saturday Club Executive Board for
their constant support and ideas.

Jan M. McAllister, *Club President*
Elizabeth L. Hinerman, *1st Vice President, Community Service*
Valerie P. Vitale, *2nd Vice President, Ways and Means*
Sandy M. Lindberg, *Recording Secretary*
Sally G. Hudson, *Corresponding Secretary*
Patty Murray, *Club Treasurer*
Nancy Gray, *Junior Advisor*
Mary C. Young, *Clubhouse Chairman*
Laurie Doghramji, *Clubhouse Rentals Chairman*

The Cookbook Committee would like to thank all our club members, families, and friends for graciously devoting countless hours to make **MAIN LINE CLASSICS II:** *Cooking Up A Little History* possible.

Junior Saturday Club:

Corinne Ackerman

Martha Aitken

Lesley Allen

Debra A. Arvanites

Libby Bailey

Mary Beth Baldwin

Kathleen Beavis

Marty J. Bedeian

Kathi Bender

Mindy Jane Berman

Debra M. Bernier

Patricia F. Bevers

Babs B. Bickhart

Barbara B. Bigford

Renee Bitterman

Lauren W. Blake

Jan S. Blynn

Jill A. Bonn

Patricia M. Brady

Deborah S. Brehm

Felicity S. Briggs

Cathy S. Buttenbaum

Diana L. Calligan

Janice Chesney

Stacy W. Clark

Sandy Claus

Susan L. Connors

Victoria Cosgriff

Lyn M. Coyne

Karen P. Dalby

Cindy C. Dautrich

Janet L. DeArmond

Laurie Doghramji

Jenifer F. Donahue

Cindy Door

Beth H. Downey

Carol M. Dressel

Celeste P. Dunlap

Lisa L. Estabrook

Betty Ann Exler

Deborah A. Fahey

Evelyn V. I. Fell

Missy B. Fennimore

Julia E. Ferguson

Liz Fitzpatrick

Gina Foley

Karen L. Forcine

Allison Fox

Vickie Frondorf

Laura Gambone

Patrice H. German

Kathy Girod

Lynn M. Gosnell

Chappy Graf

Nancy T. Gray

Rose D. Greskoff

Dana Groves

Sheila M. Grubb

Sharon K. Hamelin

Janis A. Hansen

Claire Harden

Amy Y. Hartsock

Linda D. Hawkins

Shelley V. Heaberg

Holly M. Henry

Nina M. Heppe

Ann Herron

Pamela H. Hicks

Kim D. Hildebrand

Noel D. Hill

Elizabeth L. Hinerman

Nancy H. Hirschfeld

Lori T. Horning

Donna Hosterman

Allyson S. Hotz

Sally G. Hudson

Judy Bower Huey

Jane E. Johnsen

Kay W. Joseph

Maureen F. Katona

Eddie Kennedy

Mary Kent

Julie S. Kincade

Mary Pat N. Kingsley

Diane Langton

Helenanne Lasher

Carrie G. Lawlor

Nancy P. Lawrence

Patricia V. Leidy

Sandy M. Lindberg

Nancy P. Loia

Stefanie W. Lucas

Nancy Z. MacKenzie

Mary Louise
  MacMullan

Pam Mahoney

Lisa Martin

Nancy C. Mather

Jan M. McAllister

Gail McElwee

Laurie McGrath

Teri McKee

Martha R. Mellinger

Clary E. Meyers

Elizabeth S. Miller

Paige Miller

Bobbie V. Montgomery

Dee M. Morrison

Nancy J. Muir

Patty Murray

Paula Z. Murray

Mary Murrow

Susan C. Nagy

Marita R. Needles

Helen T. Ockenden

Karen C. O'Neil

Jill Pearson

Paulette M. Petrie

Estee R. Pickens

Lisa Powers

Becky G. Pyle

Claudia Quemore

Didi Reuschel

Terri Rhodes

Tami B. Rieger

Mary R. Ring

Robin L. Roach

Sharon Roberts

Mary Kay Rocha

Ginny Rockafellow

Francie E. Rogers

Deborah Rosenberg

Jean D. Rosenberg

Paula Rothrock

Susan B. Sargent

Eve U. Sauter

Lee B. Savinar

Deb Sawin

Jean M. Schumacher

Cynthia R. Schumacker

Kathleen T.
  Schuyler

Sally M. Scorzetti

Kathryn L. Shaw

Karen B. Sheep

Carol C. Shepard

Marian W. Sieke

Carolyn C. Slota

Susan J. Smith

Jill Snyder

Ginny Spofford

Heidi L. Sproat

Corinne Stahl

Carol Stewart

Claire P. Swarr

Anne M. Taylor

Martha B. Thomson

Anne B. Toscani

Hope Ulrich

Susan Vaughn

Valerie P. Vitale

Karen K. Volpert

Jody A. Wagner

Barbara A. Weber

Mary Anne Whalen

Cynthia M. Williams

Karen S. Wymard

Elisabeth M. Yeager

Mary C. Young

Barbara C. Zonino

Other Contributors:

Louise L. Aaronson

Julia B. Alling

Carol S. Alton

Jo Asplund

Rosie R. Bainbridge

Kay K. Bell

Bud Bruno (Greenfield Grocer)

Julie Bickel-Young

George P. Bieber, Jr.
  (LaForchette)

Ida M. Bonn

Melissa Brannon

Virginia L. Campbell

Elizabeth F. Cannon

Teddy Cohen

Teddys (Spread Eagle Village)

Doren R. Connors

Sheila Connors

Peggy Cox

Paul Donnelley

Donna Eldridge

Thomas Estok
(General Warren Inne)

Jane Exler

Farmart

Feastivities Catering

Megan Florence

Irene Foley

Marie Gammello

Nancy Gary

Susan George

Eloise Gilliland

Great Harvest Bread
Company

Ray Gregg

Steve Gulkus

Gay Gunter

Michael Harkness

Ali Hartsock

Sally O. Herd

Diane Hickox

Elizabeth F. Hopkins

Louise M. Hotz

Joan Hudson

Carole W. Hupfeldt

Gloria G. Jennings

Lenora D. Johnson

Jean Kingan

Martha Laird

Josephine A. Lane

Mary I. Laroque

Sue Laskin

Jeanne Lehman

David S. Leidy

Florence R. Leidy

Margaret L.
Leshinski

Nancy Lezynski

Marion Lindberg

Jeanne Lupia

Barbara Lyons

Ed Lyons

Jane A. Lyons

Janet C. Marklund

Harry Marshall

Laura P. Melvin

Joyce P. Miller

Pat Moran

Anita Moshonas

Roxanne Moshonas

Stephen Mottram

Robert Munnich
(Noah's River Boat Cafe)

Donna M. Murphy

Kay Nothacker

Chris Oliver

Kimberly Paro

Michele I. Pension

Helen M. Penza

Daniel Powell

Susan E. Rau

Alice M. Reinl

Kelly Reynolds

Svea V. Ringquist

Megan Rooney

Wendy A. Rooney

Karen Sauter

Laura Savard

Barbara Scorzetti

Christopher B. Siegele

Julie B. Siegele

Judy Smith-Kressley

Elsa M. Spiegel

Deborah W. Stewart

Barbara Teevan

Jean Tosto

Adele Trygar

Jean C. Tullier

Theo S. Vangellow

Jacques Vitre

Deborah Vogel

Donna H. Widerman

Lisa D. Williamson

Sue York

Gertrude E. Zeager

Barbara C. Zitin

The Cookbook Committee wishes to thank
the following people for their generous assistance in proofreading,
supplying information, and finding resources:

HISTORICAL TEXT
Joseph Bonn, M.D.
Bruce Gill (Harriton House Association President)
Maureen McKew (Villanova University public relations)
Sandra L. Ormerod (Waynesborough historian)

✦

HISTORICAL RESEARCH
Ardmore Library
Bala-Cynwyd Library
Gladwyn Library
Haverford College Library
Ludington Library
Paoli Library
Penn Wynne Library
Radnor Township Library
Tredyffrin Public Library
Falvey Memorial Library, Villanova University

Any omissions or errors of the historical information in this book are an oversight.

Chester County Place Names, by Edward Pinkowski, Sunshine Press, 1962.

Early Chester County Roads, by Grace Kugler Winthrop.

Early Pennsylvania Land Records, by William H. Egle, Genealogical Publishing.

The End of the Line: Alexander J. Cassatt and the Pennsylvania Railroad, by Patricia T. Davis, N. Watson Academic Publications, N.Y., 1978.

Ever Ancient, Ever New Villanova University, by David R. Contosta, Ph.D. and Rev. Dennis J. Gallagher, O.S.A., Ph.D., Villanova, 1992.

Exploring Pennsylvania, by Sylvester K. Stevens, Harcourt Brace & Co.

Five Tales For All Hallow's Even, by Robert Goshorn, T/E Quarterly, October, 1979.

General Wayne Inn, Pamphlet, by J. Robert Mendte, ca. 1976.

Historic Lower Merion and Blockley, by Dora H. Develin, G.H. Buchanan Co., 1922.

Historic Wayne, by The Graphics Center, Argus Printing Co., Wayne, PA, 1975.

Historic Waynesborough, Pamphlet, ca. 1994.

The History of Bryn Mawr 1683–1900, by Barbara A. Farrow, Bryn Mawr Civic Association, 1962.

History of Penn, by Allen C. Thomas, L. C. Heath & Co., N.Y., 1913.

Indians in Pennsylvania, by Paul A.W. Wallace, Harrisburg, 1961.

It's an Old Pennsylvania Custom, by Edwin V. Mitchell, The Vanguard Press, Inc., N.Y., 1947.

Lower Merion—A History, Edited by Phyllis C. Maier and Mary Wood, Lower Merion Historical Society, 1988.

Merion in The Welsh Tract, by Thomas Glenn, Norristown, 1898.

Mermaids, Monasteries, Cherokees and Custer, by Robert I. Alotta, Bonus Books, Inc., 1990.

The Old Eagle School, Pamphlet, by the Strafford and Deepdale Civic Associations, ca. 1993.

Old Roads out of Philadelphia, by John T. Farks, J.B. Lippincott Co., Philadelphia, 1917.

"Old St. David's—A moving force in Radnor for 250 years," by Dan J. Szczesny, Main Line Life Newspaper, April, 1995.

On the Main Line—The Pennsylvania Railroad in the 19th Century, by Edwin P. Alexander, Bramhall House, 1971.

Pennsylvania, The Colonial Years 1681–1776, by Joseph J. Kelly Jr., Double Day, N.Y.

Philadelphia, A 300-Year History, A Barra Foundation Book, W.W. Norton & Co., 1985.

"Saturday Club of Wayne marks 100 years," by The Suburban and Wayne Times, March, 1986.

Stories of Penn, by Joseph Walton, Ph.D. and Martin C. Brumbaugh, American Book, N.Y., 1897.

Tredyffrin Easttown History Club Quarterly, by the Club, Berwyn, PA 1990–95.

William Penn's Legacy, by Alan Tully, John Hopkins University Press, Baltimore, 1977.

William Penn's Own Account of the Lenni-Lenape or Delaware Indians, edited by Albert C. Myers, The Middle Atlantic Press, Wilmington, Delaware, 1970.

EQUIVALENT MEASURES

3 teaspoons = 1 tablespoon
4 tablespoons = 1/4 cup
5 tablespoons plus 1 teaspoon = 1/3 cup
16 tablespoons = 1 cup
2 cups = 1 pint

METRIC SYSTEM

The metric system is based on units of 10. The multiples of 10 are always designated by the same prefix regardless of the base unit specified. Some commonly used prefixes include:

kilo — 1000   centi — 0.01
deci — 0.1   milli — 0.001

To convert to metric the following rules will help:

1 kilogram (1000 grams) is about 2.2 times as heavy as a pound
1 liter is equal to about 1.1 quarts
100 grams is 3 1/2 ounces

To determine degrees Celsius, subtract 32 from degrees Fahrenheit and then multiply by .555

0 degrees Celsius is 32 degrees Fahrenheit
100 degrees Celsius is 212 degrees Fahrenheit

EMERGENCY SUBSTITUTIONS

Buttermilk, 1 cup	use 1 or 2 tablespoons vinegar with milk to fill 1 cup. Let stand for 5 minutes.
Chocolate, 1 ounce or square	use 3 tablespoons cocoa plus 1 tablespoon butter
Cornstarch, 1 tablespoon	use 2 tablespoons flour
Baking powder, 1 1/4 teaspoons	use 1/2 teaspoon baking soda plus 2 tablespoons vinegar
Milk, 1 cup	use 1/2 cup evaporated milk plus 1/2 cup water
Sugar, 1 1/4 cups	use 1 cup honey; reduce liquid in recipe by 1/4
Honey, 1 cup	use 3/4 cup sugar plus 1/4 cup water
Cake flour, 1 cup sifted	use 1 cup sifted all-purpose flour less 2 tablespoons

Microwave ovens vary greatly as to wattage, power settings and accessory features; therefore, it is difficult to give exact rules for adapting recipes. Use the following facts and tips as a guide as you experiment to find out what works best for your particular oven:

✦ Fat, sugar and liquid attract microwaves causing molecules to vibrate; these rapidly moving molecules in turn cause others to vibrate and thus produce heat. Because the cooking/heating takes place through this chain reaction of vibrating molecules, cooking continues to take place AFTER the food is removed from the microwave oven. This is important to understand to prevent overcooking.

✦ Heat is produced by vibrating molecules, thus porous food like bread heats more quickly than dense food such as meat.

✦ Foods absorb the microwave energy, thus the cooking time will increase only slightly as the volume of food increases (i.e. one egg cooks faster than two).

✦ Covering food being microwaved traps steam and hastens cooking.

✦ Some ingredients are particularly sensitive to microwaves and cause overcooking, curdling or "popping." These foods include cheese, eggs, cream, sour cream, mayonnaise, snails, scallops, kidney beans and mushrooms. They should be cooked at a lower setting or added part way through cooking period.

✦ To minimize differences in density, arrange food items in a circle with the thickest part of the piece to the outside.

✦ Microwaves do not brown or crisp foods.

✦ Microwaves can reheat food quickly without overcooking. Food or beverages may be reheated in the serving dish itself. Remember the quantity and density will affect the cooking time. Reheating should be done on 50% power (medium).

A food processor saves energy and time. It chops, slices and shreds almost any food, and also stirs, whips and purées like a blender. To use your processor effectively, you may have to change the order of preparation slightly.

Here are a few tips on using food processors:

◆ Work from the dry ingredients to the wet.

◆ Use a dry bowl when chopping, starting with the smallest, hardest ingredients first, like fresh ginger. Next add larger solid ingredients like onion or peppers.

◆ Smaller pieces generally process more evenly than larger ones. Pulse until food is chopped as finely as desired.

◆ Medium loads chop more evenly than large ones, so don't overload bowl.

◆ Add flour last when preparing quick breads, cakes and cookies. Pulse briefly until flour disappears. If using raisins or nuts, add just before the flour to avoid overchopping.

◆ Processors don't aerate, so they won't whip egg whites or cream.

◆ The food processor can help lower your grocery bill. You can easily chop your own nuts, onions, green peppers and parsley. It is also great for bread crumbs, mayonnaise, salad dressings, shredded cheeses and grated Parmesan cheese.

◆ Purée vegetables and freeze in ice cube trays. The vegetable cubes are excellent for thickening sauces, soups or stews.

◆ To make fresh baby food, simply simmer or steam fresh vegetables and fruits in a small amount of water, drain and purée. Process meats with the metal blade, then soften with broth or milk.

◆ Do not process hot liquids.

◆ For pastry, cut butter into 1-inch pieces and freeze; the processor will "cut" the butter into the flour more rapidly and finely.

. . . Presenting the Original

Philadelphia
Main Line Classics
A Cookbook from the historic Philadelphia Suburbs

4 cups recipes	700 kitchen-tested favorites from members, friends, celebrities and restaurants
½ cup menu plans	Suggestions for buffet or brunch, tailgate or luncheon, fun gatherings or local traditions
1 tablespoon trends	Microwave and processor tips and recipes
Dash history	Suburban Main Line Philadelphia
1 tablespoon art	Jane Curtis illustrations of historic train stations
½ cup convenience	Serving, do-ahead and freezing suggestions, comb binding

MIX all ingredients well. Savor and enjoy for years to come. Serve on holidays, birthdays, weddings or any gift-giving occasion.

YIELD: A unique cookbook that will delight the eye as well as the palate.

MAIN LINE CLASSICS II: *Cooking Up A Little History*

Please send _____ copies at ....$18.95 each $ _____
6% tax (PA residents only) ....$ 1.14 each $ _____
Plus postage and handling ....$ 3.50 each $ _____
TOTAL $ _____

MAIN LINE CLASSICS

Please send _____ copies at ....$16.95 each $ _____
6% tax (PA residents only) ....$ 1.02 each $ _____
Plus postage and handling ....$ 3.50 each $ _____
TOTAL $ _____

Name _____
Address _____
City_____ State _____ Zip _____
Phone # _____

Make checks payable to Main Line Classics and mail to:

MAIN LINE CLASSICS
P.O. Box 521, Wayne, Pennsylvania 19087

Please allow 3 to 4 weeks for delivery. Call for information on one or two day delivery.

MAIN LINE CLASSICS II: *Cooking Up A Little History*

Please send _____ copies at ....$18.95 each $ _____
6% tax (PA residents only) ....$ 1.14 each $ _____
Plus postage and handling ....$ 3.50 each $ _____
TOTAL $ _____

MAIN LINE CLASSICS

Please send _____ copies at ....$16.95 each $ _____
6% tax (PA residents only) ....$ 1.02 each $ _____
Plus postage and handling ....$ 3.50 each $ _____
TOTAL $ _____

Name _____
Address _____
City_____ State _____ Zip _____
Phone # _____

Make checks payable to Main Line Classics and mail to:

MAIN LINE CLASSICS
P.O. Box 521, Wayne, Pennsylvania 19087

Please allow 3 to 4 weeks for delivery. Call for information on one or two day delivery.

MAIN LINE CLASSICS II: *Cooking Up A Little History*

Please send _____ copies at ....$18.95 each $ _____
6% tax (PA residents only) ....$ 1.14 each $ _____
Plus postage and handling ....$ 3.50 each $ _____
TOTAL $ _____

MAIN LINE CLASSICS

Please send _____ copies at ....$16.95 each $ _____
6% tax (PA residents only) ....$ 1.02 each $ _____
Plus postage and handling ....$ 3.50 each $ _____
TOTAL $ _____

Name _____
Address _____
City_____ State _____ Zip _____
Phone # _____

Make checks payable to Main Line Classics and mail to:

MAIN LINE CLASSICS
P.O. Box 521, Wayne, Pennsylvania 19087

Please allow 3 to 4 weeks for delivery. Call for information on one or two day delivery.

MAIN LINE CLASSICS II: *Cooking Up A Little History*

Please send _____ copies at ....$18.95 each $ _____
6% tax (PA residents only) ....$ 1.14 each $ _____
Plus postage and handling ....$ 3.50 each $ _____
TOTAL $ _____

MAIN LINE CLASSICS

Please send _____ copies at ....$16.95 each $ _____
6% tax (PA residents only) ....$ 1.02 each $ _____
Plus postage and handling ....$ 3.50 each $ _____
TOTAL $ _____

Name _____
Address _____
City_____ State _____ Zip _____
Phone # _____

Make checks payable to Main Line Classics and mail to:

MAIN LINE CLASSICS
P.O. Box 521, Wayne, Pennsylvania 19087

Please allow 3 to 4 weeks for delivery. Call for information on one or two day delivery.

MAIN LINE CLASSICS II: *Cooking Up A Little History*

Please send _____ copies at ....$18.95 each $ _____
6% tax (PA residents only) ....$ 1.14 each $ _____
Plus postage and handling ....$ 3.50 each $ _____
TOTAL $ _____

MAIN LINE CLASSICS

Please send _____ copies at ....$16.95 each $ _____
6% tax (PA residents only) ....$ 1.02 each $ _____
Plus postage and handling ....$ 3.50 each $ _____
TOTAL $ _____

Name _____
Address _____
City_____ State _____ Zip _____
Phone # _____

Make checks payable to Main Line Classics and mail to:

MAIN LINE CLASSICS
P.O. Box 521, Wayne, Pennsylvania 19087

Please allow 3 to 4 weeks for delivery. Call for information on one or two day delivery.

MAIN LINE CLASSICS II: *Cooking Up A Little History*

Please send _____ copies at ....$18.95 each $ _____
6% tax (PA residents only) ....$ 1.14 each $ _____
Plus postage and handling ....$ 3.50 each $ _____
TOTAL $ _____

MAIN LINE CLASSICS

Please send _____ copies at ....$16.95 each $ _____
6% tax (PA residents only) ....$ 1.02 each $ _____
Plus postage and handling ....$ 3.50 each $ _____
TOTAL $ _____

Name _____
Address _____
City_____ State _____ Zip _____
Phone # _____

Make checks payable to Main Line Classics and mail to:

MAIN LINE CLASSICS
P.O. Box 521, Wayne, Pennsylvania 19087

Please allow 3 to 4 weeks for delivery. Call for information on one or two day delivery.

MAIN LINE CLASSICS II: *Cooking Up A Little History*

Please send _____ copies at ....$18.95 each $ _____
6% tax (PA residents only) ....$ 1.14 each $ _____
Plus postage and handling ....$ 3.50 each $ _____
TOTAL $ _____

MAIN LINE CLASSICS

Please send _____ copies at ....$16.95 each $ _____
6% tax (PA residents only) ....$ 1.02 each $ _____
Plus postage and handling ....$ 3.50 each $ _____
TOTAL $ _____

Name _____
Address _____
City_____ State _____ Zip _____
Phone # _____

Make checks payable to Main Line Classics and mail to:

MAIN LINE CLASSICS
P.O. Box 521, Wayne, Pennsylvania 19087

Please allow 3 to 4 weeks for delivery. Call for information on one or two day delivery.

MAIN LINE CLASSICS II: *Cooking Up A Little History*

Please send _____ copies at ....$18.95 each $ _____
6% tax (PA residents only) ....$ 1.14 each $ _____
Plus postage and handling ....$ 3.50 each $ _____
TOTAL $ _____

MAIN LINE CLASSICS

Please send _____ copies at ....$16.95 each $ _____
6% tax (PA residents only) ....$ 1.02 each $ _____
Plus postage and handling ....$ 3.50 each $ _____
TOTAL $ _____

Name _____
Address _____
City_____ State _____ Zip _____
Phone # _____

Make checks payable to Main Line Classics and mail to:

MAIN LINE CLASSICS
P.O. Box 521, Wayne, Pennsylvania 19087

Please allow 3 to 4 weeks for delivery. Call for information on one or two day delivery.